TOWARDS A SOCIALLY JUST MATHEMATICS CURRICULUM

T0384896

Drawing from many years of shared experiences in mathematics teaching and teacher education, the authors of *Towards a Socially Just Mathematics Curriculum* offer a pedagogical model that incorporates and introduces learners to new cultures, challenges stereotypes, uses mathematics to discuss and act for social justice, and develops a well-rounded and socially just pedagogy. Readers will be encouraged to reflect on their own teaching practice and to identify areas for development, creating a more inclusive and equal mathematics experience for all learners.

Split into three distinct parts and filled with practical applications for the classroom, this essential book explores:

- Translating theory into practice by engaging in education for social justice;
- Applying this theory to teaching and learning across the Early Years, primary education and secondary education; and
- Reflecting on professional practice and identifying ways forward to continue providing an inclusive and equitable mathematics learning experience for all students.

This is an essential read for those interested in providing an inclusive, socially just mathematics education for their learners, including teachers, teaching assistants, senior leaders and trainees within primary and secondary schools.

Tony Cotton is a highly experienced teacher, holding over 40 years of experience working within primary and secondary schools. He is the editor of *Mathematics Teaching* and a lead tutor on the International PGCE at the University of Nottingham. He has also spent several years as an advisory teacher for anti-racist education. Tony has authored several books, including *Being a Teacher: Teaching and Learning in a Global Context* and *Transforming Teaching: Global Responses to Teaching Under the Pandemic*.

Manjinder Kaur Jagdev holds over ten years of experience teaching and as a subject lead in mathematics within a variety of multicultural secondary schools in the UK. Since 2006, she has worked in higher education teaching, supporting student teachers in primary and secondary education.

Balbir Kaur is an Assistant Professor in the School of Education at the University of Nottingham. She was previously a Lecturer in Mathematics for Primary Education Teaching in the Department of Education at Brunel University in London.

Pete Wright is currently Senior Lecturer in Education and Society at the University of Dundee. He teaches on a range of education courses at undergraduate, master's and doctoral level. He was previously an Associate Professor of Mathematics Education at UCL Institute of Education in London. Prior to that he taught for 12 years in various comprehensive schools in the UK and for three years in a rural school in Kenya. He has also held posts as a local authority consultant and curriculum developer.

TOWARDS A SOCIALLY JUST MATHEMATICS CURRICULUM

A Theoretical and Practical Approach

Tony Cotton, Manjinder Kaur Jagdev, Balbir Kaur and Pete Wright

Routledge
Taylor & Francis Group

LONDON AND NEW YORK

Designed cover image: © Getty Images. Cover design: Jo Steer.

First published 2024
by Routledge
4 Park Square, Milton Park, Abingdon, Oxon OX14 4RN

and by Routledge
605 Third Avenue, New York, NY 10158

Routledge is an imprint of the Taylor & Francis Group, an informa business

© 2024 Tony Cotton, Manjinder Kaur Jagdev, Balbir Kaur and Pete Wright

British Library Cataloguing-in-Publication Data
A catalogue record for this book is available from the British Library

Library of Congress Cataloging-in-Publication Data
Names: Cotton, Tony, author.
Title: Towards a socially just mathematics curriculum:
a theoretical and practical approach / Tony Cotton,
Manjinder Jagdev, Balbir Kaur and Pete Wright.
Description: Abingdon, Oxon; New York, NY: Routledge, 2024. |
Includes bibliographical references and index.
Identifiers: LCCN 2023051501 (print) | LCCN 2023051502 (ebook) |
ISBN 9781032421650 (hbk) | ISBN 9781032421636 (pbk) |
ISBN 9781003361466 (ebk)
Subjects: LCSH: Mathematics–Study and teaching (Primary) |
Social justice and education. | Mathematics–Study and teaching (Secondary)
Classification: LCC QA135.6 .C6749 2024 (print) | LCC QA135.6 (ebook) |
DDC 372.7–dc23/eng/20240201
LC record available at https://lccn.loc.gov/2023051501
LC ebook record available at https://lccn.loc.gov/2023051502

ISBN: 978-1-032-42165-0 (hbk)
ISBN: 978-1-032-42163-6 (pbk)
ISBN: 978-1-003-36146-6 (ebk)

DOI: 10.4324/9781003361466

Typeset in Interstate
by Deanta Global Publishing Services, Chennai, India

Access the Support Material at www.routledge.com/9781032421636

CONTENTS

PREFACE

'I think that … we should act as if the universe were listening to us …; we should act as if life were going to win. We should act as if we were attending the marriage of responsibility and delight.'

(Pullman, 2005.)

When writing about social justice it is easy to start from a deficit model. To see the injustices that are obvious in the world and in our mathematics classrooms. To see how education in general and mathematics education in particular has failed groups of learners. Perhaps Philip Pullman, someone who sits outside education, offers both a challenge and a way forward. We have the responsibility to continue to work for social justice, and we can delight in this work. In this way we may sustain any change.

The purposes of this Preface are to share with the reader both the aim of the text and what they might find in the book if they take the plunge and read on. An explanation of why this book should exist and why it should interest you. The title of the book, *Towards a socially just mathematics education: a theoretical and practical approach*, suggests that we are inviting you to join us on a journey and that this journey will involve two kinds of work. Firstly, theoretical work through which we hope to persuade you that cleverer people than us have thought very hard about the issues we discuss, that their ideas have influenced us and that we think they can influence you too. We hope that these thinkers will offer avenues for your own study and that this study will impact on your practice. We model this by exemplifying how such thinking has impacted on our own teaching.

And, secondly, practical work. We are teachers, so our work is teaching. The second section of the book offers new paths that you can choose to take and, in walking these new paths with your learners, engage them in the journey towards social justice. So perhaps this Preface is a call to action, the theoretical section offers the argument for action, and the activities we share offer you a way to take action. Finally, we share with you a vision for the next stopping point on the journey towards social justice, not an endpoint. The journey is the thing. But a sharing of where we might like to get to in the near future.

It feels apposite to reflect on what we might mean by social justice in this preface. A view that may be useful is offered by a thought experiment introduced in *A theory of justice* (Rawls, 1971) to explore my own practice through a social justice lens. He introduced me to the concept of the 'veil of ignorance.' Imagine, whilst you have been sitting in your office or a comfortable room in your house reading this book, the world outside has completely changed. When you move back outside and re-join society you do not know what position you will hold. You may still be a lecturer or teacher; or you may be the Romanian *Big Issue* seller who I see every Saturday morning outside the café I visit with my grandchildren; you may be the homeless woman we meet outside Piccadilly on our way into Manchester; or you may be one of the people struggling to get a hospital appointment.

If the society was just, you would not be concerned as to the position you had been allocated. All members of society in a just society are able to live a good life. So, how might this apply to you as a teacher or academic or both? Think of the classes that you teach, or classes of students that you visit as part of your work or colleagues with whom you engage on research. Now think of a child whom you love. If the education system was a just one, you would be perfectly happy for this child to exchange places with any of the children in that class. My guess is this might not be the case. So, an action for social justice is to explore how you might act to make that space more just for that student. And then, once you have taken that action, explore who gained and who was disadvantaged by that action and repeat.

We opened with a challenge and a suggestion for a way forward, so let us close this Preface with, perhaps, a manifesto for the book:

> When we commit ourselves to education as the practice of freedom, we participate in the making of an academic community where we can be and become intellectuals in the fullest and deepest sense of the word. We participate in a way of learning and being that makes the world more rather than less real, one that enables us to live more freely and fully. This is the joy in our quest.
>
> (hooks, 1999 p72)

References

hooks, b. (1999) *Talking back: Thinking feminist, thinking black*. New York: South End Press.

Pullman, P. (2005) 'Here lieth the delights of pity, shame and rapture,' *Times Higher Education Supplement* (22 April, indexed in the THES website).

Rawls, J. (1971) *A theory of justice*. Oxford: Oxford University Press.

ACKNOWLEDGEMENTS

Tony Cotton

I would like to thank all those who I have worked with along my educational and life journey. The children I taught at High Green School in the Eighties who taught me that a truly comprehensive, cross-curricular approach to teaching mathematics could be effective. My wonderful colleagues at the Multicultural Centre in Leicester in the Nineties, a multi-ethnic team of teachers committed to working for social justice. Cecile Wright, my tutor on the MA at the University of Leicester, and Leone Burton, my PhD supervisor, who guided me along my continuing journey searching for a route along the road to social justice through mathematics education. And, then, the students of Margaret Glen Bott School and Radford Primary School in Nottingham who put up with my continued ventures into what such a mathematics education might look like. I also need to thank Bruce Roberts at Routledge who has offered me the space to share my thinking with you. Thanks for your trust, Bruce.

Finally, I need to thank my incredible family. Helen, my partner for life's travels in and out of education and the mother of three (now grown-up) children who continue to bring joy and provide the sustenance that is needed on this journey. And then Felix, Tate, Quinn, and Wilf – our four grandsons – who show us that the journey towards social justice is both possible and necessary. They are the joy in my quest.

Manjinder Kaur Jagdev

I am grateful to my parents. Their unconditional love, support, and generosity has enabled me to enjoy a career in education. The importance of my work stems from parental influences in childhood which prioritised education. My father, Bhag Singh, graduated in mathematics from Punjab University in India, arrived in the UK in the late 1960s and worked as an engineer for 58 years. His high expectations for me to go to university have been key to my professional journey. My mother, Surinder Kaur, was a wise woman despite being denied schooling in a rural Indian village in the 1950s and took on the role of an adult as the firstborn in a family of ten children. In the UK, she worked for almost 40 years. With a strong Sikh faith and belief in service (Punjabi word: *seva*), she was a survivor, peacemaker, assertive, nurturing, affectionate, and resilient. My parents worked multiple shifts and with a strong work ethic. Despite the pushbacks, my mother remained a strong Asian immigrant woman who was resolute in her mission to do the best for her children. As my ancestors did, 'I pay it forward' to the children of the future. I appreciate the feedback, encouragement, and motivation provided to me by my family members, particularly my three loving nephews, steadfast sister-in-law and brother, and lovable Simba cat.

My gratitude extends to the teachers, colleagues, students, and community members who all play a rich part in my journey. Their positivity informs my dedication to equal opportunities for all, to make society fairer, and to celebrate diversity as a strength. As Wilson (2020) states: 'A real challenge is … balancing the teachers' role in raising awareness of social justice issues through maths with empowering learners to be able to do something about these injustices.'

Balbir Kaur

As a Lecturer in Education (primary mathematics) and Director of Equality and Diversity, my wider engagement within research and scholarship on issues of social justice in education has enabled me to make a humble contribution to this book. My contributions are based on my reflections and experiences with the aim to engage the audience to be critical, creative, and discover how to participate in the transformation of society through engagement with socially just mathematical approaches.

My thanks go to my colleagues, Tony Cotton, who made this project of writing such a book a reality and keeping us on track. I have admired his work throughout my career, and it has been an honour to work with him in this capacity. To Manjinder Kaur Jagdev and Pete Wright for the encouragement and constructive feedback received during the process: I have valued your experiences and knowledge. To all three for the friendships created.

Pete Wright

I would like to acknowledge the contribution of the five teacher researchers who collaborated with me on the 'Teaching maths for social justice' research project, which generated the ideas behind the 'Measuring inequality' and 'Counting votes' activities in Part 2, and which led to the development of my conceptualisation of mathematics teaching for social justice articulated in Chapter 2. Due to the need to protect the anonymity of research participants, they are referred to in reports of the project by their pseudonyms: Anna, Brian, George, Rebecca, and Sarah. Note that versions of these two activities and other ideas from the project are included later in this book.

I would like to acknowledge the contributions of co-researchers Caroline Hilton (UCL Institute of Education) and Joel Kelly (The Blue School, Isleworth), and the six teacher researchers who collaborated with me on the 'Primary Maths and Social Justice' research project that generated the ideas behind the 'Fair Choices' activity in Part 2. The teacher researchers are referred to in the reports by their pseudonyms: Aidan, David, Emma, Kate, Layla, Rose.

I am very grateful to the following members of the Teaching Maths for Social Justice Network for their work in generating ideas which informed the design of activities in Part 2.

Maria Esteban, Ali Ford, Ladan Sadjadi, and Max Aantjes contributed towards the design of the 'Housing and community' activity (based on the 'Community in the classroom' activity on the TMSJN website). Hafsa Farhana, Vinay Kathotia, Azadeh Neman, and Kate O'Brien contributed towards the design of the 'Investigating earnings' activity (based on the 'Growth in earnings: Fair or unfair?' activity on the TMSJN website).

INTRODUCTION TO
THE AUTHORS

Balbir

Over the years, I have realised that I cannot remove my identity from what I do and how I experience and interpret education. I am a British-born, second-generation Indian female born to immigrant parents who settled in the West Midlands in the 1960s. I grew up with gender differences, in low economic and social conditions, and experienced sexism, racism, and casteism. My interest in learning and teaching acknowledges these differences, which has guided me to explore the concept of social justice in education. I never had a plan or a set career path where I wanted to be a teacher, educator, or a lecturer in primary mathematics education. These were fortunate coincidences that I have fully embraced. As a teacher educator, I am privileged to be in a position to share my thoughts and ideas on TMSJ. Although many factors have contributed to my interest in TMSJ over the years, it has been the more recent activism demonstrated by some young people questioning educators to review their curriculums and 'decolonise' the knowledge they receive, and, as educators, how can we not respond?

My enjoyment of mathematics was present in primary school, and it was a subject I found success in. For that reason, maths was one of my favourite subjects, but also because my mother was good at it, and I saw her calculate all sorts of things on the digits of her fingers. Although I enjoyed mathematics at secondary school, it was very textbook driven. We were streamed according to our 'ability' in maths, and I was placed in the middle set throughout my secondary schooling. Looking back, that fixed stage of being in the middle set created a concrete ceiling that meant I could not access A-Level maths. I did not have the depth of knowledge needed and struggled. My enjoyment of the subject ended when I completed the AS-Level.

Going into teaching ignited the interest and passion I once had for learning mathematics. When an opening to be a mathematics co-ordinator emerged in my third year of teaching, I took on the role. My first teaching post was very similar to the primary school I attended as a child. It was a small state primary school that served a multicultural community from diverse backgrounds and cultures. It must have been the first time minority-ethnic parents encountered a minority-ethnic teacher because there was a sense of curiosity. As the mathematics co-ordinator, I instigated several home-school links and invited parents into maths lessons to learn with their children and share the maths they had learned growing up. The sharing and exchange of mathematical experiences between the school, parents, and children proved to be a powerful means to engage interest in the subject. My enthusiasm for the subject and desire to support fellow teachers led to an appointment as a regional primary mathematics lead teacher. I later went on to do some work for the local authority on engaging children who have English as an additional language in mathematics. The National Strategies drove both initiatives.

Since then, I have enjoyed a challenging yet rewarding career as a teacher educator of primary mathematics education. I spent over ten years at Wolverhampton University teaching primary mathematics across different teacher education courses, including undergraduate, postgraduate and employment-based routes. As Director of Equality and Diversity for the Education Department at Brunel University, my work on social justice forms part of the strategic plan to address the awarding gap and 'decolonise' the curriculum. On a national level, I secured a position as a panel member of the Race Equality Charter (REC) – Advance HE that reviews applications from HEIs (higher education institutions) for the REC award.

Manjinder

Born in inner-city Leicester, I attended a multicultural, comprehensive, mixed, state secondary school in the 1980s. Spurred on by my parents, I completed sixth form in the city and then went to University of Birmingham to complete a BSc Mathematics and Statistics. After completion of an MSc in Medical Informatics and working in market research, I was encouraged by a university professor to consider a career in teaching.

During my PGCE (postgraduate certificate in education) year at University of Nottingham in 1995–96, I learned from inspiring educators including Malcolm Swan, Peter Gates, and Tony Cotton. The highly rewarding experiences in the inner city, multicultural, comprehensive and state secondary placement school in which I completed my practice led me to seek my first teaching post in a similar exciting, dynamic, and rich environment. This was in inner-city Bristol, where the children were from diverse backgrounds and a multitude of home languages were spoken. A move to another city school after two years meant that I was able to provide children with more extra-curricular opportunities to take mathematics learning beyond the classroom, to other regions in England.

In 2000, I began working in a community school in the fine city of Norwich, with responsibilities for Key Stage 4 mathematics. Here, I completed my Master's in Education and Professional Development, focusing on enhancing children's learning with international practices. These ideas continued to result in increased motivation and engagement of Key Stage 3 and 4 pupils in the next school, where I was Head of Mathematics. Also, I learned that children became more interested when introduced to the ideas of historical and cross-cultural roots of mathematics. They become keen to share stories of their own home languages and those they had learned from holidays abroad. They were fascinated by how mathematics has evolved over thousands of years, throughout ancient history, with contributions from cultures across the globe. Also, I used current statistics on social justice themes, from around the world, to teach data handling on the English national curriculum. Children were enthusiastic about sharing their views on these topics.

After ten years of secondary school teaching, in 2006 I was offered a lectureship in higher education, working with secondary postgraduate secondary student teachers. Since then, I have worked in different universities in the UK and as a visiting lecturer. Because of the positive experiences with pupils, I introduce ideas of critical mathematics education to my primary and secondary student teachers. These students are vocal about social justice issues affecting different people both in the UK and around the world. As they develop into critical and reflective practitioners, they demand lesson activities and practical examples for their children in classrooms, which are centred on fairness, truth and justice. Following recent conferences at York St. John university where I now work, students have created lesson ideas on antiracism, decolonial practice, and climate change.

Contributing to this book provides an opportunity to share this work and encourage other educators and student teachers to trial the suggested activities and/or consider planning others with their children/learners. I hope that readers will find the process as rewarding, motivating, and creative as I have, and the experiences will be beneficial for all interested in pursuing social justice in education.

Pete

Throughout my career in education, initially as a secondary school teacher and more recently as a teacher educator and researcher, I have been interested in mathematics teaching for social justice. In this section I reflect on events and life experiences that generated and maintained this interest for me over the past 35 years. A recurring theme for me has been how engaging with theory, during my PGCE studies in 1986-87, during my Master's level studies in 1994-95, and during my doctoral studies from 2010, enabled me to make more sense of past experiences and generate greater insight into my own professional practice (see Chapter 2). Applying theory in this way led me to challenge assumptions and practices around teaching and learning mathematics which I had not previously questioned, resulting in modifying my stance or approach in some areas. However, it also reinforced my commitment to certain principles around equity and social justice, which I had previously felt were instinctively 'right,' but which I could now support with a stronger theoretical justification. I hope that recounting some of these experiences, and sharing the ideas and activities in this book, might enable others to gain greater insight into teaching and learning mathematics through a similar process of theory-informed critical reflection on personal experiences.

My own experiences of learning mathematics were mixed. At primary school, I remember working through maths problems independently, in a small group, on a table in the corner of the classroom, whilst other students worked in groups on different projects or other areas of the curriculum. At secondary school, mathematics learning was much more traditional, with rigid setting in place, everyone seated on single desks arranged in rows, and the teacher going through examples on the board before setting exercises for us to complete from the textbook. Whilst mathematics was never my favourite subject, I did well in the subject and experienced success based on getting higher marks in tests than many other students. This success encouraged me to study mathematics at A-Level and degree level, although I can honestly say that I enjoyed the subject less and less as I progressed through different phases of education. It was only during my PGCE studies that I developed a genuine passion for mathematics, when I began to appreciate how fun and engaging it could be when learned through collaborative and investigative approaches. Since then, it has struck me as grossly unfair and unfortunate that many students, due to the dominance of traditional teaching approaches, are never given the opportunity to appreciate just how interesting mathematics can be.

I spent more than 15 years teaching in a variety of schools in London, Newcastle-upon-Tyne, Kenya, and Sussex, many of which were located in areas of relatively high deprivation. This has enabled me to develop an empathy with learners facing greater levels of challenge than their more privileged peers. Combined with my engagement with theories around equity and social justice, it also helped me to appreciate some of the structural inequities that exist within school systems. For example, I have witnessed how the most alienated, and the lowest-attaining, students can benefit enormously from progressive teaching approaches that employ more collaboration, discussion, exploration, and problem-solving, and draw on relevant and meaningful contexts. And yet these very students are more likely to be denied access to such approaches as other people assume they are better suited to a diet of more prescriptive teaching. I have been fortunate enough to spend most of my teaching career in mathematics departments that favour mixed-attainment grouping and have consequently witnessed the positive impact this has on students' achievement and attitude towards the subject. I therefore find it frustrating that most school managers still adhere unquestioningly to a belief that setting students by prior attainment raises attainment. This is contrary to the research evidence which also highlights the damaging social impact setting has on many students.

My career in education has included taking on the positions of Advanced Skills Teacher and Head of Department. Other roles include five years working as a curriculum developer for SMILE Mathematics, two years as a local authority mathematics consultant and 11 years as a teacher educator at UCL Institute of Education, where I was a tutor on a range of ITE (initial teacher education) programmes including PGCE and Teach First. Thus, I have had an abundance of opportunities to work alongside classroom teachers in reflecting upon existing practice, developing innovative teaching approaches, and designing new classroom activities. These experiences have helped me to appreciate the importance of teacher agency in transforming pedagogical thinking and classroom practice. This appreciation was strengthened through my engagement with participatory action research methodology, which I have employed extensively in conducting my research (see Chapter 2).

Since attending university, my strong beliefs around equity and social justice have inspired me to become actively involved as a trade unionist and in several campaigning organisations including the Anti-Apartheid Movement, Amnesty International and Global Justice Now (previously called the World Development Movement). Spending over three years working as a volunteer mathematics teacher (with VSO: voluntary service overseas) in a rural school in Kenya also provided me with a more global perspective on education and life in general. An increasing appreciation of the socio-political nature of mathematics education gained through my studies has prompted me to identify more and more areas where developing mathematical understanding can be closely linked to generating students' awareness of the growing social, economic, and environmental challenges facing our society (see Chapter 2). I see working collaboratively with colleagues in promoting mathematics teaching for social justice as the most effective way of using my experiences and expertise in contributing towards tackling some of these challenges.

Tony

This story perhaps starts in the headteacher's study at Ormskirk Grammar School sometime in 1975. I had been called to see the head as a result of the options I had written on the form for choosing A-Level subjects. I had suggested I might study English, history, and mathematics, and very much in that order. The head, without looking up, as I remember, said, "Cotton, you appear to have mixed up the arts and the sciences. I have put you down for mathematics, further mathematics, physics and chemistry. Goodbye." It appeared that being a boy the expectation was that I would study the sciences. And so I studied mathematics, went to university to study mathematics and became a teacher of mathematics. A path that seemed selected for me and dictated by my background. I studied at Sheffield University from 1977–81, a rich time politically and musically with the two often coinciding. I spent much of my time in an independent bookshop near the University reading Freire and *Race Today*. I listened to Linton Kwesi Johnson and The Clash. I came to the conclusion that every choice we made was political, and as I progressed through my teacher education I came to understand that this included the choices I made about teaching, both in terms of content and pedagogy.

The second school I taught at on an estate on the outskirts of Sheffield taught through all-attainment teaching. That is why I applied for a job there. I became head of department and realised that, through discussion and modelling, colleagues could be encouraged to develop and that learners could be included in innovating the curriculum. The school implemented a fully integrated curriculum for the 11–12-year-old learners. A team of five teachers taught the whole curriculum to their tutor group. We supported each other in developing subject knowledge across the curriculum. Mathematics was taught in a three-hour lesson on Friday mornings. I introduced an idea or a concept to the whole year group: 96 students. Each teacher then described the approach they would take to exploring this idea or concept in their space. The students then chose the space that they wanted to learn in, the approach they felt suited them best, and spent the rest of the morning with this teacher. Each group fed back on their learning at the end of the morning. No bells, breaks when needed, and the most inclusive and rich environment for learning mathematics I have encountered. It was here that I learned how we might develop a curriculum within a disadvantaged, predominantly white student body that worked towards social justice for all.

I moved from there to the Multicultural Centre in Leicester where I joined a multi-ethnic team of teachers supporting all schools in Leicester and Leicestershire in developing a curriculum appropriate for the multicultural and multilingual society that made up the populations of the schools. I also became Chair of Governors at my daughter's school, another school rich in its diversity. The head there, Jasbir, and I had worked together at the

Multicultural Centre and we could put our ideas into practice. The story of this school is told in *Improving Primary Schools, Improving Communities*, first published by Trentham Books. I think this experience confirmed my belief that a multicultural society offered richer experiences for us and that institutional racism could be tackled but had to be acknowledged in order for such structures to be dismantled. This school was the location for my PhD research, also exploring social justice and mathematics education.

After time working with commercial publishers developing mathematics resources for primary students, I moved into teacher education, firstly at the University of Nottingham. The eagle-eyed amongst you will have spotted that I was a tutor on Manjinder's teacher education course. Then I moved to Nottingham Trent University and became engaged with several local community organisations which helped us in terms of diversifying the student population on our teacher education courses. This continued with my move to Leeds Metropolitan University (now Leeds Beckett) as head of teacher education. The final Ofsted report before I left included the statement, 'trainees' commitment to inclusion and disapproval of stereotyping is strong.' This is something I am very proud of. Some of the activities later in this book are drawn from this experience.

I left the university in 2011. There are currently three main foci for my work. I teach on an international teacher education course for teachers in South East Asia. My current group of tutees come from eight different countries and now teach in another six different countries. This is a joy as we all get to draw on a huge diversity of experiences in education. I edit the journal *Mathematics Teaching* (MT) for the Association of Teachers of Mathematics and continue to learn and develop my practice around teaching for social justice through the articles submitted to MT. Indeed, that is where Pete's and my paths first crossed. Currently I am working with the government of Belize to provide materials and training for their primary teachers. They are teaching what decolonising education looks like in practice.

How you might use this book

Well - you have met the authors. You know what our aims are. What next? We do not think this book demands to be read from beginning to end in one go. There are choices to be made. You may have taken an interest in a particular author. Why not start at their theoretical chapter? You may be interested in a particular phase of education. Why not start exploring the activities that we offer for your particular phase of education?

I guess what we are saying is that if you are interested in the practice start there: try something out. Our hope would be that this interests you enough to draw you into the theory. Or, start with the theory. Our hope here that the arguments will persuade you to try something with the learners in your care.

You will notice a range of stopping-off points. We would encourage you to annotate this book. Make it your own. If we sit across from you on a train and see you annotating the activities or underlining key points in the theoretical arguments, we will be delighted. Don't worry, we won't interrupt.

So, before we move into the 'Theory into practice' Section here is the first stopping-off point.

REFLECTIONS

When did you first notice injustice in school? How did you respond?

What is it in your personal history that influenced your aims and beliefs about learning and teaching?

PART 1
Theory into practice

Introduction

The next four chapters set the theoretical context which underpins the practical activities we share in Section 2. All four chapters move between theory and practice, so the practical nature of the book, and the encouragement for you to take action in your classrooms, is to the fore even in this theoretical section. We would suggest that there is a flow through these chapters. Firstly, Tony introduces the historical context for current debates around mathematics for social justice making connections between the activism underpinning classroom practice coming from the anti-racist movement in the seventies and eighties and the Black Lives Matter movement and decolonisation of the curriculum which are currently impacting education. All of this explored through activities Tony has used with a range of mathematics learners across the years.

The discussion takes a more mathematics-specific focus in Pete's chapter. Pete takes an ethnomathematical approach, exploring the ways in which mathematics has developed within and out of cultures around the world. Certainly, no sense of mathematics as a product of Western societies here. Indeed, Pete uses this exploration to question a Western absolutist view of mathematics. He develops this argument to argue that teachers can be agents of change in the move towards a more socially just mathematics education.

We move into teacher education with Balbir's chapter. Balbir shows us how teacher education programmes can be developed to model the principles of teaching mathematics for social justice. She carefully unpicks recent scholarly activity around issues of social justice in mathematics focusing on Gutstein framework for social justice.

Finally, Manjinder moves us more particularly towards the practical, offering her interpretation of how the current theoretical debates impact on her curriculum planning and the responses of her teacher education students in their planning in response to a teacher education programme with social justice at its heart.

You may notice that we are taking care with our use of terminology. In the above we talk about 'students' and not 'trainees.' This is a choice which we think is to do with social justice. We are not engaged in training 'trainees', which suggests a lack of agency in those with whom we work. We are engaged as 'teachers' and 'students' and can share our experience and knowledge, but we do this in the understanding that we are engaged in education and not training. We also prefer to use the term 'mathematics for social justice' rather than

DOI: 10.4324/9781003361466-1

anti-racist mathematics or decolonising the curriculum. This is not to disrespect those that prefer those terms, and we try to explore similarity and differences between the viewpoints in the text. We prefer the term 'mathematics for social justice' as it suggests a forward movement on the journey to justice rather than a reaction or response. We accept that, whatever terms we prefer, we are all on the same journey.

We also acknowledge the overlaps between the chapters and that occasionally we cover very similar ground. We have deliberately left these overlaps in as connections between the chapters. We hope that you see these four chapters as four different perspectives, four different voices, exploring the issues of mathematics for social justice from a particular social, historical, and personal context.

As we suggested in the Introduction, you can, of course, read these chapters in any order you like. It may feel appropriate to you to take a specific focus, read that chapter, and move directly into the activities in Section 2. You may have already explored some of the activities in the next section and be visiting this section for some theoretical justification.

So, let us start with Tony's reflection on the historical context of the current debates and his own educational journey.

1 A personal history of mathematics education for social justice

A rationale in three stories

Tony Cotton

February 1982

I am a young mathematics teacher. About six months into my first teaching post. I am teaching at a large secondary school in a Northern industrial city. Suffering, as many Northern cities are doing, from the closure of mines and steel works taking away what had been secure employment from many families. It is a bright day, I remember, I am walking down the 'Maths' corridor about to turn into my teaching room. Along the corridor I see a Year 9 student, or third year as it was called back then. I'll call him Dwayne. He is one of two brothers from the only Black family in the school. Another student, I'll call him Steve, turns just in front of me and shouts racist abuse back at his fellow student. I have never taught either of these students.

I show my anger: I grab hold of Steve and shout at him, "Don't ever let me hear that sort of thing ever again." Steve looks more surprised than threatened or frightened. He shrugs me off and disappears. Dwayne has already left the corridor. A few days later Steve comes to find me in my teaching room at break time. It's my turn to look surprised, "What do you want?" Not so angry this time. Steve pauses and then asks, "Is it true that you're married to an Asian woman?" My turn to look surprised. "No," I reply. Another shrug, "Oh, it's just that everyone says you are."

It is only later that I realise Steve was trying to rationalise why a teacher would pick him up on his racist behaviour. It must be that I have a particular emotional reason for taking an anti-racist stance. This was not the sort of behaviour he had come to expect from his teachers.

Forty years later

My wife is having a telephone conversation with a young South African man, I'll call him Kgabu, who has recently moved out after having lived with us for six months. She looks distressed. After the telephone call she tells me that one reason Kgabu decided to move was the covert and overt racism he had grown to expect on the 30-minute bus-rides into and back home from the city nearest to the Yorkshire market town in which we live.

Twenty-five years previously

My wife is working at a small secondary school in a multi-ethnic Midlands city. The ethnic mix in the school is representative of the diverse population. I have been working with her

DOI: 10.4324/9781003361466-2

on a production of a play dealing with issues of racism. There has been a recent incident of racism directed at one of the class, and I am sitting in a circle with my wife and the whole drama group. We have been discussing the recent event and other issues of racism in the school. One of the students, a 16-year-old called Sohm with whom we are still in contact, leaps to her feet: "It's all about education, Miss," she shouts.

First steps

Whilst I was studying for my Post Graduate Certificate of Education (1980), it was the time of 'Rock against racism,' of the rise of the National Front, and the protests against them. I wrote my final assignment about the media and its coverage of the New Cross fire documented in Steve McQueen's 'Small Axe' television series in 2022. In the early nineties, after ten years as a mathematics teacher, I moved to Leicester to take on a role with the title 'Advisory teacher for anti-racist education,' working out of the Multicultural Centre and delivering a cascade model of training to every school in Leicester and Leicestershire. This was the time of the Stephen Lawrence murder and the Macpherson Report which brought the phrase 'institutional racism' into the national repertoire. In 1999 I completed my PhD, 'Towards a curriculum for social justice in mathematics education.' In some sense it already felt as if the debates in mathematics education had turned towards finding a one-size-fits-all teaching strategy for mathematics in our schools: the national curriculum, the numeracy strategy, and most recently a 'mastery' curriculum as defined by the National Centre for Excellence in the Teaching Mathematics (NCETM) and imposed by the Office for Standards in Education (Ofsted).

Then, on 25 May 2020, a 46-year-old Black man was murdered by a White police officer in Minneapolis. The Black Lives Matter (BLM) movement, which had been formed seven years earlier in response to the murder of another young Black man, Trayvon Martin, seemed reenergised, and there were protests around the world. Schools and Universities began to explore responses variously termed 'decolonising the curriculum,' 'developing a curriculum for social justice,' or an 'anti-racist education.'

In 2021, I was asked by the Association of Mathematics Education Teachers (AMET) to lead an online workshop exploring issues of social justice in mathematics education. This was the first time I had been asked for such a workshop. As a result of this workshop, I was asked to repeat the session for several Universities, both for educators and for initial teacher education students. In some ways this took me back to the Multicultural Centre in Leicester.

So, this is my context, and, to some extent one story of the current historical and social context. My aim for this chapter is to explore the issues around a mathematics education for social justice by developing this personal history in the form of four activities I have used in a range of mathematics classrooms to unpick what might be meant by the terms 'decolonising the curriculum,' 'anti-racist mathematics,' and 'mathematics education for social justice.' During this discussion I will draw parallels between the debates of the 80s/90s and the current debate. It is perhaps useful, initially, to explore some terminology as the debate can become obscured by what appears to be very specialised vocabulary.

Some terminology

This is neither an exhaustive nor definitive list. Rather, it is an acknowledgement that for many people the vocabulary around these debates can obscure rather than clarify the issues. It is a starting point for discussions and further exploration, and, hopefully, permission to use such vocabulary tentatively and with respect. We develop our understanding of the different perspective through an interrogation of such vocabulary rather than through condemnation of colleagues who we may feel use the vocabulary incorrectly.

Antiracism: During the 1980s there was much debate around antiracism and multiculturalism. Multiculturalism was seen as acknowledging the rich contributions that the diverse communities making up the population of Leicester brought to the classroom. It was about overtly celebrating that diversity. For many of us, antiracism included a celebration of diversity but also aimed to challenge the structures in education that served to oppress students from what were termed minority groups. This term is in itself problematic, other terms such as 'student of colour' or 'global majority' might now be used. Reflecting on this, Pranav Patel (2022) in the book *The Antiracist Educator* asks teachers:

> How do we, in the words of Dr Ibram Kendi, consistently identify, describe and dismantle racism? How do we challenge the racist structures in which we were brought up, taught by our own teachers and now continue to propagate? As educators, this process begins with us looking inwards to our own actions and our complicity.
>
> (p. 9)

Education for social justice: Another contested and complex term. Several UK Universities have developed research centres which use the term 'social justice' in their title. The mission statement of the Institute for Social Justice at York University suggests its purpose is to:

underpin [the University's] mission 'to stand up for social justice' … through developing collaborative research and practice that … identify, expose and address … the inequalities, injustices and challenges facing society today. [We seek] to work *with* people, … partners and … communities in a manner which seeks **participation**, **implementation** and **change** as vital parts of its mission. [Original emphasis.]

In a sense, education for social justice includes recognising and working to remove discriminatory structures, both overt and institutional, and offers ways in which these structures can be challenged.

Institutional racism: To return to 1999 and my time at the Multicultural Centre in Leicester. The Macpherson Inquiry into the police response to the murder of Stephen Lawrence found that the London Metropolitan Police Force was institutionally racist and that this impacted the investigation. The report defined institutional racism as:

> The collective failure of an organisation to provide an appropriate and professional service to people because of their colour, culture or ethnic origin. It can be seen or detected in processes, attitudes and behaviour that amount to discrimination through

prejudice, ignorance, thoughtlessness and racist stereotyping which disadvantage minority ethnic people.

(Paragraph 6.34)

The debate continues. In 2021, a UK Government report written by a government commission on 'race and ethnic disparities' concluded that institutional racism was not present in UK institutions. This finding has been widely challenged.

Decolonising the curriculum: The decolonising the curriculum movement emerged from the 'Rhodes must fall' protests at the University of Cape Town, which called for the removal of the statue of Cecil Rhodes. Both the arguments around memorials and around decolonising the curriculum spread to the UK. Many UK Universities now have policies referring to 'decolonising the curriculum.' The Runnymede Trust commissioned a piece written by Martin Johnson and Melissa Mouthaan from Cambridge Assessment. They suggest that decolonisation involves 'critically examining the influence of colonial legacies on education systems … and sub-components such as knowledge and curriculum.' They offer a series of recommendations for those wishing to engage in 'decolonisation.' These are:

- Confront issues of racism directly – this includes awareness raising around racism and colonialism and critical self-reflection around individuals' positionality in systems of race.
- Explore the resources that are being used in teaching to enable diverse learning.
- Understand that decolonisation is a process.

It is interesting that many University statements around decolonisation focus on teaching materials and the content of the curriculum rather than how institutional structures perpetuate inequalities. We would argue that an education for social justice would encapsulate both.

Critical Race Theory

The term was coined in the 1970s and 1980s amongst legal scholars in the USA. It was introduced into educational studies in 1995 by Gloria Ladson-Billings and William Tate. For the purposes of this chapter, I will reproduce the definition given by David Gillborn and Gloria Ladson-Billings in their 2010 paper.

> A multidisciplinary approach that combines social activism with a critique of the fundamental role played by White racism in shaping contemporary societies.

For me there are echoes of the anti-racist approach from the 1980s and 1990s in the UK in this statement. A purely multicultural approach was criticised as a 'saris and samosas' curriculum in which 'other' cultures were celebrated in ways which could be seen as patronising and exoticising with no attention paid to the structural inequalities which mitigated against social justice.

You will have realised that the preferred term for the authors of this book is 'education for social justice.' For us, this term combines and synthesises the key tenets of all of the above. It offers a way to investigate the content of the curriculum on offer to our learners and it suggests appropriate pedagogical approaches such as collaboration, hearing the voices of the previously silenced or marginalised, and demanding participation of all communities. It also acknowledges institutional systems which act against justice in education and expects action to create new structures which do not discriminate in this way.

What has mathematics got to do with it?

So far, I have been making the argument that education, in general, has a role to play in developing a more socially just society. The vignettes with which I opened the chapter, whilst taking place in schools, even in the 'mathematics corridor,' did not refer to or involve either mathematics itself or the teaching of mathematics. Why should teachers of mathematics engage with these ideas and can we claim that mathematics itself plays a role in either reproducing unfairness, or injustice, in society or that, the discipline itself can play a part in constructing a more equitable society?

So, what connects 'anti-racism,' 'decolonising the curriculum,' or our preferred term 'social justice' and mathematics? Perhaps more importantly, what makes mathematics a special case? It may seem counterintuitive. For example, I was recently running an online webinar on teaching primary mathematics and noticed that the audience included teachers from Ukraine and Russia. I commented on the power of the internet to form groups of people who might not normally be expected to be working together and the reply came back in the chat that "Education is beyond politics." Similarly, I was once talking to a colleague from the Czech Republic, and they remembered enjoying going into mathematics lessons and doing a mathematics degree because "it was the only place that ideology did not intrude."

In the 1980s when I was working at the Centre for Multicultural Education in Leicester there was much talk of 'political correctness gone mad.' A precursor of the current 'anti-woke' agenda perhaps. At the Conservative Party conference in 1987, Margaret Thatcher announced:

> And in the inner cities—where youngsters must have a decent education if they are to have a better future—that opportunity is all too often snatched from them by hard left education authorities and extremist teachers. And children who need to be able to count and multiply are learning anti-racist mathematics—whatever that may be.

Here we see Thatcher setting mathematics teaching, and particularly the teaching of arithmetic, as diametrically opposed to teaching for social justice. We cannot see this attitude as dated. Much more recently it was reported in the *Guardian* that Oliver Dowden, who was at that time the Conservative Party chairman, had said that a West 'confident in its values' would not be 'obsessing over pronouns or indeed seeking to decolonise mathematics.' But success in high-stakes examinations in mathematics carries with it access to higher paid careers. So differential success in mathematics across different groups of leaners can either replicate current inequalities in society or lead to greater equality. I would also argue that a confidence in mathematics allows us greater control over our lives. Perhaps an example of this might be the recent Covid-19 pandemic. A report of the Women and Equalities Committee, a standing committee of the English Government (House of Commons, 2020), noted that 'underlying inequalities made the impact of the pandemic far more severe for BAME (Black and Minority Ethnic) people than their White counterparts' (p. 3). Later on the same page the committee comments that 'It is vital that Government guidance is accessible to everyone so that individuals can stay informed and prevent contraction or transmission of the disease.' And, of course, much of this information was presented in the form of mathematical data. The more confident we were in our mathematical understandings the greater sense we could make of the data in terms of deciding how we might live our lives more safely. Here, mathematics is tightly embedded in politics. David Gillborn also reminds us of the ways in which we organise and structure our education system and within that system our mathematics classes:

> In the education system racism is figured in in the distribution of material and educational resources and even in teachers' notions of ability and motivation.
>
> (Gillborn, 2008)

Thanks to Balbir for pointing out that a more recent study that investigated setting found the detrimental impact of streaming for those in the lower sets to include most Black pupils. It also noted the impact of teacher assumptions that Black and some Brown pupils were not good at maths and put those children in lower sets (Francis et al., 2017).

What is mathematics for social justice?

Earlier in this chapter I shared a quotation from the then UK Prime Minster, Margaret Thatcher, where she suggested she did not know what anti-racist mathematics might be. Around the same time I had my first article published in the journal of the Association of Teachers of Mathematics (Cotton 1990). In fact, I wrote this partly in response to her widely publicised comment. I suggested that Anti-Racist mathematics should:

- Recognise pupils' cultural heritage.
- Develop pupils understanding of cultures other than their own.
- Counter bias in materials and teaching styles.
- Develop anti-racist attitudes through mathematics.
- Draw on pupils' own experience.
- Employ a variety of teaching styles.

The piece expanded these bullet points using examples from my own teaching and making connections to the (then) new National Curriculum for Mathematics. There is much I can agree with myself on 32 years later. In fact, I still use this list as an aide-memoire to support my writing whenever I am working on classroom materials. More recently Dixson and Anderson (2018) examined Critical Race Theory (CRT) in education. What follows is their definition for the application of CRT to education. They state that:

- CRT in education argues that racial inequity in education is the logical outcome of a system of achievement premised on competition.
- CRT in education examines the role of education policy and educational practices in the construction of racial inequity and the perpetuation of normative whiteness.
- CRT in education rejects the dominant narrative about the inherent inferiority of people of colour and the normative superiority of white people.
- CRT in education rejects ahistoricism and examines the historical linkages between contemporary educational inequity and historical patterns of racial oppression.
- CRT in education engages in intersectional analyses that recognize the ways that race is mediated by and interacts with other identity markers (i.e., gender, class, sexuality, linguistic background, and citizenship status).
- CRT in education agitates and advocates for meaningful outcomes that redress racial inequity. CRT does not merely document disparities. (p122)

I would argue that a mathematics for social justice could act at a classroom level in the ways I suggested in 1990 and at an institutional level in the ways suggested by Dixson and Anderson. In fact, CRT could be used as an analytical lens through which to examine how successful the school's approach to mathematics for social justice was. And mathematics would be needed to carry out such analysis, particularly the relative achievements of different groups of students.

What follows returns to the historical narrative lurking under the surface in this chapter. I outline five activities I have used over the last 35 years using the discussion above to make connections to my 1990 definition of anti-racist mathematics and the Dixson and Anderson application of CRT.

What can I do - what have I done?

But they're all different

When I worked at the Multicultural Centre in Leicester every school in the local authority, which then included all schools in the surrounding Leicestershire area, was required to send a member of staff for training. This teacher was expected to cascade the training to all the staff in their school. The staffing at the Centre was representative of the diversity of students in all Leicester schools. Training was always delivered by one member of staff from a White UK background and one member of staff from a Black Ethnic Minority background. Care was taken to ensure that the training was delivered collaboratively with neither of the trainers taking on a leading role.

As was common in many training sessions the day would begin with a discussion about what the participants hoped to 'learn' as a result of the training. Without fail the teachers would ask to learn about how particular groups could be supported by teachers. They would hope to achieve this understanding by 'learning more about other cultures.' So we would ask which 'cultures' the teachers wished to learn about. They would usually reply with the main religious groups in Leicester: Sikhs; Hindus; Muslims. They would also add 'African-Caribbean' as there was a large community of students with this heritage to the south of the city. This was also an opportunity to discuss language use as many White teachers would be uncertain as to the 'labels' they might use. We would emphasise how important it is to have conversations about appropriate terminology and how terminology is constantly changing. This remains the case.

The teachers were then asked what they wanted to understand better about each group. Another list was generated – perhaps 'religious beliefs,' diet, dress, 'other cultural beliefs,' 'countries of origin.' We could now create a grid and the teachers would work as a group to complete the grid by pooling their knowledge. We also provided books and other resources for further support. At some stage during the activity, I would go around the groups and ask if I could add another religion to the grid: Christianity. The teachers often looked a little confused at this.

When groups fed back on the results of their collaboration they would have been able to complete the grid and so felt as though they had met their own aims for finding out more about 'other' cultures. However it was very rare for groups to complete the 'Christianity' section. When we asked why the response was always the same, the answer would be "Well, Christians are all different, aren't they?" As this statement was made there was sudden realisation that, whilst it may be helpful to have an understanding of cultures other than the ones we are most familiar with, this very knowledge carried with it the danger of stereotyping. For the trainers this was the key message along with the realisation that we are all individuals within broader groupings and we only come to greater understandings of each other through conversation.

Relating this activity back to the earlier definitions of a mathematics for social justice and CRT in education I would argue that there was an exploration both of 'cultures other than our own' and 'an awareness of our own culture.' There is also tacit acknowledgement that White culture has been normalised and this is to be challenged. Through this activity teachers began to realise how educational policy at an institutional level was implicated in the construction of racial inequalities.

Staff at the Multicultural Centre were contractually obliged to teach in the 'summer holidays.' Summer schools were organised to support students from BAME communities who were not achieving as well as their White peers, and all staff taught at these summer schools. All staff were expected to take on a role as a school governor or a magistrate to support the struggle for racial equality at a societal level. There were also regular meetings to discuss the racism we observed (as White members of staff) or experienced (as Black and Asian members of staff) and how we could and should respond to these incidents.

Here, the role of teacher went well beyond the classroom.

Nottingham – Counting to six million

I chose the above activity as it exemplifies the argument that teaching mathematics for social justice would include teachers (of mathematics) taking roles outside of the mathematics classroom to engage in other activities which work more broadly for social justice. This would certainly be the case according to CRT. Later in my career I moved to work on a secondary mathematics postgraduate teacher education programme. I had continued my commitment to involvement outside my day-to-day work and had continued to work as a school governor and as a trustee for local community organisations. However, ideas of mathematics for social justice continued to influence my day job as well. I include this activity as several colleagues whom I taught at the time or who I shared the activity with at other workshops have told me how influential they found it.

The activity is very straightforward – I simply ask, "how long would it take to count to six million, if you counted each number out loud?" What usually follows are random guesses, then. Trying to calculate how long six million seconds is – about ten weeks. Then a realisation that, as the numbers get larger, it takes longer than a second to say each number … and so on. There is some discussion about whether we should include rests, and how long these rests should be. Eventually we will agree on a figure or more likely a range of figures. This activity also poses an alternative view of mathematics and the students' role in the classroom. The student is expected to make decisions about how they will approach a problem. There is no single approach or strategy that is expected. The outcome of the investigation will be impacted by these choices, but the student is in control. There is also no single correct answer: the choices we make will impact on the answer. But we can check the reasonableness, in collaboration with others.

At this point I share with the participants the fact that six million is the figure often used as the number of Jewish people murdered by the Nazis during the Holocaust. At this point there is a shift in the atmosphere in the room. Participants realise that they have not been engaged in a purely mathematical activity but that I am using mathematics to ask them to make sense of the world in a different way. Or perhaps to make better sense of a very large number. We talk about how difficult it is to visualise or make practical sense of very large numbers. I have used other large numbers in different contexts. The United Nations suggests that more than 15 million people were victims of the slave trade (see https://www.un.org/en/observances/decade-people-african-descent/slave-trade). 25 March is the International Day of Remembrance for these victims. Maybe on the next 25 March you could work at this activity with your students. To analyse this activity against our previous criteria, I would argue this places racism at the centre of a mathematics lesson and though discussion could develop anti-racist attitudes. I would also argue that it places racial inequalities at the centre of the content of the mathematics curriculum too. (For a more detailed discussion of this activity see Noble (2023). Jim Noble was a student of mine back in the nineties when I used it on my mathematics PGCE course and has used it with every class he has taught ever since.)

What is normal?

As a way of reflecting further on the definition of CRT as the 'perpetuation of normative Whiteness' and how we might offer activities which might encourage social activism I will share an activity that I first used as an introductory activity at an Association of Teachers of Mathematics conference. The first evening of the conference always invites all participants to work together on a piece of mathematics. Doing mathematics as a collaborative activity, here, is seen as a way of developing the collaborative and community building ethos that underpins the conference.

I had been using a book called *If the world were a village of 100 people* in classrooms, and this inspired an opening activity. There were approximately 200 people in the large room. I asked a series of questions and asked the participants to arrange themselves in groups in the room to represent different sets of data. The first set of data was the percentage of the population of the world that live in North America, South America, Europe, Africa, Asia, and Australasia. After much discussion about which countries would constitute which region and relative populations, the participants settled onto a virtual world map. I then shared the percentages stated in *If the world were a village* .... These are

North America	5
South America	8
Europe	12
Africa	13
Asia	61
Oceania	1

I have used this particular activity many times in many parts of the world. It is usual that people overestimate the percentage of the world population in both North America and Africa. We wondered why this might be. Perhaps media reports of over population in Africa bias our thinking; maybe the huge influence of the USA in our media leads us to think a large proportion of the world's population lives there. This begins to question our understanding of the world and how everyday 'norms' become embedded in our thinking. (For a more developed discussion of using *If the world were a village of 100 people* see page 99.)

We moved on to explore other data. The relative populations of England, Wales, Scotland, and Northern Ireland; the percentages of the UK population in different age bands and then the ethnic make-up of the UK population. This showed a lack of knowledge of the ethnographic make-up of the UK, even in a group of people who would regard themselves as well educated. And it revealed misconceptions – particularly around the number of people in different ethnic groups. There was a huge overestimation of these numbers, perhaps still influenced by negative press headlines. I think we were all surprised, although I shared with the group a report from Refugee Action (2012) which stated that over 50% of respondents to their survey had overestimated the number of immigrants in the UK. This, in turn, led to a discussion about how we might define 'immigrant.' The Refugee Action survey suggested that about 40% of respondents thought about 10% of the UK population were refugees when the figure in 2012 was less than 0.4%. Within our group of 200 this was represented by one-quarter of a person!

The next stage again drew on data, this time data gathered from all the participants at the conference. As participants registered, we asked them to complete a questionnaire. This asked for information on participants: age; gender; ethnicity; age group of which they were a teacher; distance travelled to the conference; mode of travel to the conference; and country of birth. Prior to the session we had found the modal range, or category, for each of these items. One by one I read out the modal range from a category which I selected randomly. Any participant who was not in the modal range sat down. This was repeated until only one person remained standing – the 'most normal' person in the room. This activity successfully questioned the idea of 'normal.' Indeed, many participants came up to me throughout the conference saying that they had noticed themselves avoiding using the word 'normal' after the activity.

The first time that mathematics has meant anything

I am now working at Leeds Metropolitan University. I am the Head of School but have insisted that I carry on teaching. Maybe because I enjoy it. Maybe because I hope I can model ways of working that I want to encourage. I am teaching a whole-cohort lecture to around 100 second-year undergraduates on a primary teacher education programme. As part of the lecture, I ask students to work in small groups on the following piece of mathematics.

How many boxes measuring 50cm × 50cm × 2m could you fit in a space measuring 2m × 2m × 35m?

After working on the calculation we discussed the mathematics involved. We discussed how we could use this activity to teach specific skills and, in particular, the range of diagrams that students had used to support them in their calculations. I then shared this image (Figure 1.1) and text. It is commonly known as 'The Brooks Slave Ship.'

By April 1787, the diagram was widely known across the UK, appearing in newspapers, pamphlets, books and even posters in coffee houses and pubs. An image had rarely been used as a propaganda tool in this way before and it proved to be very effective in raising awareness about the evils of the slave trade

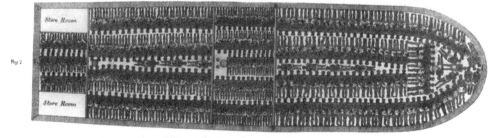

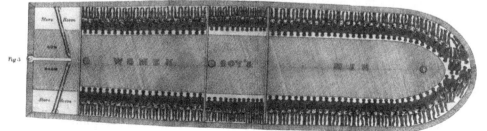

Figure 1.1 The Brooks Slave Ship.

As with the counting to six million activity, the atmosphere in the lecture theatre changed as students came to the realisation that the calculation they had worked on modelled calculations owners of slave ships must have carried out. And how those involved in and profiting from the Slave Trade could only function by seeing fellow human beings as figures in a calculation.

Later that morning one of the few Black students in the group poked her head round my office door. "Thanks for that session this morning," she said, "It's the first time I have ever really connected with mathematics."

If you came all that way of course you would try to cross the Channel

Whilst the main aim for the chapters in this opening section has been to offer a theoretical overview of social justice and mathematics education it seemed important to exemplify the theory with exemplars drawn from across my personal educational journey. The Association of Teachers of Mathematics (ATM) has been a constant on this journey. I first joined in 1981 as a beginning teacher and have drawn on their resources throughout my career. This final example for this chapter, which is developed in more detail in Section 2 of this book, draws on a workshop from a recent ATM Easter Conference. This final example again emphasises that mathematics can challenge racist narratives. I completed the first draft of this chapter on 1 November 2022. Yesterday, the Home Secretary for the English Government referred to the numbers of refugees arriving in small boats on the South Coast as an "invasion." Such inflammatory language was followed by a fire-bomb attack on a 'processing centre' for those seeking asylum in England.

The workshop explored the refugee journey from Syria to Calais. After calculating how long it would take to walk from Aleppo to Calais, participants were given the data on the proportions of refugees in each country on such a journey. The vast majority of refugees remain in the countries which neighbour Syria. At the time of the workshop less than 0.5% of the refugees fleeing Syria travelled as far as Calais. The group had created a scale map of the journey and 100 clay figures that they had modelled were placed on the map to represent the percentage of the refugees in each country. The group refused to pull apart one of their 'people' but agreed that the single person placed at the Channel was an over-estimate. The scale map of the journey on the floor of the large room we were working in stretched most of the way across the room along a diagonal. When we calculated the width of the channel to the same scale it approximated to the width of the tape measure we had been using. One of the participants stood back, looked at the journey, looked at the solitary figure placed by the tape measure and said, with tears in his eyes, "Well, if you had travelled all that way, of course you would try to cross the Channel."

Conclusion

My aim in this chapter has been to use my personal educational journey to offer a theo-retical exploration of a mathematics education for social justice and exemplify these theo-retical ideas through activities that I have used in a variety of contexts with a variety of learners. It is the task of the second section of the book to offer a more fully developed set of activities for readers to explore in their own contexts.

But why should teachers, why should readers of this book, work towards a mathematics education for social justice? I choose to end this chapter with a vision for education from a colleague, Maresa MacKeith. These are the closing paragraphs of a piece she wrote originally for a collection on ethics and mathematics education and then for a special issue of *Mathematics Teaching*.

> My vision is to have a world where we all know how to listen to each other and care for each other. To get there, we need to grow up with each other. It therefore makes sense to have schools where we all learn together. Many of us have additional needs to the basic human needs for food, water, shelter, love and belonging. Some of us have physical needs we cannot meet by ourselves, such as eating, getting dressed or communicating. Others of us have additional needs for help with vision or hearing, and many of us have ways of learning that are not always understood.
>
> All these needs could be catered for in ordinary life. They are all ordinary needs in the spectrum of diversity. At present there are artificial dividing lines between what are seen as 'ordinary needs,' additional needs' and 'special needs.' One definition of a 'special need' is that we do not know how to meet it, so we hide it away, and the person having the need becomes isolated from the ordinary world.
>
> My vision is that we create a system of learning that prioritises our relationships with each other, rather than how we achieve in competition with each other. In that way we could learn about each other's needs, as *ordinary* needs, which we could find ways of meeting. I think that within a generation of having a learning system without competition, we could have a world where people are valued for what they can give, which is ultimately who they are. Those who need the most care could be seen as giving the opportunity to others to get close and understand the commonality of vulnerability. This, in turn, could make us all feel safe about our own vulnerability. Real inclusion, for me, is about the promotion of peace and equality.
>
> (MacKeith, 2021)

Maresa communicates using 'facilitated communication.' A piece of card with a keyboard printed on it sits on her knee as she sits in her wheelchair. A personal assistant holds her hand and feels as she moves towards each letter to spell out words. When Maresa was 14 and had spent most of her time isolated in empty classrooms throughout her schooling, her mother sensed that she was trying to communicate and created the keyboard. The first words Maresa spelled out were,

> Why has it taken you so long?

I opened this chapter with a vignette from 1982. It is now 2022. Forty years. Why is it taking us so long?

References

Cotton, T. (1990) Anti-racist mathematics teaching and the national curriculum. *Mathematics Teaching*, No. 132, pp. 22-25.

Dixson, A. D. and Anderson, C. R. (2018) Where are we? Critical race theory in education 20 years later. *Peabody Journal of Education*, Vol. 93, No. 1, pp. 121-131. London: Taylor and Francis.

Gillborn, D. (2008) *Racism and Education: Coincidence or Conspiracy.* London: Routledge.

House of Commons (2020) *Unequal Impact? Coronavirus and BAME People: Third Report of Session 2019–21.* https://committees.parliament.uk/publications/3965/documents/39887/default/. Accessed 12th October 2022.

MacKeith, M. (2021) Breaking the cycle of isolation and ignorance. *Mathematics Teaching 279.* Derby: The Association of Teachers of Mathematics.

Noble, J. (2023) *Mathematics Lessons to Look Forward To: 20 Favourite Activities and Themes for Teaching Ages 9 to 16.* Didcot: Routledge.

Patel, P. (2022) *The Antiracist Educator.* London: Sage.

Refugee Action (2012) *More than Half of the British Public Overestimate Number of Immigrants in the UK.* https://www.refugee-action.org.uk/half-british-public-overestimate-number-immigrants-uk/#:~:text=Only%20one%20in%20eight%20people,of%20immigrants%20in%20the%20UK. Accessed 27 October 2022.

Before we move into a more mathematics-specific exploration with Pete, take a moment to reflect on moments in your personal history, in and out of education, which have impacted on your thinking about a mathematics education for social justice. Do you have stories you can tell similar to those which opened this chapter?

My personal history in education for social justice: two stories

Key readings

A handbook of narrative inquiry by Jean Clandinin. Sage Publications, London.

If you are interested in the narrative approach that I have taken in this chapter, then this book offers a theoretical background for you. I would recommend it for anyone interested in developing their own research through studying, rigorously, the stories we tell about our lives.

"Breaking the cycle of isolation and ignorance" by Maresa MacKeith in *Mathematics Teaching 279*. Derby: The Association of Teachers of Mathematics.

Maresa offers a powerful and persuasive view about what education could be like. If schools worked towards her vision they would be better places for all learners. I also hope that you might be tempted to join the Association of Teachers of Mathematics. I think there will be much in their journal, *Mathematics Teaching*, to interest you.

Mathematics lessons to look forward to: 20 favourite activities and themes for teaching ages 9 to 16 by Jim Noble. Routledge, London.

This book is not explicitly focused on social justice but is focused on the joy that teaching mathematics can bring. Anne Watson has talked about the importance of both caring for the learners we teach and the mathematics we share with them. This book has care of mathematics at its heart.

2 The mathematics curriculum and concerns for social justice

Pete Wright

Introduction

Completing a PGCE Mathematics course and starting out as a secondary mathematics teacher in 1987 prompted me to reflect critically on my own experiences as a mathematics learner (having studied mathematics up to degree level). At the time, I had naively assumed that the mathematics I had already learnt, together with the pedagogical strategies I would learn on the PGCE course, would prepare me fully for the role of secondary school mathematics teacher. Luckily, I was prompted on the PGCE course to re-examine my own prior assumptions about mathematics, which led to two revelations in my thinking.

Firstly, I began to appreciate for the first time the fallible and value-laden nature of mathematics, that is, that the development of the discipline over time was dependent on argument and debate amongst the community of mathematicians. My eyes were opened to how powerful mathematical knowledge could be used to pursue both desirable and undesirable outcomes, including presenting a Eurocentric view of the subject which ignores contributions from different cultural and philosophical perspectives.

Secondly, teaching in schools in relatively deprived areas of inner-city London helped me to realise how students face an unlevel playing field in learning mathematics. I began to appreciate the extent to which my own relatively privileged background gave me a head start in developing positive dispositions towards learning the powerful mathematics knowledge that would extend my horizons. I contrasted this with the high levels of disengagement and alienation from mathematics I encountered amongst many students in the classroom, particularly those from marginalised groups.

These experiences prompted me to continue to ask questions related to the nature of mathematics, and the inequitable challenges faced by some learners, during my 15 years as a classroom teacher, seven years as a teacher educator and other time spent as a curriculum developer and local authority consultant. These questions are crucial to consider in striving to decolonise the mathematics curriculum, move towards a more socially just mathematics curriculum and widen access to a high-quality mathematics education for all students.

The nature of school mathematics

Mathematics as a discipline has developed over millennia prompted by the need for humans to survive and flourish in their local environments. The earliest mathematics evolved from

DOI: 10.4324/9781003361466-3

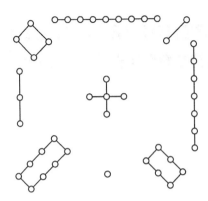

Figure 2.1 Lo Shu magic square, attributed to Ts'ai Yuan-Ting, China, 12th Century (SMILE Mathematics, 2001, p. 10)

recognising patterns in the position and movement of the sun, moon and stars that helped farmers to predict the seasons and hence identify the best time to plant crops (Rogers, 2014). Babylonian astronomers (circa 1600 BCE) adopted 360 days as the length of a year and established 360 degrees in a circle by calculating that the sun moves by about 1 degree relative to the stars each day. By 700 BCE, they had developed a theory for the motion of the planets and by 500 BCE they had adopted 12 months (based on a twelve-constellation zodiac) of 30 days each in a year. Mathematics knowledge was generated by different cultures and peoples from all around the world including, in the case of generating magic squares, China (see Figure 2.1) and Nigeria (see Figure 2.2), and, in the case of the 'Babylonian Algorithm' (see below), from modern-day Iraq (you might like to think about whether it always works and why).

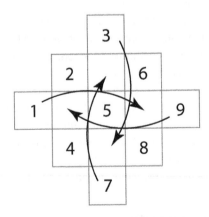

Figure 2.2 Method of generating magic square, attributed to Muhammad ibn Muhammad, Northern Nigeria, 1732 (SMILE Mathematics, 2001, p. 16)

Babylonian Algorithm (Mesopotamia, circa 500 BCE) for finding two numbers, given their sum and product:

> Take half the sum, square it, from this square subtract the product, find the square root of the result, and add or subtract this result to half the sum, to find the two numbers.

(Rogers, 2014, p. 110)

Various mathematical ideas reappeared in different parts of the world as they were shared through ancient trading routes. Many of these ideas have been attributed to European mathematicians who may have been the first to formalise them into written manuscripts. Applications of what is known nowadays as 'Pythagoras' Theorem' have been identified in Northern India (Sulbasutras, circa 800–600 BCE) and Egypt (Hieroglyphics, circa 2560 BCE) long before they were attributed to Pythagoras (Rogers, 2014). The Shulba Sutras (or Śulbasūtras) are Vedic texts which contain discussion and non-axiomatic demonstrations of cases of the theorem and 'Pythagorean triples.' Egyptian engineers used a 3-4-5 'Pythagorean triple' to construct right angles by knotting a rope into 12 sections that stretched out to produce a 3-4-5 triangle. It is interesting to note that Pythagoras (569-500 BCE) travelled widely in Egypt where he learnt mathematics. There are many more examples of mathematical ideas originating from other parts of the world being appropriated by European mathematicians, e.g., Pascal's triangle which originated in China.

Mathematics has been practised around the world for different purposes, often spiritual and aesthetic in nature. Geometric patterns have been used widely in Islamic architectural design, e.g., in tiling patterns in the Alhambra (a Moorish palace in Granada, Spain), and in the design of Rangoli patterns (used to celebrate festivals) and Yantras (used for meditation purposes) in India and other parts of the world. Indian and Chinese cultures traditionally had a different style of reasoning to Western mathematics, which "aims for deeper understanding rather than 'proof,' and generalisation rather than abstraction" (Rogers, 2014, p. 117). However, as Western European powers colonised much of the world, schools and curricula became vehicles for the colonial powers to maintain control over the people they ruled over. Formal schooling replaced more traditional methods of passing on knowledge from one generation to the next with those lucky enough to attend (schools were only made available to an indigenous elite) being trained to work in the interests of the colonial administration. Different mathematical ideas and applications practised by peoples around the world became devalued and the origin of mathematical ideas often became completely hidden in an increasingly abstract and formalised Western school curriculum (Rogers, 2014).

The 'Euclidean' version of mathematics, based on the absolutist view of mathematics as a system of logic, deduction and truth, gained an increasingly privileged position within the Western school curriculum. Meanwhile, the fallibilist view, which recognises how mathematical knowledge (including that which is subsequently proved formally) is generated through a process of inquiry, conjecture and peer scrutiny amongst humans, became increasingly ignored (Ernest, 1991). As a consequence, Boaler (2009) argues that students' experiences of school mathematics are impoverished because they are so far removed from the work of real mathematicians, leading to widespread disaffection amongst students who see the subject as lacking meaning and relevance.

This 'Euclidean' version of mathematics, which was dominant in Europe in the 16th and 17th centuries, was imposed on the rest of the world through the process of colonialisation (D'Ambrosio, 2006). This accompanied the replacement of local culture, religion, language and communal values with those of an increasingly individualistic and materialistic Western Europe, often dictated by the commercial and militaristic needs of capitalist economies (D'Ambrosio, 2008). The Industrial Revolution and the rise of capitalism compounded the situation with education, both in the colonising powers and colonised countries, becoming more geared towards producing docile and compliant workers with the skills needed to service the economy (Gutstein, 2006; Skovsmose, 2011). The class system that permeated Western Europe and North America ensured that only a privileged minority (destined to become leaders) received the type of high-quality education needed to become independent decision makers and problem solvers.

The function of the school curriculum as a means for powerful groups to dominate others has survived colonialism with many countries that gained independence modelling their education policies on those of the former colonisers. This was apparent to me in the three years I spent in the 1990s teaching mathematics at a rural girls' school in Kenya (which gained its independence in 1963, before I was born) to students from families with relatively modest incomes (the poorest families could not afford to send their daughters to secondary school). The layout of the classrooms was modelled on those that might have been commonly found in schools in Victorian England, and corporal punishment was commonplace. Textbooks were the main pedagogical tool and, despite being written by Kenyan authors, these frequently reflected Western cultural contexts rather than local contexts. For instance, the probability chapter of the book in use at the school where I taught had multiple references to playing cards, dice games and spinners with which the students had very little familiarity.

In modern-day capitalist economies, politicians tend to prioritise the need for education to contribute towards economic growth and national competitiveness and appear less concerned about the impact of education on the welfare of individual learners or the common good of society. In England, over the past 35 years, the increasing involvement of politicians in educational policy making has led to a shift towards curriculum content being determined by the needs of the economy, rather than educational discourses (Wright, 2012). Increased spending on mathematics education has been justified by individuals' higher levels of wealth creation and ability to contribute towards economic growth; hence financial literacy is promoted at the expense of mathematical agency. The mathematics curriculum needs to move away from one primarily determined by the needs of employers and wealth creation, towards one that enables all learners to develop the powerful knowledge they need to contribute actively towards all aspects of society.

School mathematics and inequity

Many researchers have drawn attention to the persistent correlation between family wealth and attainment and participation in mathematics (Boaler, Altendorf, & Kent, 2011). Teach First (2019) highlighted how 38% of students living in the poorest postcodes in England failed to reach Grade 4 (defined as a 'standard pass' by the Department for Education) in GCSE Mathematics, compared with 20% of students from the richest postcodes. Similarly, in 2019, 13% of the poorest students attained the top three grades (7, 8 or 9) in GCSE Mathematics, compared with 26% of the richest students. Mathematics acts as a 'critical filter' with examination results in mathematics (along with English) determining children's future opportunities for accessing higher status education courses and better-paid employment. Therefore, these differences in achievement serve to limit the social mobility of children from poorer backgrounds. Hence, mathematics makes a major contribution to the reproductive function of schools in perpetuating the existing unequal power relations within society and in reproducing inequity from one generation to another (Jorgensen, Gates, & Roper, 2014).

Differences in attainment based on socio-economic status appear to be larger than those based on other characteristics. For example, the gender difference in 2021 was modest with 56% of girls achieving Grade 5 or above in English and mathematics compared with 48% of boys. Whilst the percentage of all students achieving this threshold was 52%, the figure for White students was 51%, for Black students 49%, and for Asian students 61%. Thus, socio-economic background continues to be the strongest factor affecting students' achievement in school mathematics in England (Jorgensen, 2016), despite numerous policies designed to address this attainment gap such as the 'pupil premium' introduced in 2011. To fully understand these attainment differences, it is necessary to look carefully at structural causes of inequality such as the tendency for students from poorer backgrounds to receive a lower quality mathematics education.

Despite numerous calls from mathematics educators, over the past 30 years or more, for a more engaging curriculum, focusing on problem-solving and sense-making rather than answer-getting (Boaler, 2009; Schoenfeld, 2012; Swan, 2006), mathematics teaching appears to have changed very little. Many mathematics lessons are still characterised by the teacher modelling a closed mathematical method or procedure to students, who are then given a series of almost identical closed exercises to answer before being tested on their understanding (or more accurately their ability to recall the methods). Skovsmose (2011) describes how this 'exercise paradigm,' which is evident in mathematics lessons throughout the world, cultivates a 'prescription readiness' in students, thus preparing them for work practices which involve following instructions unquestioningly. Similarly, Gutstein (2006, p. 10) argues that such a disempowering mathematics curriculum reflects the need to produce low-skilled compliant and obedient workers to service the needs of capitalist economies. Perhaps one reason why mathematics teaching has proved to be highly resistant to change is that the current system serves the interests of powerful groups within society, many of whom have navigated the system with a certain amount of success. Most mathematics teachers have themselves been successful learners of mathematics, and may therefore be less invested in seeking change (Wright, 2021).

Indeed, teacher-centred approaches, including 'direct instruction,' 'explicit instruction,' and 'mathematics mastery,' have enjoyed something of a resurgence in popularity in England over recent years (Wright, Fejzo, & Carvalho, 2022). These approaches are based on the premise that learning is most effective when teachers present a series of mathematical concepts in a highly structured and unambiguous way. Examples are carefully selected and explained in sequence, avoiding cognitive overload by minimising conceptual steps, thus enabling learners to draw correct inferences. The emphasis is on maintaining a fast pace, providing regular guided practice to consolidate learning, and using routine testing to correct students' errors (Doabler & Fien, 2013; Rosenshine, 2012). However, teacher-centred approaches such as these have been shown to cause widespread damage to students' engagement with mathematics, leading to increasing levels of anxiety towards, and alienation from the subject (Foster, 2013; Hudson, 2018; Williams & Choudry, 2016). They also prevent students from developing mathematical agency by discouraging them from taking any responsibility for their own learning or making decisions about the direction it might take.

Given that teacher-centred approaches such as those described above are often advocated primarily for use with lower attaining students and those from disadvantaged backgrounds (Doabler & Fien, 2013), this has worrying implications for gaps in attainment and equity of access to high-quality mathematics teaching. These concerns are exacerbated by the predominance of setting within schools in England (in which students are grouped together according to prior attainment), sometimes from a very early age, with a disproportionate number of students from lower socio-economic groups being placed in lower sets (Taylor et al., 2017). Research has shown that students placed in lower sets are more likely to receive a more prescriptive and lower quality of teaching, and to be exposed to more limited curriculum content, thus denying them the possibility of catching up with their peers at a later stage (Wilkinson & Penney, 2014).

Carr (2003) warns of the danger of implementing research findings based solely on 'what works' protocols, without taking into consideration wider educational principles. He argues that, even if there was evidence to suggest that direct instruction and setting might result in higher attainment for some students (which is questionable), this should be outweighed by legitimate concerns over students' wellbeing, equity, and social justice. He draws a parallel to corporal punishment which, although it might be shown to improve behaviour, is now considered morally indefensible in many parts of the world. It is important for teachers to take account of empirical research findings. However, they should resist pressure to apply recommendations derived from these studies in a technical and uncritical way, for example through the setting of targets as part of performance management processes within schools (Hammersley, 2004). Instead, they should exercise principled reflection in determining whether these recommendations are ethically sound or morally justified (Carr, 2003). Making judgements about 'what works' is meaningless without considering purpose, i.e., what it is that implementing the recommendations is aiming to achieve. Biesta (2015) highlights the imperative for teachers to consider the broader educational aims of enculturating children into society and empowering them to interact with the world, alongside the narrower aims of acquiring knowledge, skills and dispositions, when making judgements.

Accepting setting as beneficial to students' learning without question is one of several 'discourses of inequity' permeating the field of mathematics education, by which I mean assumptions and beliefs that have come to be accepted by the majority of mathematics teachers as true, but which are not founded on research evidence or critical reflections on practice (Francis et al., 2017). During my career in mathematics education, there have been countless occasions when I have overheard comments, from teachers of mathematics and other subjects, parents, students and student teachers, which reinforce one or more of these 'discourses of inequity.' These include beliefs that mathematics is neutral and value-free, mathematical ability is an innate gift or talent, the mathematics classroom is a level playing field, and success in mathematics is all about getting as many correct answers as possible in the shortest possible time. I would like to think that I have challenged these comments wherever I could, although I am sure I have missed many opportunities to do so and may well have been guilty of inadvertently making such comments myself. However, most of the time these 'discourses of inequity' are either reinforced by school policies or go unchallenged due to pressures faced by teachers, including excessive workload, pressure to cover excessive curriculum content, performance management of teachers and high-stakes examinations.

Transforming the mathematics curriculum

In moving towards a more empowering and socially just mathematics curriculum, attention needs to be given not just to what is taught in mathematics classrooms but also to how it is taught. The content of the curriculum needs to be reviewed to ensure that it reflects the wide diversity of cultural and philosophical perspectives that have contributed towards the development of mathematics as a discipline. Questions such as 'What is mathematics?' and 'How was mathematics developed?' and 'What is the purpose of mathematics?' need to become a routine part of discussions in mathematics classrooms. This will enable more learners to see the subject as meaningful and relevant to their own lives and to appreciate its fallible nature. Appreciating how mathematics has been developed by human beings to make sense of their everyday experiences and solve real-life problems will encourage students to engage more with the subject and lead to lower levels of mathematics anxiety and alienation (Rogers, 2014).

Recent historical events, including the Covid-19 pandemic, the 2020 US presidential election and the Brexit referendum, have demonstrated how statistics can be used to promote particular viewpoints, and how misleading media reports and adverts can influence the voting habits and behaviour of millions of people. There is a growing appreciation of how numbers and data can be presented and represented in different ways in order to portray very different pictures of a situation. This highlights the need for citizens to develop a critical understanding of mathematics and to be willing to question the mathematics they encounter as part of arguments presented to them, so that they can avoid being exploited by others and exercise their democratic rights in an informed way.

International educational policy-making organisations (OECD, 2018; UNESCO, 2015) are increasingly calling for a review of school curricula with a greater focus on developing the individual knowledge and skills, critical understanding, and collective agency, that are required to tackle the environmental, economic, and social challenges facing our global society. Mathematical understanding has a crucial role to play in this process as it underpins so many issues facing the world, such as climate change, misinformation, inequality, global trade and democracy. For learners to be able to change the future direction of the world, education must be genuinely empowering, with students' increased levels of under-standing accompanied by a growing appreciation of their own situation and place within society (Freire, 1974). Mathematics can play a central role within a school curriculum that aims to address the social, economic and environmental challenges we face as a global soci-ety. To make this happen, students need to learn how to use mathematical ideas effectively in generating their own arguments for change.

My research career began during my final year of teaching when I had the opportunity to begin my doctoral studies (in 2010). I soon became aware of the abundance of theoreti-cal papers in the world of academia that relate the teaching of mathematics to issues of equality and social justice. However, I noticed that there was relatively little guidance on what a socially just mathematics curriculum might look like in practice. Given my own inter-ests in teaching mathematics and issues of equity and social justice, and my experience of working with practising teachers in developing their practice and curriculum materials, it seemed natural to focus my research on bridging this gap between theory and practice. In collaboration with teacher researchers, I have conducted three research projects that have identified four essential elements of mathematics teaching for social justice:

- Employ collaborative, discursive, problem-solving, and problem-posing pedagogies which promote mathematical sense-making and the engagement of all learners with mathematics.
- Promote mathematical inquiries that resonate with learners' real-life experiences and that help them develop greater understanding of their social, cultural, political, and economic situations.
- Facilitate mathematical investigations that develop learners' individual and collective agency, enabling them to take part in future social action for the public good.
- Challenge common myths surrounding school mathematics, expose processes that lead to the marginalisation of some learners, and open up to scrutiny what it means to be successful.

You may find it interesting to compare this schema with the model for anti-racist teaching shared by Tony on page 8. The findings from my research (Wright, 2016a; Wright, 2021; Wright, Fejzo, & Carvalho, 2022) have demonstrated how teaching approaches based on these principles can have a significant impact on students' mathematical engagement and agency, and their appreciation of what it takes to be successful in the mathematics classroom, particularly for those students from disadvantaged backgrounds and those who were previously alienated from mathematics. A collection of teaching ideas and activities developed through these projects can be found in a book entitled *Teaching Mathematics for Social Justice: Meaningful Projects for the Secondary Mathematics Classroom* (Wright, 2016b)

Many of the teachers who participated in these research projects showed an initial hesita-tion to devote significant curriculum time to the types of teaching approaches and learning activities described above. This is understandable given the pressure to prepare students for high-stakes mathematics exams that can determine the future life opportunities available to them, which is seen as particularly important for those from disadvantaged backgrounds. However, after witnessing the impact of providing a more meaningful mathematical curriculum and cultivating agency on students' engagement with mathematics, the teacher researchers became more and more enthusiastic about adopting these new practices. Advocates of 'self-determination theory,' including Ryan and Deci (2020), highlight the importance of teachers providing greater levels of support to students in becoming autonomous learners. They argue that this is more likely to result in students recognising learning activities as valuable and worthwhile, hence increasing their levels of intrinsic motivation, confidence, and self-esteem, leading ultimately to higher levels of attainment and participation.

My research has also highlighted the potential of adopting a participatory action research (PAR) methodology for enhancing teachers' agency, encouraging them to reflect critically on existing practice, and enabling them to overcome constraints they face in addressing social justice in the mathematics classroom. More conventional approaches to research have been criticised for claiming to be objective and bias-free, thus ignoring the power-relationships that permeate the field of mathematics education (Valero, 2004), and being conducted in settings that do not reflect typical classroom situations (Skovsmose, 2011). This might explain why they have had little impact on addressing issues of inequity in the mathematics classroom. In contrast, PAR is overtly political in nature, focuses on challenging existing norms and assumptions underlying practice, and seeks to bring about positive social change (Brydon-Miller & Maguire, 2009). It involves genuine collaboration between academic researchers and teacher researchers, recognising teachers' in-depth knowledge of students and the classroom situation (Atweh, 2004). It can lead to transformations in teachers' thinking and classroom practice in contrast to other models of professional learning which neglect teacher agency, the development of teacher identity and collaborative modes of professional development (Boylan, Coldwell, Maxwell, & Jordan, 2018).

Many new entrants to the teaching profession, including mathematics teachers, share an enthusiasm for a humanistic vision of education that promotes human rights, diversity, respect, equality, and social justice. This can be seen from the comments by Manjinders' students in the last chapter in this section. However, it is too easy to lose sight of these ideals given the constraints teachers face on a day-to-day basis, including the high-stakes nature of examinations, increasing levels of workload, commercialisation, and performativity in schools. Such pressures can result in teachers feeling obliged to conform to existing practices and avoiding initiating change or experimenting with 'high-risk' teaching strategies in their classrooms. Biesta (2021) argues for a 'world-centred' education, in which teachers 'point' (or direct) students' attention towards the world in which they live. An education that enables future generations to make sense of the world, and what the world demands of them, is vital given the increasing social, economic, and environmental challenges facing global society. I have already highlighted how the mathematics curriculum and mathematics teachers have an important role to play in such a 'world-centred' education.

Despite the constraints that they face, teachers occupy a crucial position as agents of change given that those in privileged positions (including many policy makers) are unlikely to initiate change that erodes their own power. Socially just mathematics teachers and their allies need to establish networks and mutual-support mechanisms that will enable them to overcome the multitude of constraints they face in implementing the strategies advocated in this book. They need to engage in principled and critical reflection on existing thinking and classroom practice. They need to challenge discourses of inequity they encounter and take account of wider purposes of education that relate to empowering the next generation to bring about a better, safer and more just world for themselves and for others. In doing so, they will begin to address some of the tensions in their professional identities as they re-engage with the reasons why they came into teaching in the first place. Evidence from the collaborative research I have conducted with teacher researchers demonstrates that once they have started to do this, the increased levels of agency, engagement, and mathematical achievement exhibited by their students will only encourage other teachers to climb on board as their joint enterprise gathers momentum.

References

Atweh, B. (2004). Understanding for change and changing for understanding: Praxis between practice and theory through action research in mathematics education. In P. Valero & R. Zevenbergen (Eds.), *Researching the socio-political dimensions of mathematics education* (pp. 187-205). Dordrecht: Kluwer.

Biesta, G. (2015). What is education for? On good education, teacher judgement, and educational professionalism. *European Journal of Education, 50*(1), 75-87.

Biesta, G. (2021). *World-centred education: A view for the present.* New York: Routledge.

Boaler, J. (2009). *The elephant in the classroom: Helping children learn and love maths.* London: Souvenir Press.

Boaler, J., Altendorf, L., & Kent, G. (2011). Mathematics and science inequalities in the United Kingdom: When elitism, sexism and culture collide. *Oxford Review of Education, 37*(4), 457-484.

Boylan, M., Coldwell, M., Maxwell, B., & Jordan, J. (2018). Rethinking models of professional learning as tools: A conceptual analysis to inform research and practice. *Professional Development in Education, 44*(1), 120-130.

Brydon-Miller, M., & Maguire, P. (2009). Participatory action research: Contributions to the development of practitioner inquiry in education. *Educational Action Research, 16*(1), 79-93.

Carr, D. (2003). *Making sense of education: An introduction to the philosophy and theory of education and teaching.* London: Routledge.

D'Ambrosio, U. (2006). *Ethnomathematics: Link between traditions and modernity.* Rotterdam: Sense Publishers.

D'Ambrosio, U. (2008). Peace, social justice and ethnomathematics. In B. Sriraman (Ed.), *International perspectives on social justice in mathematics education* (pp. 37-50). Charlotte, NC: Information Age Publishing.

Doabler, C., & Fien, H. (2013). Explicit mathematics instruction: What teachers can do for teaching students with mathematics difficulties. *Intervention in School and Clinic, 48*(5), 276-285.

Ernest, P. (1991). *The philosophy of mathematics education.* London: Falmer Press.

Foster, C. (2013). Resisting reductionism in mathematics pedagogy. *The Curriculum Journal, 24*(4), 565-585.

Francis, B., Archer, L., Hodgen, J., Pepper, D., Taylor, B., & Travers, M.-C. (2017). Exploring the relative lack of impact of research on 'ability grouping' in England: A discourse analytic account. *Cambridge Journal of Education, 47*(1), 1-17.

Freire, P. (1974). *Education for critical consciousness.* London: Sheed & Ward.

Gutstein, E. (2006). *Reading and writing the world with mathematics: Toward a pedagogy for social justice.* New York: Routledge.

Hammersley, M. (2004). Some questions about evidence-based practice in education. In G. Thomas & R. Pring (Eds.), *Evidence-based practice in education* (pp. 133-149). Maidenhead: Open University Press.

Hudson, B. (2018). Powerful knowledge and epistemic quality in school mathematics. *London Review of Education, 16*(3), 384-397.

Jorgensen, R. (2016). The elephant in the room: Equity, social class, and mathematics. In P. Ernest, B. Sriraman, & N. Ernest (Eds.), *Critical mathematics education: Theory, practice and reality* (pp. 127-146). Charlotte, NC: Information Age Publishing.

Jorgensen, R., Gates, P., & Roper, V. (2014). Structural exclusion through school mathematics: Using Bourdieu to understand mathematics as a social practice. *Educational Studies in Mathematics, 87,* 221-239.

OECD. (2018). *The future of education and skills: Education 2030.* Paris: Directorate for Education and Skills – Organisation for Economic Co-operation and Development (OECD).

Rogers, L. (2014). History of mathematics in and for the curriculum. In D. Leslie & H. Mendick (Eds.), *Debates in mathematics education* (pp. 106-122). Abingdon: Routledge.

Rosenshine, B. (2012). Principles of instruction. *American Educator, 36*(1), 12-19, 39.

Ryan, R., & Deci, E. (2020). Intrinsic and extrinsic motivation from a self-determination theory perspective: Definitions, theory, practices, and future directions. *Contemporary Educational Psychology, 61,* 1-11.

Schoenfeld, A. (2012). Problematizing the didactic triangle. *ZDM Mathematics Education, 44*(5), 587-599.

Skovsmose, O. (2011). *An invitation to critical mathematics education.* Rotterdam: Sense Publishers.

SMILE Mathematics. (2001). *Bridging units from SMILE mathematics.* London: RBKC SMILE Mathematics.

Swan, M. (2006). *Collaborative learning in mathematics: A challenge to our beliefs and practices.* Leicester: National Institute of Adult Continuing Education.

Taylor, B., Francis, B., Archer, L., Hodgen, J., Pepper, D. T., & Travers, M. (2017). Factors deterring schools from mixed attainment teaching practice. *Pedagogy, Culture and Society, 25*(3), 327-345.

Teach First. (2019, August 21). *GCSE subjects reveal stark unfairness faced by disadvantaged pupils.* Retrieved August 18th, 2022, from Teach First Press Releases: https://www.teachfirst.org.uk/press-release/New-investigation-into-GCSE-subjects-reveals-the-stark-extent-that-disadvantaged-pupils-are-being-left-behind

UNESCO. (2015). *Rethinking education: Towards a global common good?* Paris: United Nations Educational, Scientific and Cultural Organisation.

Valero, P. (2004). Socio-political perspectives on mathematics education. In P. Valero & R. Zevenbergen (Eds.), *Researching the socio-political dimensions of mathematics education* (pp. 5-23). Dordrecht: Kluwer Academic Publishers.

Wilkinson, S., & Penney, D. (2014). The effects of setting on classroom teaching and student learning in mainstream mathematics, English and science lessons: A critical review of the research literature in England. *Educational Review, 66*(4), 411-427.

Williams, J., & Choudry, S. (2016). Mathematics capital in the educational field: Beyond Bourdieu. *Research in Mathematics Education, 18*(1), 3-21.

Wright, P. (2012). The Math Wars: Tensions in the development of school mathematics curricula. *For the Learning of Mathematics, 32*(2), 7-13.

Wright, P. (2016a). Social justice in the mathematics classroom. *London Review of Education, 14*(2), 104-118.

Wright, P. (2016b). *Teaching mathematics for social justice: Meaningful projects for the secondary mathematics classroom.* Derby: Association of Teachers of Mathematics.

Wright, P. (2021). Transforming mathematics classroom practice through participatory action research. *Journal of Mathematics Teacher Education, 24*(2), 155-177. https://doi.org/10.1007/s10857-019-09452-1

Wright, P., Fejzo, A., & Carvalho, T. (2022). Progressive pedagogies made visible: Implications for equitable mathematics teaching. *The Curriculum Journal, 33*(1), 25-41.

In the next chapter Balbir explores further models for teaching mathematics for social justice. Before embarking on that chapter we invite you to take another moment for reflection.

What is the same and what is different about the models for teaching mathematics for social justice offered by Tony on page 8. And Pete on page 26. How do these models relate to your own experiences of teaching and learning mathematics?

Key readings

Reading and writing the world with mathematics: Toward a pedagogy for social justice, by Eric Gutstein. New York: Routledge.

Drawing on the work of Paulo Freire, Eric describes projects carried out with students in his own classroom that enabled them to investigate, critique, and challenge inequalities and injustices which they, their families, and communities experienced on a daily basis.

An invitation to critical mathematics education, by Ole Skovsmose. Rotterdam: Sense Publishers.

Ole provides a theoretical justification for how school mathematics contributes towards the reproduction of inequity from one generation to the next. He coined the term 'critical mathematics education' to describe an alternative view of mathematics and mathematics teaching that seeks to empower learners.

"Social justice in the mathematics classroom," by Pete Wright. London: UCL Institute of Education. *London Review of Education*, 14(2), 104–118. Open-access article available at: https://uclpress.scienceopen.com/hosted-document?doi=10.18546/LRE.14.2.07

This paper reports on the findings from my doctoral research study that aimed to support secondary school mathematics teachers to translate theories around teaching mathematics for social justice (including those of Gutstein and Skovsmose) into classroom practice.

Teaching mathematics for social justice: Meaningful projects for the secondary mathematics classroom, by Pete Wright. Derby: Association of Teachers of Mathematics.

This is a collection of seven projects designed to address social justice in the secondary mathematics classroom. It is based on ideas generated by the teacher researchers I worked with in my doctoral research study.

3 Anti-racist and decolonial practice in mathematics education

Balbir Kaur

Purpose of the chapter

This chapter is inspired by several factors that gave me the courage to share my thoughts on teaching mathematics for social justice (TMSJ). The first is the call to decolonise the curriculum provoked by student activism, both globally and nationally. Taking inspiration from the global protests for greater social justice (SJ), students across the UK have led campaigns such as 'Why isn't my professor Black?', 'Why is my curriculum White?' '#LiberateMyDegree' led by the UK's National Union of Students and the Rhodes Must Fall Oxford (RMFO) campaign that challenges the Eurocentric domination and lack of diversity in curricula across UK universities. In response, I have re-evaluated my position of privilege and power as a teacher educator and critically reflected on the diversity of the curriculum I designed and the approaches to pedagogy I advocate. I have reflected on how I used content formation and subject knowledge of the mathematics curriculum to support socially just practices in mathematics education. The second motivating factor is the expression of interest as voiced across several mathematics associations and communities that seek further guidance on how to embed TMSJ practices into teacher education programmes. I share some ideas from my practice and experience that colleagues may find helpful in adapting and using. Finally, as a woman of colour, a second-generation immigrant, and an ethnic-minority teacher educator, I write as one who wishes to share her identity, cultural diversity, and roots through the creative expression of mathematics.

In this chapter, I present some modifications in the design and structure of a teacher education mathematics programme to make space for a more socially just approach to teaching mathematics. In the following sections, I provide some models and frameworks on how teacher educators could design mathematics education curricula that support a SJ approach. The following examples are discussed from an initial teacher education (ITE) perspective, but school teachers and mathematics coordinators can adapt the ideas for school curricula. Although the methods and approaches of in-depth self-reflection and examination of the curriculum will be familiar to many educators, what may have been absent is the application of socially just lens when discussing how learning, teaching, assessment, and outcomes are put together and how they may foster inequalities in how mathematic is taught and received by some students.

DOI: 10.4324/9781003361466-4

Policy and reforms: The ideology of the 'turn away' from issues of social justice in mathematics education

Reflecting on the title of this book and many other similar subject-related teacher education books and articles that centralise the topic of SJ in their work, the words 'towards, turn, rethinking' or other associated synonyms are often used. These words drew my attention to the fact that, for some time, educators may have moved away from certain principles and core ideas associated with 'good' learning and teaching that go beyond treating everyone equally. How as mathematics teachers and teacher educators, we may have drifted in a direction that has lost consciousness of how mathematics education contributes to issues of SJ or even injustices in society. How the discourse and thinking on the purpose of education may require some adjustment or a rebalance in the recognition that schooling contributes to social immobility and social exclusion of some marginalised groups (Gates and Jorgensen, 2009). It also questions the role of educators and teachers in how learning and teaching, specifically in mathematics, is represented in learning spaces, and how relations of power, access, and equity are lived in and through mathematics education in classrooms, interactions, and teacher education programmes.

Over the decades, there has been a growing body of scholarly activity focusing on issues of SJ and equity in education and, more recently, in the preparation and education of mathematics teachers (Larnell et al., 2016). Even with the attention on SJ within mathematics education, there appear to be very few studies that have explored the preparedness and understanding of SJ practices across teacher and mathematics education in the UK or how the discourse around race, racism, and racialisation is realised in mainstream education (Lander, 2014; Larnell et al., 2016). Despite the growing scholarship surrounding SJ in education, the response to the action in addressing these issues by the teaching profession has been slow (Dover et al., 2020; Guyton, 2000). Larnell (2017) further argues that although some principles of SJ are adopted within mainstream education, such as research regarding teachers' beliefs about what constitutes quality content knowledge in mathematics and how it is enacted as quality classroom instruction in diverse learning spaces, they are often not evaluated with a critical lens that may examine unconscious perceptions and actions when working with linguistic-minority and other politically, socially, and economically marginalised students. Often, these perspectives are implemented at a moderate level, based on slight amendments to the curriculum and classroom environments, with little to no consideration given to the social and structural realities faced by marginalised pupils outside of school and how mathematical opportunities for success and failure are situated in those social realities (Gorski and Dalton, 2020).

There are several reasons for this lack of activity as discussed by Pete in the previous chapter. Education, over the last few decades, has become increasingly more politicised to favour a conservative restorative 'back to basics' approach (Mukhopadhyay and Greer, 2015). Ball (1993, p. 196) discusses the neo-liberal and neo-conservative education policy dominance as re-valorising traditional forms of education and a 'cultural restoration of New Right political thinking.' The associated political agendas and complex web of performativity mindset policies and educational reforms of accountability, standardised curriculum, high-stakes assessment, standardised pedagogy, and nationalised teacher preparation have diverted attention from issues that support SJ and equity in teacher and mathematics education (Dover et al., 2020; Mukhopadhyay and Greer, 2015).

Within the confines of teacher education programmes, many scholars have expressed concerns about how 'Whiteness' and the ideas of the dominant cultures are activated (Bhopal, 2015; Jett, 2013; Lander, 2014). The result has become the normalisation of hegemonic structures and systemic inequalities that uphold 'Whiteness' to the detriment of marginalising issues of equity and SJ (Henry, 2014). In response to addressing some of the political agendas as described above, integrating SJ perspectives throughout teacher preparation programmes rather than confining it to a single course is strongly advocated.

One of the challenges to embedding SJ perspectives into education is associated with a limited understanding of how the socio-political and economic systems of oppression permeate the schooling system and mathematics education. The countless combination of educational policies, reforms, curricula, and interventions proposed by various governments over the decades have been ineffective in managing the widening gap between social groups in education, particularly in mathematics achievement. Connections between social class, gender, race, and language and the intersectionality of these and many other identities and educational underachievement have been the focus of research by many scholars, as outlined in previous chapters. The turn or rethinking of mathematics education is an attempt to better understand the relationship between politics, knowledge, and power and the purpose of mathematics education in a democratic society (Cochran-Smith et al., 2009; Larnell et al., 2016). Ernest (1991, p. 207) refers to this as the 'public educator ideology of mathematics education,' where knowledge is seen as the key to 'action and power' that leads to social change. This public educator ideology is based on a critical epistemological viewpoint in which 'knowledge, ethics, and social, political, and economic issues are all intertwined.' Knowledge, in particular, is seen as the 'key to action and power, and not separate from reality' (Ernest, 1991, p. 197). In accordance with TMSJ, the goals of public educator ideology include liberation, equity, and social change. Larnell et al. (2016, p. 20) refer to such mathematics education as 'critical mathematical literacy' (or education) or social justice mathematics education (see Frankenstein and Gutierrez, 2013; Gutstein, 2006) that focuses on addressing socio-political injustices in society (see previous chapters for a more detailed debate).

In this chapter, I ask that we put on our critical lens and consider how we might engage and work with prospective teachers on issues related to TMSJ by re-examining our position on these matters and how they are enacted in our teaching. As argued by Gutstein (2006, p. 7), if we approach the learning and teaching of mathematics from a non-critical perspective, we have failed to examine the 'structural inequalities that perpetuate oppression,' reducing the purpose of mathematics education to nothing more than functional.

This point further supports the debates made in the previous chapters in that some of the responsibilities associated with TMSJ challenge existing structures and require a re-evaluation of the experiences that lead to the failure and disengagement from learning for some pupils. Research has shown that promoting SJ, particularly in mathematics education, can support democracy, increase young people's political participation, enhance their political knowledge, and foster tolerance and social cohesion for democratic citizenship (Ellis and Malloy 2007; Trent et al., 2010). Applying an SJ lens to maths education is to reassess how the subject contributes to a world in which students at all levels of education can become agents for change, contributing to greater equity, respect difference and play a part in protecting the environment.

An in-depth examination or analysis of a topic: Positioning social justice, anti-racist and decolonial perspectives in mathematics education

A practical place to begin addressing matters related to the TMSJ is to employ a critical reflective lens that scrutinises how the mathematics curriculum has been constructed. This can be achieved by embracing the concept of deep dives. A 'deep dive' is a method in which an individual or team conducts a thorough investigation and an in-depth analysis of a specific problem or subject. The application of multiple perspectives and lenses is required to capture diverse views on how an area of the curriculum is taught. Although most educational institutions associate deep dives with Ofsted inspections in England, they have been used more widely in other professions as part of strategic and innovative thinking. It often requires scrutinising and analysing the relationships revealed through quantitative (evaluation data) and qualitative evidence (focus group discussion). In my context, the question that prompted the application of a deep dive of the ITE mathematics curriculum was to review the presence or lack of SJ perspectives and question the effectiveness of these perspectives. The other interpretation is to examine how socially unjust the mathematics curriculum is when compared against a set of definitions and frameworks that advocate for SJ education.

Critical reflection

The process of enacting a 'deep dive,' engages in the need for critical reflection. John Dewey (1933) pioneered the concept of critical reflection in teacher education. Dewey questioned the extent to which reflective thought must consider larger historical, cultural, and political contexts when framing and reframing problems for which solutions are sought. He referred to this process as critical reflective thinking, which fosters democratic processes that are both educative and transformative (Ingram and Walter, 2007). Critical reflective thinking has evolved to include being more analytical of established truths, which includes questioning the foundation of truth claims, such as 'the assumptions underlying assertions, and the interests that motivate people to promote particular positions' (Ryan, 2005, p. 11, cited by Ingram and Walter, 2007, p. 30). As we are all products of cultural conditioning, critical reflection calls into question the rigidity that gives views and beliefs the appearance of certainty (Ingram and Walter, 2007). However, the deconstruction of such a schema is a time-consuming process that begins with self-analysis of our values, beliefs, and attitudes.

Creating a safe, respectful, and supportive environment for critical reflection must be considered because deconstructing historical, political, and socioeconomic perspectives can be challenging, as our knowledge and understanding of what influences our personal systems and who we are as people. For instance, Gutstein (2006) talked about the opposition and controversy that arose when he asked teachers to describe how shifting the ideological foundation of mathematics education threatened their status as teachers and their cultural membership. Similarly, Weissglass (2000) developed a series of equity workshops for maths teachers and discovered that activities aimed at altering instructional strategies did not alter teacher practice, unless they addressed participants' implicit ideological assumptions. In summary, a personal reflection on one's beliefs, biases, stereotypes, influences, values, and affiliations, as well as through shared experiences with others, leads to cultural consciousness, which must be established in educators' everyday practices (Ingram and Walter, 2007, p. 31).

In this section, I detail my approach of how a 'deep dive' can be used in the context of an ITE primary mathematics curriculum. Although the example I share is a personal reflection of my practice that is specific to my setting, the process can be applied to all mathematics curricula across the different stages of education to include secondary and primary sectors and can be approached as a team.

Stage 1: Definitions and principles

Before embarking on an in-depth examination, having a collective understanding of what is meant by socially just mathematics education through which to view the curriculum provides a point of reference. As a guiding principle, it can inform learning, teaching, and assessment and how this work may shape student teachers' identity in classrooms. As discussed in previous chapters, agreeing on a definition of SJ is highly disputed in the literature. The multiple definitions and enactments make the term calculable and dependable in how it can be mobilised to shape and determine economic and political relations. The precarious nature of these contested terms adds to the challenge of embedding this work in teacher education. As mentioned earlier, reviewing the current landscape, scholarship, and pedagogy to interrogate the different articulations of socially just mathematics education that may exist will further inform the scope and criteria of the deep dive.

Although SJ and related terms have been discussed in previous chapters, my activism towards the decolonisation of knowledge and my support for student activists who are championing this agenda has required a personal acknowledgement of my understanding of decolonisation. The 'coloniality of power' can sometimes be overlooked when talking about issues of SJ. Tuck and Yang (2012, p. 21) argue that 'decolonialisation is not a metonym for social justice.' Studies and theories of decolonialism have developed concepts, such as 'coloniality of power,' a phrase developed by Quijano (2000), to describe how the legacies of European colonialism are still practised in modern social structures and forms of knowledge. The term 'coloniality of power' refers to the sexual, racial, political, linguistic, and social hierarchies imposed by European colonisation that reserve value to some people and their knowledge while excluding others. Decolonisation is often framed as the 'destruction or disassembling of colonisation' (Sathorar and Geduld, 2018, p. 4). In mathematics education, decolonisation requires challenging dominant pedagogical structures and strategies that promote singular world views, such as the Eurocentric, dominant Western perspective, while disenfranchising the knowledge of other cultures. The impression implied by such perspectives suggests that mathematics education is independent of culture (Iseke-Barnes, 2000; Parra and Trinick, 2018; Sathorar and Geduld, 2018). These interests link decolonial struggles to the field of epistemology, which can be understood as a theory of knowledge that investigates how people acquire knowledge and the various ways in which it is transmitted and transformed. Epistemology also investigates how cultures recognise specific knowledge as legitimate and appropriate and has been identified as a key issue in mathematics education regarding the specificity of mathematical knowledge (Ernest, 1991; Hersh, 1997, cited in Larnell et al., 2016). As argued by Larnell et al. (2016), a decolonial perspective can shed light on some of the issues mentioned by exploring topics, such as how mathematics is generated, taught, and learnt by opening up a new range of research and practice opportunities.

As discussed in the previous two chapters, TMSJ entails using mathematical thinking to help students become aware of social injustices that occur in society and their own lives while increasing their mathematical understanding. In the context of the generalised statement that underpins socially just mathematics education, I identified the following principles that informed my analysis, based on the work of Gutstein (2006), who draws on Paulo Freire's theory that views mathematics as a tool for critical consciousness.

Stage 2: Theoretical frameworks for socially just mathematics education

Gutstein's (2006) framework for SJ is divided into two broad goals. The first goal explores how the curriculum develops mathematical pedagogical knowledge and supports the view that all students need a solid foundation in quality mathematics education to be a full part of society and make sense of the world. The second goal requires an analysis of how the curriculum uses students' experiences to explore SJ issues in mathematics. This goal uses mathematics as a critical tool to understand social life and explore the position students hold as members of a society where there are issues of power, agency, and oppression. Although it is beyond the scope of this chapter to discuss Gutstein's framework in detail, I will provide a brief overview and relate it to the primary mathematics ITE curriculum.

The first goal of mathematical pedagogical knowledge recognises that all children need high-quality mathematics. Gutstein (2006) identifies three components that are situated under this goal.

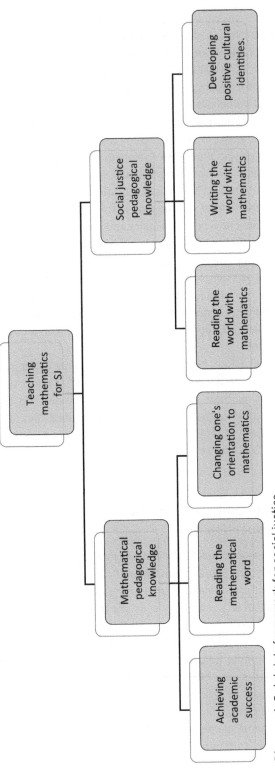

Diagram 1: Gutstein's framework for social justice

1. The first is 'reading the mathematical word' and developing 'mathematical power' (2006, p. 29). Gutstein argues that limited mathematical knowledge and understanding may prevent students from fully comprehending significant political concepts. Many people do not consider economic survival to be an academic issue. However, research and government data identify students from marginalised groups and those from working-class and low-income backgrounds as disproportionately affected by educational underachievement. Their life circumstances suffer the most. The broader issues of learning opportunity, access, and equity all require that marginalised students have the opportunity to develop mathematical power, which is particularly important to transform society successfully.

2. The second is academic success and achieving on standardised tests and exams so that access to advanced mathematics and opportunity to mathematics-related careers is possible. This component focuses on having access to the type of mathematics included in schools that is essential for academic success in the traditional sense of passing exams and the mathematical literacy required to function in society. Although regarded as highly important, this component alone will not change inequitable relations of power that continue to create injustices. This type of mathematics operates as functional literacy, designed to make adults in a given society's workforce and community more productive. Even though it may appeal to economic mobility, the concepts of culture, power, and critical thinking central to critical literacy become less embracive (Giroux, 1983, cited in Gutstein, 2006).

3. The third component is a change in orientation to mathematics that uses mathematics to investigate real-world problems.

Gutstein's second goal of SJ pedagogical knowledge involves a greater emphasis on mathematical thinking to help students become aware of the social injustices in their lives and society and improve their mathematical understanding. The three components associated with SJ pedagogical knowledge identify:

1. Reading the world with mathematics requires understanding the socio-political, cultural-historical conditions of one's life, community, society, and world. It requires students to reflect on their lives through political lenses and learn more about the conditions of their lives and society. Gutstein (2006) understands:

   > Reading the world with mathematics means to use mathematics to understand relations of power, resource inequities, and disparate opportunities between different social groups and to understand explicit discrimination based on race, class, gender, language, and other differences. Further, it means to dissect and deconstruct media and other forms of representation. It means to use mathematics to examine these various phenomena both in one's immediate life and in the broader social world and to identify relationships and make connections between them.
   >
   > (Gutstein, 2003, p. 45, cited in Gutstein, 2006, p. 6)

2. Writing the world with mathematics means using mathematics to change the world. Gutstein (2006) viewed this component as a developmental process in which one

begins to believe one can make changes. The students' gradual development is cap-tured by a 'sense' of social agency and a dialectical relationship between how people see and believe in themselves and the actions they take. The process requires a deeper understanding of the world by fighting for changes in their own lives while making a change to society because they have a better understanding of it by actively participat-ing in social change (Gutstein, 2006).

3. Developing positive cultural and social identities firmly rooted in their home languages, cultures, and communities while also being able to appropriate the resources they need to thrive in the dominant culture. Mathematics is frequently regarded as universal and acultural (Felton-Koestler, 2020). On the other hand, scholars have identified signifi-cant ways mathematics is a cultural practice. One line of work within these perspec-tives is primarily concerned with connecting mathematics to students' lives, including their cultural identities and practices outside the classroom. This includes recognising and utilising learners' knowledge resources, such as family or personal areas of inter-est, community resources, and so on, making mathematics instruction more cultur-ally relevant and relating it to students' actual experiences. Celebrating the numerous ways mathematics has been used throughout human history. This may help students connect with their cultural identity, while in other instances, it will expose them to diverse practices (Felton-Koestler, 2020).

Stage 3: Rethinking the teacher education mathematics curriculum: Mathematical pedagogical knowledge

To offer some context to the mathematics element of the primary PGCE (Postgraduate Certificate in Education) programme I work on. Many student teachers are local to the northwest Greater London area, mostly female and about 70%+ come from diverse racial and ethnic backgrounds. Based on the early analysis of primary PGCE student teachers' experience of learning mathematics over the years, many describe their relationship with mathematics as ever changing, moving from a positive relationship towards a negative emotion when learning maths. Some describe the fear and anxiety of doing mathematics and their low self-confidence and low self-efficacy in the subject.

The document analysis of the mathematics curriculum and a review of the end-of-course student survey and module/subject review data provided an opening for further examina-tion. Scrutiny of the documentation and data opened up points for reflection that required a change to the curriculum content, reading lists, and assessments, how I engaged student teachers to apply critical lenses across their mathematics teaching practice and how I scaf-fold those experiences. Gutstein's framework and a shared understanding of the termi-nology associated with SJ within mathematics education provided criteria to frame the analysis. The findings from reviewing the ITE primary mathematics curriculum indicated an emphasis on all three components under the 'mathematical pedagogical knowledge.'

The mathematical evaluations of a core curriculum-based module indicated student teachers developed confidence in their subject and pedagogical knowledge and how to support pupils' mathematical learning. Overall, the majority of student teachers indicated a change in orientation regarding how they viewed mathematics from one in which they considered the subject as a collection of disconnected procedures to be memorised and rehearsed to one in which they viewed it as a powerful instrument for analysing and comprehending real-world problems. Many student teachers had transformed their beliefs about mathematics and had greater confidence to teach the subject by the end of the programme.

The goal of developing 'mathematical pedagogical knowledge' across the ITE primary mathematics curriculum is highly successful, providing a solid foundation of quality mathematics education that is necessary to be a full part of society and make sense of the world. The emphasis is on teaching traditional or functional mathematics as described by the national curriculum and adapting the supporting pedagogical approaches, strategies, and resources. Greenstein and Russo (2019, p. 7) relate 'reading the mathematical word' to the five strands of mathematical proficiency: 'conceptual understanding, procedural fluency, strategic competence, productive disposition, and adaptive reasoning.' This involved engaging student teachers in complex mathematical tasks, demonstrating flexibility in problem-solving and communicating mathematical ideas flexibly through developing their subject, content, and pedagogical knowledge. In effect, the ITE primary mathematics curriculum, to some extent, mirrored the approaches to teaching mathematics used in most schools, based on the mathematics mastery reform introduced in England in 2014 to raise standards in mathematics. However, having secure mathematical pedagogical knowledge, although crucial, will not assist in overcoming social injustices caused by racism, sexism, and classism (Olawale et al., 2021). Having dismantled the contents of the taught sessions, it became apparent that the ITE primary mathematics curriculum offered a narrow and hegemonic perspective of mathematics. This was also evident in the lesson observations and feedback on taught mathematics lessons that student teachers received from their mentors and assessment tasks they were required to complete. Upon reflection, the ITE primary mathematics curriculum offered methods of teaching and understanding mathematics that did not challenge how the subject can contribute to societal injustices. Greater critical awareness of how to advocate for equitable opportunities through developing 'social justice pedagogical knowledge' was required.

Stage 4: Rethinking the teacher education mathematics curriculum: SJ pedagogical knowledge

Mathematics and SJ are often considered as two different ideas in opposition to each other and, therefore, a challenge to integrate (Larnell et al., 2016). Critics have claimed that a greater focus on TMSJ means less importance is placed on traditional education that emphasises mathematics subject knowledge matter and teachers' responsibility for pupils' learning. The emphasis on teachers' knowledge, particularly during the early stages of training, has questioned the forms of knowledge and experiences student teachers are expected to have to develop into good teachers of mathematics. Most student-teacher education curricula are fixed around theoretical frameworks that emphasise pedagogical content knowledge, such as the one presented by Lee Shulman in the late 1980s. However, teaching mathematics for SJ includes identifying specific mathematical objectives to increase understanding and knowledge of mathematics while critically examining the environment for greater democracy and equitable opportunities.

Shulman's (1986) framework identified three types of knowledge required by student- teachers for teaching – pedagogical knowledge, content knowledge, and subject knowledge (PCK model). According to Shulman (1986), teachers who possess PCK can efficiently

- construct representations of concepts,
- recognise pupils' preconceptions and misconceptions regarding the material, and
- sequence the curriculum to improve pupil learning.

The PCK model became a popular framework and one of the most influential paradigms in teacher education (Dyches and Boyd, 2017). It ran parallel to the rising importance given to teachers' knowledge of mathematics that was seen critical in improving pupils' academic outcomes in mathematics. Although the framework has evolved to include many other important aspects that require specialised professional knowledge, the foundational principles of the framework are still widely used vis-a-vis educating mathematics student teachers. Most lesson observations and reflections will focus on how student teachers demonstrate PCK during their teaching and how their knowledge of the subject impact's pupils' learning outcomes in mathematics. As a basic and essential function of teacher education, it significantly impacted on the teacher education landscape for thirty years and formed a powerful ideology. Despite its foundational qualities, the framework leaves some unexplored elements in that there is no designated area for SJ or reference to the cultural expertise of the teacher to teach diverse pupils in the paradigm. To address this gap, Dyches and Boyd (2017) propose a teacher preparation model that divides knowledge into three domains, Knowledge of Social Justice, Pedagogical Knowledge of Social Justice, and Content Knowledge of Social Justice (SJPACK), that also supports Gutstein's SJ pedagogical knowledge goal (Dyches and Boyd, 2017).

SJPACK model based on Dyches and Boyd (2017)

Dyches and Boyd (2017) give particular attention to Shulman's idea of the activity of when the teacher translates knowledge for students as part of the learning process.

They argue that the act of translating that knowledge is inextricably linked to one's SJ beliefs, whether they be advanced or limited in scope. As a result, the theoretical SJPACK model proposes that having SJ knowledge, or lack thereof, 'profoundly shapes teachers PCK practices' (Dyches and Boyd, 2017, p. 479). With reference to Freire (1868/1970) the SJPACK model draws attention to the fact that educational processes, at all stages, are never apolitical (cited in Dyches and Boyd, 2017). Associatively, no component of PCK is neutral: at every stage, teachers make instructional decisions that either foster a more equitable society, or, under the pretext of neutrality, perpetuate hegemony. They further argue that PCK practises are always shaped by politics, the realms of SJ knowledge and PCK are intricately linked, and PCK can never be separated from SJ knowledge. Claiming to be ideologically neutral is thus an ideological attitude in and of itself. SJPACK explicitly challenges teachers to teach for SJ rather than merely within its confines. The model encourages teachers and students to recognise and challenge oppression, and it views pedagogies, resources, and material as tools for doing so. It necessitates an understanding of SJ theory and requires experience of a variety of freeing pedagogies in order to teach equitably (Dyches and Boyd, 2017).

To further investigate student teachers' understanding of TMSJ I collected qualitative data. Students were asked to comment on their understanding of TMSJ. The use of an online interactive tool enabled students to respond anonymously and the posts provided a stimulus for further discussion in class. Using the qualitative data, I reviewed the mathematics programme and built-in sessions that included knowledge of SJ in mathematics education and SJ mathematical content and pedagogical knowledge. Diagrams 3, 4, and 5 provide some initial ideas of how each domain, as identified in Dyches and Boyd's (2017) SJPACK model, can be transformed and Gutstein's (2006) framework can be applied. Feedback from students provided a steer of how I needed to modify my curriculum and be responsive to the experiences, beliefs, and views of the students.

Knowledge of TMSJ

Cochran-Smith's (2010, p. 7) understanding of SJ examines power disparities between groups and the mechanisms that support privileges. All pedagogical and curricular decisions under SJPACK are based on one's knowledge of SJ. What the SJPACK model emphasises is that teaching techniques are always politically motivated, and that impartiality is a thinly veiled charade to maintain the status quo (Dyches and Boyd, 2017). My engagement with wider reading and my discussions with student teachers (see quotes that are representative of the majority of the cohort) indicated that student teachers were neither impartial nor politically motivated; they were unaware of the connection between SJ and mathematics education. Part of this unawareness can be attributed to the fact that inequity is difficult to eradicate because social injustices are embedded in everyday actions. SJ knowledge requires an understanding of how everyday acts contribute to reinforcing hegemony that reproduces racism, classism, sexism, heteronormativity, xenophobia, ableism, and other issues.

As shown in Diagram 3, the mathematics programme was modified in several ways to embed knowledge of teaching mathematics for SJ. A lead session on TMSJ was included; SJ knowledge cannot be taught in a single session and requires integration throughout the mathematics curriculum to support student teachers' teaching philosophies and actions. Although a dedicated session is allocated to discuss SJ theories and frameworks for TMSJ, the themes introduced in the lead session are revisited in other sessions that focus on planning, adaptive teaching, and assessment. Throughout these sessions, students are required to reflect on how the actions that drive PCK in mathematics may influence and sustain oppressive systems in existence, as well as how actions may address and overcome such structures.

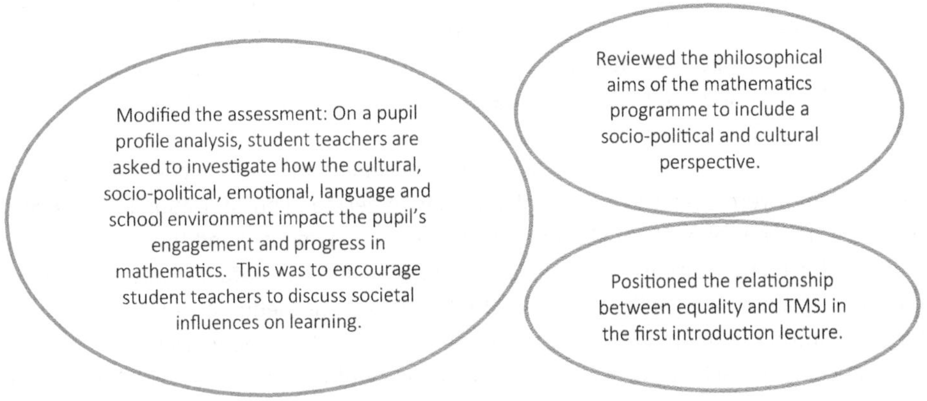

Modified the assessment: On a pupil profile analysis, student teachers are asked to investigate how the cultural, socio-political, emotional, language and school environment impact the pupil's engagement and progress in mathematics. This was to encourage student teachers to discuss societal influences on learning.

Reviewed the philosophical aims of the mathematics programme to include a socio-political and cultural perspective.

Positioned the relationship between equality and TMSJ in the first introduction lecture.

Diagram 3: Embedding Knowledge of TMSJ
"I've not experienced maths in a social justice context"
"I have no understanding of how mathematics can be taught for social justice"
"Social justice was never mentioned in the maths I learned"
"Mathematics has no social connotations"
The quotes above are from primary PGCE student teachers to the question.
'What is your understanding or experience of learning and/or mathematics for social justice?'

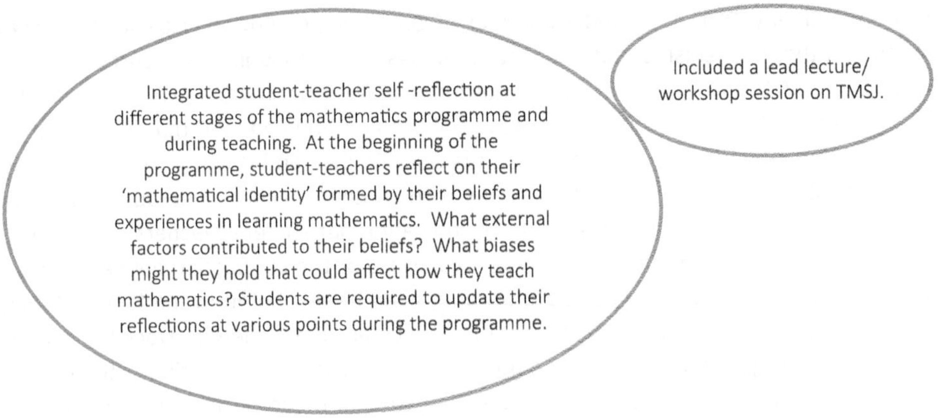

Integrated student-teacher self-reflection at different stages of the mathematics programme and during teaching. At the beginning of the programme, student-teachers reflect on their 'mathematical identity' formed by their beliefs and experiences in learning mathematics. What external factors contributed to their beliefs? What biases might they hold that could affect how they teach mathematics? Students are required to update their reflections at various points during the programme.

Included a lead lecture/ workshop session on TMSJ.

The understanding that if practitioners are to act as change agents and SJ knowledge is to be successfully translated into SJ practice, developing a personal understanding and a plan for contributing to a fairer society must begin with self-reflection. Learning about SJ requires examining one's autobiographies and socialisation to develop critical consciousness, an understanding 'that our ideas come from a particular set of life experiences' (Hinchey, 2004, p. 25). Teachers who want to teach for SJ must know themselves and how they relate to others. This includes thinking about how their beliefs about teaching and learning mathematics are influenced by the cultural, historical, and economic contexts in which they grew up and understanding other people's perspectives and experiences so that they could think about how their own biases might affect how they teach (Bartell, 2013). As part of SJ knowledge, reflection is defined as recurring, contextual, and shaped by social and cultural factors that help student teachers to consider how their positionality influences their interactions with culturally and linguistically diverse pupils. In the SJPACK mode, reflection entails evaluating one's positionality and how this orientation affects how learning is designed.

Gorski and Dalton (2020) provide a valuable Typology of Approaches to Reflection in Social Justice Teacher Education (see Table 1). The typology identifies three approaches to critical reflection – conservative, liberal, and critical across five levels.

1. The conservative approach, which they refer to as 'Amorphous cultural reflection' (p. 363), places a vague focus on culture but avoids topics such as racism, heterosexism, or other justice concerns.
2. The liberal approach is split into two levels, one that requires students to reflect on personal identities and the other on cultural competence reflection. Liberal approaches prepare teachers to have an awareness of and sensitivity towards diversity, particularly through the examination of their personal biases. It equips teachers with knowledge and practical skills to implement SJ curricula and incorporate a range of pedagogical strategies but fails to prepare them to understand or respond to ways power and inequity are exerted in schools. With reference to race, it can be argued that, even from a liberal approach, diversity may be appreciated through a 'colourblind' lens that fails to understand how social injustice and racism is reproduced in the education system and how to confront it by engaging student teachers in critical analysis of assigned learning materials.
3. The third level is the critical approach and requires social transformation and advocacy for equity which is also split into two levels. The critical approach prepares teachers to be change agents by engagement in critical examination of systemic influences of power, oppression dominance, inequity, and injustice in all aspects of education. It encourages teachers to participate in the reconstruction of schools by advocating equity, confronting issues of power and privilege, and disrupting oppressive policies and practices.

Table 3.1 Typology of approaches to reflection in social justice teacher education

Conservative approach - Amorphous 'cultural' reflection	To reflect broadly on one's understandings of 'other' cultures, usually in an essentialising way	• Vague focus on 'culture' • Avoidance of focus on racism, heterosexism, or other justice concerns • Danger of confirming stereotypes of 'the other'
Liberal approach - Personal identity reflection	To reflect on one's personal identities without grappling with the implications of difference or power or how identities influence one's worldviews or understandings of justice	• Consideration of role of personal identity in life and school experiences • Focus on 'diversity' but not on justice or oppression • Lack of connection between identities and their impact on teaching practice
Liberal approach - Cultural competence reflection	To reflect on one's teaching practice with 'diverse learners' in light of one's identities and life experiences	• Cultural competence framing related to teaching 'diverse learners' • Absence of reflection on beliefs or actions related to oppression against or advocacy for marginalised students

Liberal approaches prepare teachers to have an awareness of and sensitivity towards diversity, particularly though the examination of their personal biases. It equips teachers with knowledge and practical skills to implement multicultural curricular and pedagogical strategies engaging with the diverse styles of all students, but fails to prepare them to understand or respond to ways power and inequity are exerted in schools.

Critical approach - Equitable and just school reflection	To reflect on one's preparedness and willingness to be an agent of social justice change in a school context	• Explicit examination of positionalities and responsibilities related to oppression and liberation in schools • Presumption of educator as a social justice change agent
Critical approach - Social transformation reflection	To reflect on one's preparedness and willingness to be an agent of social justice change in and out of school contexts and to reflect on the areas of continued growth one needs to be an agent of social justice change	• Connection between oppression and anti-oppression in schools and • outside schools Incorporation of forward-leaning reflection related to continued needs for development as social justice advocates

Critical approach prepares teachers to be change agents by engagement in critical examination of systemic influences of power, oppression, dominance, inequity, and injustice on all aspects of education. It encourages teachers to participate in the reconstruction of schools by advocating equity, confronting issues of power and privilege, and disrupting oppressive policies and practices.

The ideological approaches to SJ anti-racism and decolonialism can be considered at three levels. The three levels are taken from the works of Jenks et al. (2001) and have been expanded into five categories by Gorski and Dalton (2020 p. 363).

Content and pedagogical knowledge required for TMSJ

Shulman (1986) describes how teachers' content and pedagogy knowledge base are integrated to understand better how topics, problems, or subjects are organised, represented, and adapted to the various interests of pupils. Dyches and Boyd (2017) recognise all pedagogy, including how classrooms are organised for learning, classroom discussion, choice of worksheets and textbooks, to be political in nature and fuelled by a teacher's relationship to subject knowledge. As such, content and pedagogical knowledge for SJ should concentrate on methods that provide the best possible experiences for pupils. One approach that recognises the cultural wealth, knowledge and skills that pupils from diverse groups bring to the classroom is culturally relevant pedagogy (CRP).

CRP seeks to develop multicultural content and multiple means of assessment with the intention of connecting pupils' cultural experiences to the mathematics curriculum and align with the three components under socially just pedagogies in Gutstein's framework. It is a pedagogy that includes historical perspectives and acknowledges that many cultures and racial groups have contributed to the development of mathematics (Ladson-Billings, 1994). Taylor and Sobel (2011, pp. ix–x) describe CRP as a commitment to the success of all students, 'including students who have a diverse set of languages, cultures, racial/ethnic backgrounds, religions, economic capitals, interests, abilities, and life experiences as well as students who are members of the society's mainstream cultural, linguistic, and socioeconomic group or groups.' The key aim of CRP is to integrate pupils' and their families' funds of knowledge. It rejects deficit thinking and prevalent discourses in education, such as the notion that some pupils 'cannot learn' or that parents 'don't care' (Dyches and Boyd, 2017, p. 484).

Based on the understanding that mastery of content and pedagogical knowledge is required for effective teaching, understanding the cultural characteristics and contributions of various ethnic groups is part of this knowledge (see Diagram 4). Acknowledging different cultures in the classroom while demonstrating a willingness to learn about them creates a more effective learning environment. Creating a culturally aware classroom environment makes students from various cultures feel validated, resulting in a stronger sense of classroom community. Consideration can be given to how textbooks, worksheets, posters, and other instructional materials used in mathematics teaching represent diverse people and lifestyles. Pictures, names, images, and content of mathematics materials ought to be culturally relevant and non-offensive. Materials should include historical and present mathematicians, who may serve as role models. Regardless of the racial makeup of the student body, cultural diversity in classroom materials is essential. CRP also assist teachers in viewing cultural differences as assets rather than liabilities. Relating the curriculum to pupils' cultural experiences, establishing connections with families and local communities, and increasing pupil engagement can improve academic outcomes for students from underrepresented populations (Min et al., 2022). An example of this includes women and many racial and ethnic minorities, who traditionally have fewer opportunities and less encouragement in mathematics. This can lead to lower self-confidence, greater anxiety, and a decreased interest in mathematics for these groups. As a result, it makes sense to pay some attention to underrepresented groups in mathematics (see Diagram 5). Manjinder provides many examples of how positive cultural identities can be embedded in the curriculum in the next chapter.

Acknowledging the historical contributions made by different cultures and racial groups across the mathematics curriculum. Integrating the content with examples and content from a variety of cultures and groups to illustrate key concepts and ideas.

Measurement (some examples).
☐ origins of how and what measurement tools were used (earlier contributions from Ancient Egypt)
☐ sundials (Egypt)
☐ history of how the body ruled as a form of measurement (global contribution).

Diagram 4: Developing culturally responsive mathematical content knowledge for SJ, anti-racist and decolonial perspectives

"I always felt maths was a neutral subject"
"I agree mathematics should ideally be neutral but at times has a lot of bias towards certain genders and class"
"Maths cannot be neutral, various influences determine how and to what extent individuals or groups of people engage with it"
"I have never been in a maths lesson where I was told about the historical background of mathematical concepts and that maths originates globally"

The quotes above are from primary PGCE student teachers to the question.
'Is mathematics a neutral subject and therefore value free?'

Number and place value (some examples).
☐ Different ways of counting using fingers across cultures;
☐ origins of the number system (earlier contributions from the Indian mathematician Aryabhat).
☐ Arabic numeral system (including decimal numbers).
☐ Lattice multiplication strategies.
☐ Egyptians use of fractions.

Geometry (some examples).
☐ Babylon 3000 BC (know now as Iraq). General rules for area and volume, Pythagorean theorem, concept of astronomical geometry)
☐ India (Indus Valley 3000BC). Pythagorean theory, trigonometry.
☐ Egypt (North Africa). Approximate area of a circle)
☐ Islamic Golden Age – 9th century - Islamic mathematicians building on Indian sources contributed to trigonometry, astronomy and algebraic geometry.
Greek Classics – 12th century (via Arabic literature)
☐ Use of patterns across cultures.

Statistics (some examples).
The statistic programmes of study lend themselves to explore relationships between power and inequalities and provided the space to incorporate Gutstein's read the world with mathematics and write the world with mathematics.
☐ Interpret and discuss secondary data such as the United Nations Sustainable Goals (UNS Goals) as starting points to create lines of inquiry, also book 'Village of 100 people'.
☐ Explored the sustainable goal 'to end hunger' at a local level, in school communities, use of food banks (book 'One grain of rice')
☐ Explored the sustainable goal 'achieve gender equality and empower all women and girls'.

Used research to better understand mathematical pedagogical approaches and impact on some groups of pupils.

Exploring classroom participation structures and high-quality mathematics for all pupils that are culturally and linguistically compatible. E.g. exploring a more student-centred teaching philosophy.

Mathematical ability is fixed: Used research on mathematical mindsets that assumes each pupil is capable of understanding complex mathematical concepts and should be given opportunities to acquire academically challenging knowledge and skills. [Boaler, 2013; Dweck, et al., 2019; Francis et al., 2017; Francis, et al., 2019; Hill, et al., (2016)]

Understanding the need to know the pupils you are working with so that you can acknowledge, appreciate, and draw on the cultural and linguistic resources, as well as the interests and knowledge, of pupils.

Research on how to support particular groups, such as English Learners.

Diagram 5: Developing culturally responsive mathematical pedagogical knowledge for SJ, anti-racist and decolonial perspectives

"I see maths as a gender-neutral subject"
"Maths for me was always a male dominated subject. I have always been taught by male maths teachers and this made me feel there was no point in competing in a male dominated subject"
"I was in the higher sets the lower ability were typical troublemakers or 'problem children'"
"setting does lead to higher attainment for all".
"maths always felt like there was a ceiling to each person's ability".

Develop problem-solving strategies that teaches pupils to collaborate, communicate effectively, and value the contributions of their peers regardless of race/ethnicity, gender, or social class [Boaler, 2008; Boaler et al., 2022]

Understand a wide range of strategies for assessment and, and not rely on standardised tests as the only or main method of assessment.

Engage with mathematical networks/teams, local maths hubs to develop research-informed practices of SJ, anti-racist and decolonial practices across the mathematics curriculum.

Conclusion

The aim of this chapter was to contribute to the development of TMSJ in an ITE programme. It focused on how SJ perspectives can be implemented as a pedagogical approach within mathematics education.

As teacher educators, we occupy a position as change agents who can actively engage prospective teachers in SJ, anti-racist, and decolonial practices through our teaching and research, where we can affect change by educating new teachers in the profession. School mathematics can be thought of as a type of capital that is distributed according to gender, race/ethnicity, socioeconomic class, and other social categories. Some scholars consider it a 'critical filter' in the social stratification of communities and the social structuring of students' lives (Moses and Cobb, 2001, cited in Freitas, 2008, p. 43). Consequently, mathematics teachers and educators are deemed gatekeepers, but many are hesitant to acknowledge or become aware of the political impact of their teaching. Some studies that have challenged mathematics teachers' beliefs have been met with resistance and controversy. Other studies have found that prospective mathematics teachers were more likely than pre-service teachers to dismiss social issues in the learning and teaching of the subject (Gutstein, 2000). Although research in this field is beginning to emerge, there is still much to learn on how to prepare mathematics teachers to teach mathematics for SJ and incorporate anti-racist and decolonial perspectives (Gonzales, 2009).

The final chapter in this section offers a further example of the activities that can be used on a teacher education course to support teachers in teaching mathematics for social justice. However, maybe take a moment to consider your response to the issues raised in this chapter.

Look back to Table 3.1 on page 46, the typology of approaches to reflection in social justice teacher education. Where do you consider your current approach lies? What about the institution in which you work? Where would you hope to move to in the future? What changes would you need to make?

References

Ball, S. J. (1993). Education, majorism and 'the curriculum of the dead'. *Curriculum Studies, 1*(2), 195-214.

Bartell, T. G. (2013). Learning to teach mathematics for social justice: Negotiating social justice and mathematical goals. *Journal for Research in Mathematics Education, 44*(1), 129-163. https://doi.org/10.5951/jresematheduc.44.1.0129

Bhopal, K. (2015). *The experiences of black and minority ethnic academics: A comparative study of the unequal academy.* London: Routledge.

Cochran-Smith, M., Shakman, K., Jong, C., Terrell, D. G., Barnatt, J., & McQuillan, P. (2009). Good and just teaching: The case for social justice in teacher education. *American Journal of Education, 115*(3), 347-377.

Dewey, J. (1933). Why have progressive schools?. *Current History, 38*(4), 441-448.

Dover, A. G., Kressler, B., & Lozano, M. (2020). "Learning our way through": Critical professional development for social justice in teacher education. *The New Educator, 16*(1), 45-69.

Dyches, J., & Boyd, A. (2017). Foregrounding equity in teacher education: Toward a model of social justice pedagogical and content knowledge. *Journal of Teacher Education, 68*(5), 476-490.

Ellis, M., & Malloy, C. E. (2007). Preparing teachers for democratic mathematics education. In D. Pugalee (Ed.), *Proceedings of the ninth international conference on mathematics education in a global community* (pp. 160-164). https://www.academia.edu/1352569/Proceedings_of_the_Ninth_International_Conference_-Mathematics_Education_in_a_Global_Community

Ernest, P. (1991). *The philosophy of mathematics education.* London: Falmer Press.

Felton-Koestler, M. D. (2020). Teaching sociopolitical issues in mathematics teacher preparation: What do mathematics teacher educators need to know?. *The Mathematics Enthusiast, 17*(2), 435-468.

de Freitas, E. (2008). Troubling teacher identity: Preparing mathematics teachers to teach for diversity. *Teaching Education, 19*(1), 43-55.

Gates, P., & Jorgensen, R. (2009). Foregrounding social justice in mathematics teacher education. *Journal of Mathematics Teacher Education, 12*(3), 161-170. https://doi.org/10.1007/s10857-009-9105-4

Gonzalez, L. (2009). Teaching mathematics for social justice: Reflections on a community of practice for urban high school mathematics teachers. *Journal for Urban Mathematics Education, 2*(1), 22-51.

Gorski, P. C., & Dalton, K. (2020). Striving for critical reflection in multicultural and social justice teacher education: Introducing a typology of reflection approaches. *Journal of Teacher Education, 71*(3), 357-368.

Greenstein, S., & Russo, M. (2019). Teaching for social justice through critical mathematical inquiry. *Occasional Paper Series, 2019*(41), 1.

Gutstein, E. (2006). *Reading and writing the world with mathematics: Toward pedagogy for social justice.* New York: Routledge.

Guyton, E. (2000). Social justice in teacher education. *The Educational Forum, 64*(2), 108-114.

Henry, E. (2014). A search for decolonizing place-based pedagogies: An exploration of unheard histories in Kitsilano Vancouver, B.C. *Canadian Journal of Environmental Education, 19*, 18-30.

Hinchey, P. H. (2004). *Becoming a critical educator: Defining a classroom identity, designing a critical pedagogy.* New York, NY: Peter Lang.

Ingram, I. L., & Walters, T. S. (2007). A critical reflection model to teach diversity and social justice. *Journal of Praxis in Multicultural Education, 2*(1), 2.

Iseke-Barnes, J. M. (2000). Ethnomathematics and language in decolonizing mathematics. *Race, Gender & Class, 7*(3), 133-149.

Jett, C. C. (2013). Culturally responsive collegiate mathematics education: Implications for African American students. *Interdisciplinary Journal of Teaching and Learning, 3*(2), 102-116.

Ladson-Billings, G. (1994). What we can learn from multicultural education research. *Educational Leadership, 51*(8), 22-26.

Lander, V. (2014). Special issue race ethnicity and education: Initial teacher education: Developments, dilemmas and challenges. *Race Ethnicity and Education, 17*(3), 299-303.

Larnell, G. V. (2017). On the entanglement of mathematics remediation, gatekeeping, and the cooling-out phenomenon in education. *Mathematics Education and Life at Times of Crisis*, 654-663.

Larnell, G. V., Bullock, E. C., & Jett, C. C. (2016). Rethinking teaching and learning mathematics for social justice from a critical race perspective. *Journal of Education, 196*(1), 19-29.

Min, M., Lee, H., Hodge, C., & Croxton, N. (2022). What empowers teachers to become social justice-oriented change agents? Influential factors on teacher agency toward culturally responsive teaching. *Education and Urban Society, 54*(5), 560-584.

Mukhopadhyay, S., & Greer, B. (2015, February). Cultural responsiveness and its role in humanizing mathematics education. In *CERME 9-ninth congress of the European society for research in mathematics education* (pp. 1624-1629).

Olawale, B. E., Mncube, V. S., & Harber, C. (2021). Critical social pedagogy in mathematics teacher education. *International Journal of Higher Education, 10*(6), 93-104.

Parra, A., & Trinick, T. (2018). Multilingualism in indigenous mathematics education: An epistemic matter. *Mathematics Education Research Journal, 30*(3), 233-253.

Quijano, A. (2000). Coloniality of power and Eurocentrism in Latin America. *International Sociology, 15*(2), 215-232.

Sathorar, H., & Geduld, D. (2018). Towards decolonising teacher education: Reimagining the relationship between theory and praxis. *South African Journal of Education, 38*(4), 1-12.

Shulman, L. S. (1986). Those who understand: A conception of teacher knowledge. *American Educator, 10*(1), 9-15 and 44-45.

Taylor, S., & Sobel, D. (2011). *Culturally responsive pedagogy: Teaching like our students' lives matter.* Bingley, UK: Emerald Group.

Trent, A., Cho, J., Rios, F., & Mayfield, K. (2010). Democracy in education: Learning from preservice teachers' understanding and perspectives. *Journal of the NNER, 2*(1), 183-210.

Tuck, E., & Yang, K. W. (2012). Decolonization is not a metaphor. *Decolonization: Indigeneity, Education and Society, 1*, 1-40.

Weissglass, J. (2000). No compromise on equity in mathematics education: Developing an infrastructure. In W. Secada (Ed.), *Changing the faces of mathematics: Perspectives on multiculturalism and gender equity.* Reston, VA: National Council of Teachers of Mathematics.

Key readings

Reading and writing the world with mathematics: Toward pedagogy for social justice by Eric Gutstein. Routledge, New York.

My chapter and some of the practical classroom examples in this book are mod-elled on the theoretical framework for teaching mathematics for social justice pro-posed by Gutstein. Therefore, this selected text is core reading as it conceptualises how social justice and mathematical goals can be achieved. Situating mathematics education within a socio-political context, Gutstein argues for reading the world with mathematics, which requires using mathematics to understand power rela-tions, resource inequalities, and differences in opportunities across social groups. It also highlights how mathematics can be used to realise explicit discrimination based on race, class, gender, language, and other differences. Gutstein's definition of writing the world with mathematics is using mathematics to change the world, being capable of producing change, and having a sense of social agency. Gutstein also highlights the significance of mathematical knowledge, including mathematical goals in his framework targeted at interpreting the mathematical word and gaining mathematical power, academic success, and using mathematics to investigate real-world problems.

"Striving for critical reflection in multicultural and social justice teacher edu-cation: Introducing a typology of reflection approaches" by Paul Gorski and Kelly Dalton in the *Journal of Teacher Education*, 71(3), pp. 357–368.

This article highlights the value of critical reflection in developing equity and social justice focused educators. Based on the conceptualisation of critical reflection, the research analysed assignments and identified the essential nature of reflection incorporated in them. Based on the analysis, the study offers the beginnings of a typology of five approaches to reflection in multicultural and social justice edu-cation: (a) amorphous 'cultural' reflection, (b) personal identity reflection, (c) cul-tural competence reflection, (d) equitable and just school reflection, and (e) social transformation reflection. The typology is a practical framework to reflect on one's teaching practices in relation to the level of approaches taken when engaging in work related to social justice.

"Toward a Theory of Culturally Relevant Pedagogy" by Gloria Ladson-Billings in the *American Educational Research Journal*, vol. 32, no. 2, pp. 465

Due to word limitations I was not able to expand on the theory of culturally relevant pedagogy credited to Gloria Ladson-Billings. This article outlines the need to make pedagogy a central area of investigation when talking about improving education, teacher education, equity, and diversity. This article attempts to challenge notions about the intersection of culture and teaching that rely solely on micro-analytic or macro-analytic perspectives.

4 Diversity and inclusion in initial teacher education

Manjinder Kaur Jagdev

In this chapter I reflect on my work as a mathematics teacher educator, collaborating with primary and secondary postgraduate and undergraduate student teachers. This work focuses on developing a mathematics education that contributes to the broader sense of social justice. The chapter draws on ready-to-use teaching examples, activities, and resources which I hope will be of interest to teachers and educators seeking to embed decolonial and anti-racist principles. The classroom activities identify the key issue of bridging the practice and theory gap by engaging teachers, pupils, and teacher educators to develop their approach to teaching mathematics for social justice within the mathematics curriculum.

Ollerton and Sykes (2012) emphasise that in mathematics, 'everything is connected.' This seems to me to be ideal for those of us interested in social justice by highlighting the interconnectedness of humanity.

The second half of this chapter develops some of these ideas in more detail and the next section of the book offers a more detailed commentary on them. The ideas take the perspective of critical mathematics education which is concerned with social justice. Ernest (2021) argues for the use of ethical examples in the teaching of mathematics by using real-world examples such as Covid, global warming, pollution, health and mortality figures, and statistics on gender and race inequalities. In the context of solving these real-world problems, mathematics is used as a tool. A socio-critical approach draws on the ideas of Freire (1970) and work within ethnomathematics (D'Ambrosio, 1985). Mathematics education must take part in educating students to be critical, engaged citizens (Barbosa, 2006, p. 294). By centralising the activities described below within the mathematics school curriculum, 'othering' in terms of race can be challenged and tokenistic gestures avoided in our work with children.

I would argue that activities such as these offer ways in which links can be made between mathematics and other subjects. We can also make connections between how race inequality is evident in the curriculum and issues of gender inequality. For example, in geography, the approach of early female geographers differs from their male counterparts. Similarly, contributions from the Black majority address exclusionary and biased approaches in education. The appropriation by Europeans of contributions to mathematics, for example, Pascal's triangle and the Fibonacci sequence, developed ideas from the mathematicians in the Arabic and Indian world. This could be countered by referring to examples of the development of mathematics in India, China, pre-Columbian America, and the Arab world.

School mathematics can begin to redress injustices caused by colonisation. Working with parents and the wider community, we can co-create knowledge and activities for use

DOI: 10.4324/9781003361466-5

Table 4.1 Topics that support teaching mathematics for social justice

Area of mathematics	Possible topics
Number	The origins of numbers.
	Number systems around the world, for example: Yoruba, African, Indian languages, Egyptian, Roman, Urdu and Arabic, The Hindu and Chinese derivation of zero.
	The use of base 20 in some counting systems.
	Vedic mathematics.
	The influence of mathematicians from around the world.
Algebra	The Arabic origins of algebra.
	Links to trade and finance, including currency and taxation.
Shape, Space and Measure	Geometry in art.
	Maps (including how some exaggerate the size of Europe, for example, Mercator versus Peters).
	Mazes.
	Rangoli patterns, African patterns, and Islamic designs. Symmetry and tessellation.
	Cathedral, mosque and pyramid designs.
	Celtic knots.
	Roman mosaics.
	Chinese tangrams.
Data handling and statistics	Analysis of gender and race inequality.
	Statistics at a global level including population, health, and literacy.
	Games around the globe including the origins of chess. All relate to probability and chance.
Real-world problem solving	Explore issues such as: global warming, climate change, biodiversity and extinction, natural resources, deforestation, recycling, forced migration, mining precious metals, pandemics.

in after-school clubs and at home. This is a structural challenge to the existing relations between teachers and students. Such projects can be further developed by creating and adapting resources with children, getting feedback from student teachers, experienced teachers, and parents, for use in mathematics classrooms. Children can investigate the historical and cross-cultural aspects including key Black and Asian Global Majority (BAGM) figures such as Wang Zhenyi (astronomer, poet and mathematician) born in 1768 in China, who understood complicated arithmetic theories and at the age of 24 published a five-volume guide for beginners called *Simple Principles of Calculation*. Katherine Johnson (physicist and mathematician) born in 1918 in West Virginia, USA, calculated flight paths involving complicated geometry equations. She calculated the launch window of the 1961 manned Mercury mission and became the lead in calculating trajectory, doing most of the calculations on the path for the first manned mission to the Moon in 1969. Katherine checked the mathematics of NASA's mechanical computers. Her story is captured in a beautiful online reading of the book *Counting on Katherine* by Helaine Becker that teachers can use with learners in the classroom: www.youtube.com/watch?v=wXtTMCBpXRg. Annie Easley (computer programmer, mathematician, and rocket scientist) was born in Alabama, USA, in 1933 and used NASA's mechanical computers to start her work, stating:

'Nothing was given to minorities or women. It took some fighting to get that equal oppor-tunity, and we're still fighting today.' Maryam Mirzakhani, born in 1977 in Iran, focused on hyperbolic surfaces. Maryam created an equation to show the relationship between the number of straight lines and the length of a hyperbolic structure that is essential to under-standing curved shapes and surfaces. Maryam solved a billiard ball problem in mathematics so complicated that computers could not simulate it and which provided a better under-standing of geometry and physics. In 2014, Maryam won the Fields Medal, the first woman to do so. Teachers can find further inspirational stories to share with children in the book *Women in Science* by Rachel Ignotofsky.

An example of one primary school making changes to their curriculum to include themes of diversity and inclusion was shared at a conference at York St. John University in June 2022. The school's senior leader highlighted how the curriculum changes led to increased engagement by pupils, parents and community members, and motivation of staff. Staff at the school suggested that their 'long-term aim was to have further developed our curriculum by the end of the next academic year, so it inspires, celebrates, provides a sense of belonging and identity and also raises aspirations for all pupils...' The staff had worked with Leeds Heritage Corner, who adopt a unique creative approach that exposes hidden narratives and engages participants and audi-ences in understanding African history/heritage and connections to Yorkshire. One example of their work is the award-winning*Leeds Black History Walk*, a fascinating stroll featuring an expert cast of historical figures who bring the inspiring narratives of Africa's hidden past to life.

The school reported an increased enthusiasm amongst staff to work towards a curricu-lum for social justice as well as increased pupil enjoyment and engagement with the curric-ulum. They suggested that 'school feels better now that all cultures are regularly celebrated and represented right across the curriculum rather than just through one off events.' They described this initial year as the first year of an ongoing journey that will be continually built on. They suggested that:

> We have noticed that our Black and Asian children are taking more pride in their cul-ture and family history as a result of seeing themselves represented throughout our curriculum. They have realised that they matter too. They have a wider understand-ing that people like them have made positive contributions to events throughout his-tory and they want to celebrate that.

The pupils agreed with this saying:

> It's not just White people that I learn about, I can see how people like me have made a difference to the world. I have realised that Black people have done some amazing things and that I can too.

Another contribution to the conference involved a group of primary school pupils recount-ing the knowledge they had gained from a recent project they had completed surround-ing migration, including of members in their community, before sharing their own family migration stories with the audience. These experiences were reflective, positive, authen-tic, and genuine, from a variety of backgrounds, cultures, and countries of birth. These young students bravely stood up in front of a large audience at an academic conference and shared their stories beautifully, with maturity and confidence. The stories were insightful and powerful, revealing the multiple generations of migration present in York. This acted as an important reminder of what diverse and inclusive education can look like.

Activities I have shared with students

Algebra

The BBC Teach Class video clip on Baghdad in AD 900 provides a simple mathematics riddle for children to solve whilst learning about the golden age of Islam through this short engaging animation: www.bbc.co.uk/teach/class-clips-video/baghdad-in-900ad-the-golden-age -of-islam/zjfxpg8

> A man sends his servant to the market to buy some gifts for his daughter; flying carpets are 30 dirhams each and magic lanterns are 7 dirhams each. The servant must spend exactly 1001 dirhams. How many flying carpets can he buy?

The video captures the essence of trade, culture, knowledge and books (stored in the House of Wisdom), the building of hospitals, universities, and observatories whilst Europe experienced the Dark Ages. The animation mentions the famous Baghdad mathematician, Muhammed ibn Musa al-Khwarizmi, who termed the word 'al-jabr' (from which 'algebra' is derived), meaning 'how to solve number problems with the symbols.' There are further teacher notes for teachers to use as guidance, linked to the history. This introduction to the Islamic contributions to mathematics from AD 825 could be an insightful hook to solving puzzles and lead into teaching algebraic topics. The solution to the riddle above, I hear you ask. Well, you will have to watch the video!

World statistics

To explore topics such as gender inequality, literacy rates around the world, mortality rates, and population censuses, children can be shown real-time statistics using online resources such as *Gapminder* and *Worldometer*. These make cross-curricular links to geography, providing opportunities for rich classroom discussions which develop pupils' compassion and empathy for poorer nations.

As a classroom teacher, I provided pupils with statistics based on topics such as child labour, patents, ocean pollution, infant mortality, life expectancy, illiteracy, healthcare, division of labour, and Gross National Product. Children can apply their knowledge and understanding of statistics, interpretation of scatter graphs, pictograms, tally charts, and tables to engage with real-life data. Some of these issues are explored in much more detail in the next section.

Chinese tangrams

In my own teaching I have used Chinese tangrams to teach about shape, particularly exploring properties of shapes. I have noticed that students who have previously struggled with the more number-focused activities or who struggle when expected to work silently and on their own can excel when working on topics exploring shape. I remember one such student becoming the 'expert' in the classroom, assisting her peers who became frustrated at the puzzles. Tangrams offer opportunities for sharing knowledge, paired and group work, enabling pupils to talk mathematics and consolidate their understanding of the properties of shapes. Below (Figure 4.1) is the basic starting square of seven pieces (*tans*) that can be cut from card:

Figure 4.1 A tangram

Source: https://chinesepuzzles.org/tangram-puzzle/

I provide the seven-piece puzzle, above, in envelopes (there is a simpler five-piece version that could be used with younger children). Children can be challenged to use every piece to make the square. Depending on previous learning, questions to pose include: 'Can you name each shape?', 'What are the properties of each shape?', and 'What are the interior angles in each shape?'. Offer more detail of exactly how a teacher might use this in the classroom. There are a plethora of books and online resources that offer activities based on Chinese tangrams. Teachers can use these to create their own adaptions suitable for their children's needs. Each of these resources provide opportunities where learners must use all pieces to create a 'picture' (for example, a cat, boat or person) without overlapping the pieces. These activities support the development of visual and spatial awareness.

Vedic mathematics

This activity explores the connection between numbers and shape. I provide each student with squared paper upon which they write 1–9 horizontally and vertically as shown below (See Figure 4.2). They calculate the products to complete the table although where the answer has two digits, they add these until a single digit results. So, for example, five multiplied by seven gives 35, which leads to 3 + 5 = 8. Once children have completed several copies of these, they can discuss patterns observed. The next step is to join all the 3's or 7's or 8's etc. Different children or pairs of students can do this. I have found that children like to use different colours to do so, which helps to identify similarities between shapes created. This leads to discussion on the types of shapes created their symmetries and properties as well as connections between them. The mathematics can be developed by exploring why these patterns are formed.

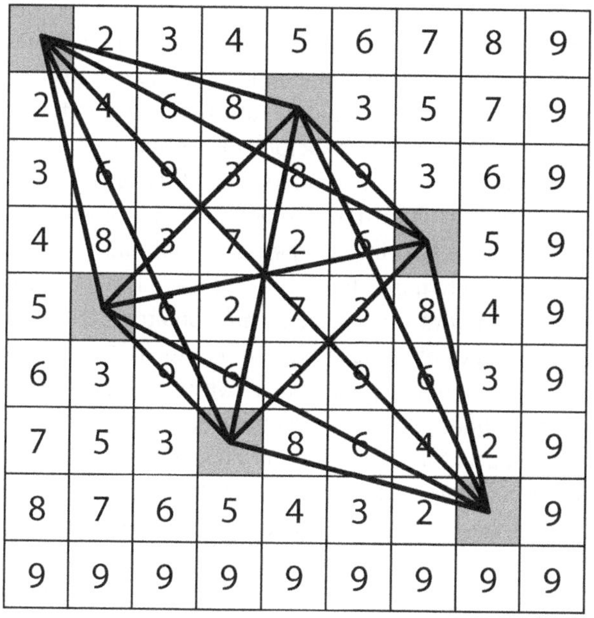

Figure 4.2

Source: Erin Bittman: https://eisforexplore.blogspot.com/2014/05/vedic-square-math-art.html

Multiplication tables in a range of languages and number scripts

I have also used multiplication tables in different languages in a range of ways with students. Below are a few examples from the Arabic, Bengali and Chinese languages. Children can look for patterns in the scripts and so gain an understanding of number concepts and multiplication. Further discussion points include the similarities and differences between these scripts. Children I have taught found it fascinating that the numbers we use today derive from the Hindu script, especially the symbols for 2 and 3. Arabic offers an insight into writing from right to left although we can see this is not the case for two-digit numbers, so the number 50 is still written with the symbol for five first, followed by the symbol for zero. In my classes, Chinese children completed the multiplication table in their language quickly. Some children were keen to have a go at writing in languages that they were not familiar with. This activity allowed discussion of languages spoken at home and those learned when on holiday abroad.

Symmetry and pattern in African textiles and Islamic art

There are rich tapestries of mathematical patterns in Native American Indian, African, and Islamic designs and Aboriginal art, Roman mosaics, and Celtic knots which can be shared with children. Along with these are stories connected to nature, animals, and the Earth. The latter can provide fruitful discussions on conservation, climate change, and ecological justice. Children can practice their geometry skills to recreate some of these designs, exploring concepts of shape in the process. The use of symmetry and tessellations can be explored as children enhance their vocabulary of mathematical language. Architecture around the world such as York Minster, the Alhambra Palace, and the Taj Mahal can provide interesting talking points, especially if children have made visits to these and other places.

I have given secondary school children the opportunity to use their instruments in their geometry sets to create signs from world religions and Islamic art and architecture, examples of which can be found in the book *Multiple Factors: Classroom mathematics for equality and justice* by Sharanjeet Shan and Peter Bailey. Also included are symmetry in Asian fashion and textile design, symbols from the Hindu faith, geometry in Botswana baskets. As a teacher, my pupils created Roman mosaics, exploring symmetry, rotation, and reflection. Photographs of Roman mosaics can be shown to pupils to inspire and there is a plethora of resources such as by Tarquin Publications: www.tarquingroup.com/geometric-patterns-from-roman-mosaics-1523.html. The mathematics of Celtic knots can be explored, with children learning how to create their own designs. Here is a wonderful activity, 'Drawing Celtic Knots,' that can be used with pupils, which includes two videos to guide learners and thought-provoking questions to provoke mathematical thinking: https://nrich.maths.org/6809. Connections can be made to Irish and Scottish culture and history, and to the meanings of Celtic knots.

I have used Claudia Zaslavsky's book *Africa Counts* for children to learn about symmetry, reflection, translation, and rotation on an axis, in African embroidered raffia cloth patterns and pottery design. Children can be given opportunities to create these geometric-strip designs and then make their own combinations. These make for a spectacular classroom display in bright colours. Cross-curricular links with the Art and Textiles department of these ideas provide exciting, rich, and three-dimensional learning to motivate children who may otherwise be disillusioned with mathematics. There are connections to exploring mathematics in contexts beyond the classroom and to other cultures in the world.

Student responses to working with these ideas

I have found that initial teacher education students are receptive to these ideas. Following a student conference on the themes of diversity and inclusion, the primary undergraduate students, were asked, "How has the conference helped to develop your understanding of inclusion and diversity?"

Here are some of their responses:

- I am going to make sure I use lots of the resources Manjinder showed us. There were so many, and I have noticed when doing my research for my wider curriculum essay many subjects, especially history and science seem to be very white male dominated.

- I have come away with a lot of strategies that I will implement in my teaching.
- It has given me a deeper understanding of each group of people/children and this has enabled me to think of ways to support them more effectively.
- [It has] left me wanting to do lots more research as I feel I have only scratched the surface of what there is to learn about the different groups.
- [The day] was filled with eye opening information which will helped inform my future practice.
- It has given me insight into the backgrounds children may have and how best to respond to this. It's broadened my knowledge on things I didn't previously have a lot of knowledge on and ways in which I can improve my teaching and outlooks.

These are some responses after a similar conference for postgraduate secondary students. I have included some comments from non-mathematicians as they seem relevant:

- I have realised the importance for the need [to] change the literary canon taught in schools.
- The links between colonialism and climate change are very interesting. Honestly, would have never made those connections before today.
- We need to push this and educate our students so they can carry it on in their journeys.
- As a History trainee, this is making me begin to feel quite ignorant in the face of diversity in my teaching. It's definitely going to make me be mindful of this going forward.
- In Music, we did a lesson on the slave trade to give context and an introduction to the origin of blues. I try to say "enslaved people/persons" rather than "slaves". thinking about the language I use. Advice on this told me that slave isn't an identity, rather a circumstance.
- This is showing me that I'm definitely not doing enough! I don't think diversity is really addressed in my lesson plans at all.

The student teachers' comments above highlight the need to include this important work of diversity and inclusion within mathematics classrooms. Often teachers are concerned with the prescriptive nature of the curriculum. However, the examples of activities provided above, and by the student teachers themselves in a follow-up workshop, show that there are ample opportunities to choose different materials which we provide to students to engage with mathematics. Indeed, such creative resources promote an understanding of people around the world, other perspectives, and views. The students' comments also show the current narrow view of school subjects, and they feel positive about empowering themselves to learn what they do not know to teach accordingly. There is acknowledgement of change in their language, understanding, and skills for their professional development.

How can equality and diversity be promoted in schools?

Deer (2020) discusses the importance of equality and diversity, how these can be promoted in school, and key principles that schools should follow considering The Equality Act 2010. In the article, "Promoting equality and diversity in the classroom," Marcel Deer (2020) offers a series of questions which can be used to reflect on our practice in terms of developing a more inclusive and diverse practice in learning and teaching mathematics. I have used these to reflect on my practice at York St John and would like to invite you to do the same.

Is the diversity of your students reflected in your lesson plans?

In my own practice, I have included the home languages of children in teaching mathematics as described in the above examples of multiplications in different scripts.

Is the language in your learning materials non-racist/sexist/discriminatory?

We can be mindful of the language we use and present to children and students. For example, I have recently found it useful to make the change from 'Black and Ethnic Minority' (BAME) to the 'global Black majority.'

Do you review your resources/lesson plans regularly?

I regularly present images of Black and female mathematicians in teaching. This allows stereotypes to be challenged and encourages children/students from under-represented groups to be see themselves in such roles.

Are negative attitudes actively challenged?

In my experience, I have found that negative attitudes often arise from ignorance and/or a fear of change. With students both in school and university, I have directly addressed racism by challenging derogatory language and highlighting meanings behind words.

Do you promote multiculturalism in lessons?

In mathematics teaching, children have learned about how mathematics has had contributions from all over the world, from many cultures over centuries. This includes the activities described earlier in this article, such as Chinese tangrams, multiplication tables in other languages, and Vedic mathematics.

Do your resources use multicultural themes?

Children have enjoyed board games from around the world. Also, my own student teachers have planned lessons on Towers of Hanoi, Sudoku, and Kenken.

Do you actively avoid using stereotypes in classroom resources and examples?

We can present images of different mathematicians to learners, as described in detail above. One such example that I have shared with my students is of Kate Okikiolu, a renowned

British research mathematician who has won many prestigious awards. After completing an undergraduate degree in mathematics at Cambridge, she went on to study a PhD at the University of California at Los Angeles.

Do you actively reference and use examples from different traditions, cultures, and religions?

Using the examples highlighted above, such as African textiles, Native American Indian designs, Aboriginal art, Celtic knots, Roman mosaics, and Islamic patterns, provides opportunities for children to discuss mathematics in new ways. In my own practice, children have positively engaged with activities which involve using the instruments in geometry sets to recreate symbols from different faiths.

Are you doing your best to challenge society's stereotypes?

We can all do more to challenge society's pre-conceptions and stereotypes on the themes of diversity and inclusion. We have made progress although there remains further work to tackle inequalities in relation to gender, race, sexuality, health, etc. For example, in my own experience, children are far more aware of issues relating to LGBTQ+ and race than we might expect. As a mathematics educator, I am inspired and excited by the student teachers, school-teachers, and children who are engaged in anti-racist and decolonial practice and indeed can take the lead on these issues to work towards a more humane mathematics education.

Notes

Some of these ideas were shared and discussed with colleagues at The Association Mathematics Education Teachers (AMET) webinar on 2 March 2022. The materials can be found at www.ametonline.org.uk/resources/.

References

Barbosa, J. C. (2006) Mathematical modelling in classroom: A socio-political and discursive perspective. *ZDM*, 38(3), 293-301.

D'Ambrosio, U. (1985) Ethnomathematics and its place in the history and pedagogy of mathematics. *For the Learning of Mathematics*, 5(1), 44-48.

Deer, M. (2020) Promoting equality and diversity in the classroom [online]. https://cpdonline.co.uk/knowledge-base/safeguarding/promoting-equality-and-diversity-in-the-classroom/.

Ernest, P. (2021, February 24) The ethics of mathematics and its uses in education and society [webinar presentation]. The Association Mathematics Education Teachers of Mathematics.

Freire, P. (1970) *Pedagogy of the Oppressed*. Continuum.

Ollerton, M. and Sykes, P. (2012) *Getting the Buggers to Add Up* (Third edition). London: Continuum.

As we come to the end of this 'theoretical' section pause for a moment. Use the key principles from the end of the chapter to think about your current practice.

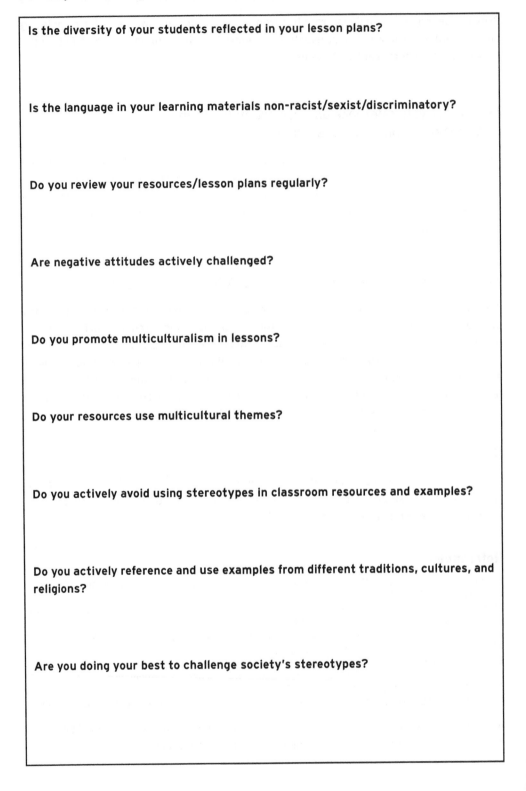

Is the diversity of your students reflected in your lesson plans?

Is the language in your learning materials non-racist/sexist/discriminatory?

Do you review your resources/lesson plans regularly?

Are negative attitudes actively challenged?

Do you promote multiculturalism in lessons?

Do your resources use multicultural themes?

Do you actively avoid using stereotypes in classroom resources and examples?

Do you actively reference and use examples from different traditions, cultures, and religions?

Are you doing your best to challenge society's stereotypes?

Key readings

Ernest, P. (2021, February 24). *The ethics of mathematics and its uses in education and society* **[Webinar]. The Association of Mathematics Education Teachers.** https://www.ametonline.org.uk/resources/

This resource is freely available from the AMET website and addresses ethics in mathematics, maths tests as critical filters, negative attitudes to the subject, seeing the world mathematically, humanising and reforming mathematics, and teaching critical citizenship via the subject.

Ignotofsky, R. (2017) *Women in Science.* **London: Hachette Children's Group.**

This wonderful and colourful book is a celebration of the contributions throughout history of trailblazing women to mathematics, science, engineering, and technology. Use with children and adults of all genders to inspire the next generation.

Shan, S. and Bailey, P. (1994) *Multiple Factors: Classroom mathematics for equality and justice.* **Chester: Trentham Books Limited.**

An exciting and inspirational book packed with practical activities for any classroom. Ideas include Vedic mathematics, global statistics, geometry of faith symbols, number in international recipes, patterns in dance, world economics, class projects, and more to challenge racism.

Zaslavsky, C. (1990) *Africa Counts.* **Chicago: Lawrence Hill Books.**

A beautiful book capturing the contributions of African peoples to mathematics, including number systems, geometry, art in textiles and crafts, architecture and games. A creative resource to aid activity planning with, and for, learners.

PART 2
Practice drawing on the theory

The following three chapters contain a series of practical examples for teachers and university tutors. We hope that tutors and teachers will be able to make immediate use of these activities in their teaching, whether working with early career teachers or students in school. Each lesson or activity is presented in the form of a case study, as they all draw on activities the authors have used in their teaching. Each activity shares the resources you will need, sometimes in the text and sometimes through a link to the companion website.

We recognise that some readers may have chosen to start their journey through the book at this point, preferring to start with the practical rather than the theoretical. We would hope that the exploration of ideas of social justice through trying out practical activities will encourage you to explore the theory which underpins this practice at a later date. We believe that the theoretical perspectives offered in the first section offer the foundations on which these activities are built and will help you to better understand the rationale behind them. And we believe that this theory illustrates why these are more than activities to be used as curriculum enrichment or enhancement. Rather they are the bedrock on which all mathematics curricula should be built. The theory argues that a socially just curriculum provides a better educational experience for all.

While individual activities were developed by individual authors, the final versions are the result of collaboration and discussion between the four authors and other specialists in the field. We hope that this might mirror the way in which the reader might draw on the activities. Working for social justice is often more effective, and certainly more fun, if we develop and evaluate our teaching in collaboration with colleagues and those we are teaching. In this spirit of collaboration there is a space on the companion website for you to share your experiences of working with these activities. We would love this space to be a place where teachers, tutors, and students of all ages can share their experiences. There is also a space for you to offer your own ideas for activities.

Each activity uses the same form. There is an introductory section which sets the context for the activity both in terms of the issue that is explored and the mathematics that will be drawn on and developed in the activity. This is followed by the starting point for the teacher or tutor; this is a suggestion about how you might introduce the activity. The next section offers you ways in which you can develop the learning throughout the activity followed by possibilities for further exploration of the ideas, both mathematical and in terms of the issue being analysed.

DOI: 10.4324/9781003361466-6

While this section is split into stages, it is recognised that many of the activities are suitable for use across phases. The following is an overview:

Chapter 5: Mainly Early Years

1. Waste and recycling: Classifying waste to explore if it can be reused or recycled. Classification and counting
2. Equality or equity: Equal and fair sharing of snacks. Division as equal distribution. Human bar charts.
3. A teaspoon? Exploring a range of cultural practices using non-standard measures.
4. 100 squares in different scripts: Exploring 100 squares in a range of different scripts. Number and place value and valuing and acknowledging a range of linguistic backgrounds.

Chapter 6: Mainly Primary

1. Gender equality: Exploring representation of women and girls in children's books. Data handling and analysis using fractions and percentages.
2. Race equality: Similar to above. Exploring representation in books drawing on diverse backgrounds and ethnicity.
3. If the world were a village of 100 people: Based on the book of the same name. Uses interpreting data to examine issues of inequality and social justice at the global level. Includes developing understanding of large numbers.
4. Nutritious lunches: Examines school lunches to see if they meet the requirements of the 'Food for life' quality mark. Data handling and analysis using fractions and percentages.
5. Water use and conservation: Investigating how much water children use in a day. Measurement, capacity in particular.
6. Food miles: Exploring distances that different types of food travel before they are purchased.
7. Plastic waste: Estimating the quantity of plastic in the class. Exploring recycling
8. Wildfires: Mathematical modelling of the way wildfire spread.
9. Fair choices: Exploring different ways to vote. Which gives the 'fairest' result?

Chapter 7: Mainly Secondary

1. Child labour: Interpreting data in graph form about child labour around the world. Understanding percentages and proportion.
2. Counting the votes: Understanding different voting systems.
3. Housing and community: Interpreting data to explore different types of housing and home ownership. Developing understanding of how graphs can be misleading.
4. Investigating earnings: Investigating the inequalities in earnings across different ethnic groups. Interpreting and analysing data.

5. Measuring inequality: Using economic theory to explore and generate measures of global inequality.
6. Refugee journeys: Developing ideas of scale to create scale maps of refugee journeys. Using percentages to explore how many refugees reach different countries.
7. Epidemics: Mathematical modelling of the spread of epidemics. Using probability to estimate rates of increase.

5 Mainly early years

Creating a mathematically rich and a mathematically just environment

Education in the Early Years may well look very different from the experience of education as children get older. Indeed, we would argue that it should look different. The early years should not be seen as simply preparing children to start formal education. This is not to argue that a mathematics education for social justice is not appropriate for our youngest learners. There is a large body of research that shows that children develop and are aware of gender and racial stereotypes around the age of six (see, for example, Brown and Bigler, 2005). So, we would argue, social justice should be a key component of Early Years practitioners' planning and practice. This chapter opens with a more broad discussion around the environments in which our children learn as we accept and hope that many Early Years settings will be operating on a model that follows a child-initiated and a child-centred philosophy. And, as with the rest of the book, we think all teachers can learn from other phases of education. Perhaps this is even more true of teachers of older children learning from the Early Years.

So, in the spirit of reflection, let us start with a thought experiment. Try to remember a time in which you felt you were really learning something. When was the last time you had that feeling of exhilaration and joy that learning something new brings? Can you take yourself back to that place and the people around you? Try to recall:

Where did the learning take place? Were you inside or outside?
Who were you with? Did these people take the roles of teachers or collaborators in learning?
What equipment were you using? Did you require specialist resources?
What had motivated you to become engaged in this particular learning?

The answers to these questions will begin to unpick for you what a rich learning environment looks like for you. You can use this thought experiment to think about what a mathematically rich and a mathematically just environment might look like. Of course, your learning may not have been mathematical, and you may not see it related to social justice, but it gives you a starting point.

In order to think about mathematics and social justice more directly we will return to the Rawlsian 'veil of ignorance' described by Tony on page vii. Think of your usual planning

DOI: 10.4324/9781003361466-7

for mathematical activities for young children. As you reflect on this, think of the learners who seem to have the least connection with these ideas or who are least able to access the activity. Ask yourself why it is that these learners are less able to access the mathematics learning than the others. How might you change the learning environment so that these learners become as engaged in the lessons as their peers? While acknowledging that many key drivers of inequality are built into an inequitable education system, this approach allows teachers and Early Years practitioners to act in the areas in which they have agency.

A rich learning environment is made up of people, places, and objects. These three are connected but can be explored separately. Each of them have an impact on the richness of the mathematical environment and the contribution that such an environment can make to social justice. The people who engage in mathematics with young learners are models of mathematicians for the young learners. As such, it is important that children see positive models of people engaging with mathematics. If they see adults enjoying mathematics, being successful in mathematics, and using mathematics to explore interesting questions, they will learn that this is the nature of mathematics. This will include creating an environment in which it is fine to have a go and make mistakes. Teachers and Early Years practitioners can model how we learn from errors and how these should be embraced as learning opportunities. Many children are put off mathematics through fear of making mistakes (and being humiliated), so how we respond to errors is critical in establishing a rich learning environment.

Ideally children will see the diversity of the population of the UK in the practitioners they work with. The model they see here is that mathematics is available to all and not the property of particular groups. Everyone can be successful in mathematics whatever their background. If your setting struggles to recruit diverse practitioners then draw on the local communities around your school to support the mathematical experiences.

In terms of the places in which we learn, the message for mathematics and for social justice is that mathematics takes place and can be learned in all the different spaces we inhabit. This might be the classroom, it may be an outside space, and it definitely includes children's homes, places of worship, places that they visit for recreation, or places that they visit for holidays or when visiting family. There is a social justice dimension here as we can learn from each other's environments and appreciate the range of mathematics that might be available to others in environments that we may not normally visit.

Finally, the resources that we draw on will include specialist mathematics resources but can also include objects which children are familiar with from home. These resources will vary from home to home and from community to community. We can take advantage of the richness which this diversity will bring. The four activities that follow exemplify these ideas, but we hope that this section gives you food for thought in terms of the changes you could make to the learning environment regardless of the activities that are taking place.

Reference

Brown, C.S., and Bigler, R.S. (2005) Children's perceptions of discrimination: A developmental model. *Child Development*, Vol 76, Issue 3, pp. 533-553.

What changes can you make immediately to the learning environment to make it a more mathematically rich and a more just learning environment?

Activity 1: Waste and recycling

Introduction

The social justice element in this activity is linked to waste and recycling and addresses the 12th United Nations Goal, 'Ensure sustainable consumption and production patterns' (See https://sdgs.un.org/goals/goal12). It addresses how we can look after our environment by understanding how we can recycle and reuse waste. It begins by exploring how children can recycle waste and rubbish in their classroom space and their contribution to the environment. Learning can be shared with the rest of the school in an assembly or through displays around the school.

In this activity, children apply and develop their knowledge of counting to ten or more, use vocabulary more than, less than, equal to, and sort and classify. Mathematics within this activity is better taught within a thematic or cross-curricular approach to learning and teaching, which is often the approach taken within most Early Year settings.

The activity below provides a blueprint to be used as a scaffold to personalise the activity to your school and setting. The activity is presented as a problem-solving and problem-seeking task to address a social justice issue and uses child-initiated and child-centred pedagogies. We think the activity is most effective when:

- Teachers adopt a guided inquiry approach using key questions to scaffold children's mathematical thinking.
- Teachers encourage collaborative group work and social interactions between children and the teacher throughout the lesson in order to develop mathematical thinking, problem-solving, and dialogue.

Prior mathematical knowledge required for this session broadly falls into the areas of classifying, sorting, measuring, and counting. However, this subject knowledge is further developed throughout the activity, building on the differing experiences that learners bring with them.

Starting point

This activity is effective when links are made to other curriculum subjects, such as 'the world around us,' that discuss the topics of waste, recycling, and reuse. This will provide some background knowledge and understanding of the topic for application in mathematics lessons. It can be useful to have a hook to get children interested in the topic, such as a video or book such as *Hey, that's not trash! But which bin does it go in?* by Renee Jablow. These stimuli can be a useful starting point to then pose a problem for the children in the class such as, 'How good is our class at reducing the waste/rubbish we throw away?' Try to build on the responses of the children and steer questioning towards how waste can be recycled. For example, you could create a compost bin or find ways to reuse some items. It would be helpful if children are familiar with and have some working knowledge of what the terms *recycle* and *waste* mean. For example, do they know what a compost bin is? If the school already has a compost bin this could be used as a teaching resource.

Development

Make sure you have followed all health and safety requirements. It might be best to do this activity in the afternoon once the class has accumulated rubbish. It can be done outdoors where you have space and you can clear up easily. Following on from the starting points above, consider classifying the rubbish as follows:

- we can recycle this rubbish,
- we can put this rubbish in a compost bin,
- we can reuse this rubbish,
- this rubbish, we must throw away.

Shapes can be drawn on the floor to classify the rubbish. Using a litter collector or gloves, children can move rubbish into various sections. Discuss the concept and purpose of classification.

Diagram 1: Sorting rubbish

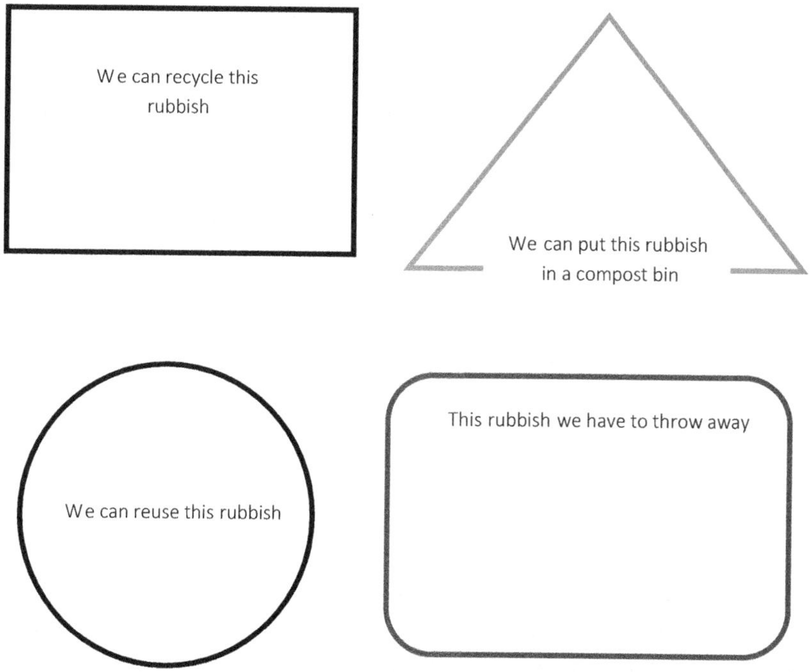

We can recycle this
rubbish

We can put this rubbish
in a compost bin

We can reuse this rubbish

This rubbish we have to throw away

Move the discussion on to how to measure each section. How can we find out the mass of how much of the rubbish we recycle, we reuse, we keep for the compost bin, or we get rid of as waste? Introduce or remind children of the balance scale. It would be useful if your outdoor space had a balance scale that children were familiar using with non-standard units of measure.

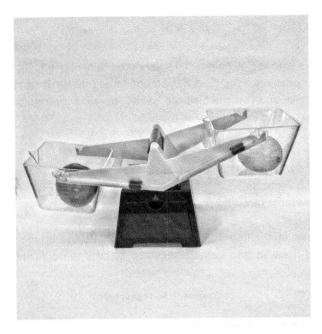

The whole class can take responsibility by dividing the children into groups assigned to each classification and each group records the number of non-standard units

As children measure the mass of each classified rubbish, they focus on counting (using appropriate units of measure, bears, multilink cubes, blocks, etc.).

- Emphasise one-to-one correspondence of the non-standard unit used for measurement.
- If you have a number square or number line in the outdoor space, ask children to find that number in those visual images.
- With chalk, ask children to write out that number on the floor.
- Repeat the task with the different rubbish classifications, and give each group the mass measurement of the rubbish in a sentence, for example, our class recycles nine blocks of rubbish.
- You can move onto asking questions about how the class has more or less rubbish to recycle than rubbish that is waste.
- The numbers and representations from the above task can be used in the classroom, such as counting up to nine or finding nine multilink cubes to represent the data.
- The activity can be repeated over the week, with the aim that each day the children think carefully about how they can reduce the rubbish waste. They can also compare the measurement with the previous day and discuss whether it is more or less than before.
- Each day, children can create a visual 3D block graph. As a class the data can be recorded on a chart.

Other possibilities

These activities can be used to encourage young learners to take an activist stance. For example:

Can the children invite the head teacher and ask if the school has a recycling system? What strong argument can they use from the data they collected to indicate the importance of recycling?

Can the children find out if the school has a compost bin? If there is none, is this something that the school can start up? Can the children find a strong argument using the numbers they collected to indicate why this would be a good idea?

At home, ask children to help with recycling some rubbish. Find out the special bins in the area, and remind children that the bin is for all recycled rubbish.

Resources

Hey, that's not trash! But which bin does it go in? by Renee Jablow and Mike Byrne. London: Little Simon. This is a 'board book.' That is, it is interactive, and children can press out pieces in the shapes of everyday objects to sort. There is a YouTube video of the book available.

The United Nations website contains many resources which will be helpful for planning. See www.un .org/sustainabledevelopment/sustainable-development-goals/.

Another useful online resource is 'Kids against Plastic': see www.kidsagainstplastic.co.uk/alismap/. This resource for litter classifies the different types of plastics that are thrown away in your area. Although a little ambitious for Early Years, it could be a useful resource to use as a school to campaign for reducing plastic.

Activity 2: Equality or equity?

Introduction

The concepts of equality and equity relate to the evolving philosophies of distribution of wealth and services. Both equality and equity aim to promote fairness and justice. However, equality works if everyone starts from the same point and needs the same things, whereas equity is based on the needs of individuals, groups, and communities. As a result, equity and equality permeate all aspects of the UN Goals and are not fixed on any specific UN goal.

While this activity is aimed at the Early Years phase, it can be used across all age groups in the primary sector. The activity below offers a basic structure and idea of how teachers can explore the ideas of equality and equity in mathematics. It has been written to offer a useful bank of ideas and examples of how mathematical learning can be used to explore a social justice theme. The activity is presented as a problem-solving and problem-seeking task and is child-centred. It requires teachers to use culturally responsive pedagogies and teaching, to draw on their knowledge of the children they teach, their own subject knowledge around early number, and confidence to draw out issues of social justice when planning and teaching. We think this activity is most effective when:

- Teachers adopt a guided inquiry approach using key questions to scaffold children's mathematical thinking.
- Teachers encourage collaborative group work and social interactions between children and teachers.
- Prior mathematical knowledge required for this session broadly falls into the areas of counting and early addition, subtraction and counting, and the concept of division as sharing. However, this subject knowledge is further developed throughout the activity, building on the differing experiences that learners bring with them.

Starting points

Activity 1: Sharing and division as equal distribution

Most schools have snack time in the form of fruit or vegetables offered to children. During snack time:

- Ask children how to share the snack fairly with everyone in the class. Unpick the language of 'share' and invite other words from children. The mathematical symbol of equals/balance can also be introduced.
- Ask, "How many snacks do we need so that we all get one?" Count the children and teachers in the class, and find that number on a number line.
- Ask children to give examples of what would be an unfair sharing of the snack, and work with the ideas provided.
- Ask what would happen if we always distributed the snacks unfairly based on examples provided by children.
- Carry out whole-class counts using the 1:1 principle as the snack is being shared.

Activity 2: Distribute the leftover snack fairly

- Make sure there is some snack left over. Once children have eaten the snack, count the number of snacks left over: I have five snacks left over (for example). Find that number on a number line.

- Ask, "What can we do with the leftover snacks? Throw them away, share them equally, or give them to another class?" Children make suggestions and then vote on a choice. Children physically arrange themselves into a human graph. Count the number of children in each category, 1:1 counting, and match the number to the symbol. In each category, can children give a reason for their choice?

  We think we should throw the snack away because...

  We think we should give the snack to another class because....

  We think we should share the leftover snack equally in class because....

  The human graph can generate some simple addition and subtraction calculations for children to work out.

- How can we distribute these five snacks fairly among the children in our class? Discuss the responses provided by the children.

- Ask, "What if the snacks could not be cut? How can the five snacks be shared fairly in this class?" Use the suggestions posed by the children. These suggestions could be based on giving the snacks to children who like that snack. Use them as criteria for sorting: "I like this snack and I do not like this snack." The children can physically arrange themselves into a human graph.

- Count how many children do not like eating this snack, and count how many do like eating the snack. Find that number on the number line. Use questioning related to how many more children like eating the snack than those who do not. Subtraction as a difference can be shown on a number line or found physically with the children.

- Discuss the statements, "I like this snack" and "I do not like this snack." Discuss whether it would be fair to give the second snack to those children who like eating that snack. Pose the question: "are we being equal?"

- The group who like the snack may still be too big. Discuss how you can fairly distribute the five snacks. For example, "Does everyone in that group need to have a second helping of the snack?" Discuss what might be a need to have a second helping of a snack. Use children's responses, and build on thinking based on giving the snack to those who like eating the snack and did not have a proper or no breakfast that morning, or those children who are hungry, or those who like eating the snack but do not buy this snack at home/or do not eat this snack at home. Discuss whether that would be fair.

- Use the above to raise the bigger question, "Is that equal? Is fair and equal the same?"

Other possibilities

These activities can be used to encourage young learners to take an activist stance. For example:

- As a class, decide the fairest way to share leftover snacks. Have that as a reminder statement displayed in the class for all snack times.

- Investigate what happens to leftover food in the school kitchens at lunchtime.

- Investigate what happens to leftover food in places that sell food. Some takeaway out-lets and supermarkets give leftover food to charity, and others give to good causes or to those who need it. Discuss who or what the good causes might be. Discuss whether it is fair to give free food to those causes.

Children could organise an assembly to the school and parents on how they fairly share leftover snacks in their class. They could talk about some food places that also give leftover food to those who need it. In order to do this the children might need to investigate this in the local area and invite people to be part of the assembly.

Resources and links

What is equality and social justice? is a useful 'BBC Bitesize' video that can be shared with children. Available at www.bbc.co.uk/bitesize/topics/znbrpg8/articles/z42khbk

A lovely story about equality and equity called *Fair is fair*, and based on food, is available at www .youtube.com/watch?v=kVqZzLN9eQU.

Information about the *Too good to go* app which sells leftover food at a reduced price and sometimes gives away free leftover food at the end of the day is available at www.toogoodtogo.com/en-gb.

As well as helping the environment, this app helps those families who do not have enough to eat. The class could share the app as a notice in the school newsletter to parents.

Activity 3: How much is a teaspoon?

Introduction

This activity came out of working with parents from the local Asian communities in Leicester. My daughter attended a primary school which was rich in cultural diversity. The school drew on this diversity in many ways including a community café at lunchtime which many parents, including me, enjoyed. We took it in turns to prepare the lunchtime meals and I noticed that the mums I was working with measured out the spices they were using with their hands rather than teaspoons or tablespoons or weighing them.

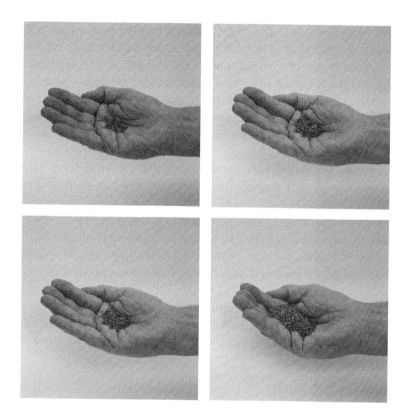

The children in the school helped with the cooking. This would often involve the children of the parents who were preparing the food. The children of many of the school staff also attended the school including the headteacher's two girls and the chair of governor's daughter. I was chair of governors at the time.

Two of the areas that are encouraged in the Statutory Framework for the Early Years Foundation Stage (EYFS) in England are:

- Partnership working between practitioners and parents and/or carers.
- Equality of opportunity and anti-discriminatory practice ensuring that every child is included and supported.

Involving parents of the whole community in this way ensures that everyday mathematical practices from home are valued and built on within school. It also allows the informal conversations between parents and practitioners which are so important to take place.

Starting point

Activities involving measuring are best carried out actively. We learn to measure by measuring. We learn to measure accurately by measuring in context. In this context, if we measure inaccurately, we impact the flavour of the food we are eating. This activity can be replicated across the age ranges. For the purpose of the book I will focus on the Early Years initially.

As with all Early Years' activities this should not be seen as a one-off activity which 'teaches' measurement. Rather, it is a starting point from which activity can be developed on an ongoing basis as part of continuous provision. I have found that the most motivating starting point, the starting point which best engages young learners' curiosity, is to invite parents in to the setting to cook a dish which they would regularly prepare at home. Clearly a diverse classroom offers a wider variety of choice for tasty dishes. If you are unfortunate enough to work in a monocultural classroom take yourselves on a world tour and try out dishes that are new to you.

Create recipes on laminated card (laminate is important when cooking ingredients are around – it is as messy as art!). Measure out the ingredients aloud. Model different ways of measuring. Use a teaspoon – tip the teaspoon into your hand. Notice what it looks like. Use the vocabulary of, "how much..?" and "how many?" As you can imagine there is a lot of counting involved. I will talk about clockwise and anti-clockwise as we stir.

After cooking and eating the dish, continuous provision can include a cooking corner where children role-play preparing food for each other using a range of dry pulses of different sizes.

Children enjoy counting out the measures, and this makes a link between measures and spatial reasoning. It also makes direct connections between mathematics and cultural awareness. To select from the Early Learning Goals, I have noticed evidence of all of the following during this activity:

- Working cooperatively and taking turns
- Forming positive attachments to adults and friendships with peers
- Using a range of small tools
- Reading words
- Recall number bonds up to five
- Subitise up to five

Unfortunately, in September 2021 the Early Years Mathematics Curriculum was considerably impoverished by the removal of measurement from the statutory curriculum. I would argue that measuring activities such as this both support the development of the understanding of number and are important in their own right. The language of comparison is developed through asking children for 'more' or 'less' of an ingredient and so on.

Finally, Paragraph 1.13 in the statutory guidance suggests that:

> For children whose home language is not English, providers must take reasonable steps to provide opportunities for children to develop and use their home language in play and learning.

What a great way activities involving measurement are to meet this requirement.

Development

You can develop this idea by extending into how many of one measure can fill another measure.

- How many teaspoons fill a small cup?
- How many handfuls fill another container?
- How many small containers in a large container?

This can lead to activities exploring the conservation of measure. Provide a range of containers of different shapes and sizes. Ask children to place them in order by estimation and then compare them by filling them using a smaller cup.

Other possibilities

As children get older they can create more complex meals and follow more complex recipes. They can also use ratio and proportion to adapt recipes that they are given. They can even prepare meals for special events with parents and make decisions around budgets and how much to charge for meals at a charity event.

Older learners can create tables such as this one.

Hand comparisons

1. 1/8 teaspoon = 1 pinch between thumb, index, and middle fingers.
2. 1/4 teaspoon = 2 pinches between thumb, index, and middle fingers.
3. 1/2 teaspoon = Cup your hand, pour a quarter-sized amount into your palm.
4. 1 teaspoon = Top joint of index finger.
5. 1 tablespoon = Entire thumb.

Bibliography

Department for Education (2021) *Statutory framework for the early years foundation stage: Setting the standards for learning development and care for children from birth to five.* London: DfE. https://assets.publishing.service.gov.uk/government/uploads/system/uploads/attachment_data/file/974907/EYFSframework-March2021.pdf

Activity 4: 100 squares in diverse scripts

Introduction

I have often heard teachers refer to the 100 square below, or numbers written using Hindu-Arabic script, as 'normal' numbers. They are, of course, only normal to people who use this script to write numbers. Assuming this norm does great disservice to the large populations of the world that use other scripts to both write and to write numbers. This includes large numbers of students to whom different scripts are not at all unusual. This assumption of a false norm can also lead to confusions. I have travelled in the Middle East and often notice Arabic-speaking passengers being unable to locate their seats on planes as the seats are all numbered using Hindu-Arabic script rather than the Arabic script they are familiar with.

Once, when asked to run a series of parents' workshops at a school in inner-city Leeds, I realised that in the group of 12 parents there were five different languages spoken. My starting point for this workshop was to ask a representative of each home language to teach us all to count to 20 in their language. We explored similarities and differences and discussed the roots of some of the number words. This produced a fascinating discussion and a way of easing tensions and worries at the start of such a workshop.

I first used this activity in the 1990s in primary schools in Leicester and have repeatedly used it with groups in primary and secondary schools as well as teacher education students since.

Starting point

The starting point is straightforward. I photocopy each of the 100 squares in a different colour and create jigsaws by cutting up the square. Each jigsaw is then placed in an envelope. Before the students enter the room, I distribute the jigsaw pieces around the room, making sure that each group, or table, has a range of different jigsaw pieces.

The first phase is the students rearranging themselves so that they are sitting with other students who have the same colour jigsaw piece. They can then attempt to create the jigsaw. I encourage the students to talk, articulating the decisions they are making while they are solving the jigsaw. I note some of the phrases that people use on the whiteboard.

Once the jigsaws are completed the groups describe the process by which they completed the jigsaws. They explain how they used their knowledge of the 100 square to help with this solution. We also notice how working in another script makes it more difficult for us to show the mathematics skills that we possess and that observers may assume we are less skilled in place value than we really are – if assessed in a different way.

I have run this session many times, and every time at least one person in the room can count in languages other than English. It is rare that one of the group does not work in a script other than English. At this point I will ask this student to teach us all to count in this other language. Again, we note the clues and cues we use to memorise the new number names.

Development

The 100 squares can be used to support simple calculations using the script of the 100 square. This models the importance of having representations of the number system to support learners, particularly learners working with English as an Additional Language.

Other scripts can be explored and examined and other 100 squares created. This is particularly powerful when members of local communities who use scripts other than English create 100 squares for the class and visit the class to teach students how to count in this language. This is also a good opportunity to be taught nursery rhymes from that language and other counting traditions. For example, this image shows a Chinese finger counting system.

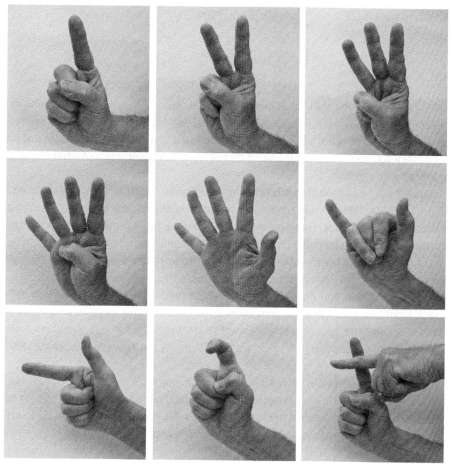

In some Indian cultures, segments of fingers are used to count so each finger represents four and a hand 20. This is another ripe area for research.

Other possibilities

The history of number development is a very rich area for exploration and raises the profile of the mathematics of the Islamic world and offers opportunities for introducing students to mathematicians from many different cultures and backgrounds. This is also an activity that lends itself to Black History Month.

6 Mainly primary

We want to acknowledge that for some readers, particularly those of you teaching in primary schools, this may be the point at which you open the book. We are also aware that many of you will have spent considerable time reading and thinking about ideas of social justice before you reach this point and so do not want to repeat much of what has already been shared with readers.

We hope it will be sufficient in this brief introduction to reiterate our understanding that there are many factors outside of our classrooms which mitigate against a mathematics education for social justice. However, we believe that we have some agency in the spaces in which we teach and can make choices within our planning and pedagogical approaches which are supportive of the fight for social justice. To some extent we can model the society we would like to see outside our schools in our classrooms.

Whilst we hope that you find the activities which follow useful, and would love to have feedback from you through the companion website about the ways in which you have used these activities in your practice, we want to start the chapter with a reflection on the broader pedagogical approaches which we think support the move to a more socially just mathematics education.

On page 48–49 Balbir Kaur offers a schema which suggests ways in which teachers and schools can develop 'culturally responsive mathematical pedagogical knowledge for social justice, anti-racist and decolonial perspectives.' A useful starting point might be to reflect on these questions before planning to teach any of the activities which follow.

- To what extent have I researched how my pedagogical choices impact different groups of children?
- Have I explored which classroom participation structures are culturally and linguistically compatible? For example, have I explored how child-centred my practice is?
- Do I model my belief that mathematical ability is not fixed? Do all the children in my classroom believe they can be successful mathematicians?
- Do I know the children in my classroom as individuals? Do I understand their culture and beliefs? Do I appreciate and draw on their cultural heritage in my mathematics teaching?
- Have I explored how I can use mathematics to develop the linguistic skills of all the children in my class no matter what their linguistic background is?

DOI: 10.4324/9781003361466-8

- Do I draw on problem-solving strategies to teach children to collaborate and communicate effectively and value all contributions regardless of their peers' backgrounds?
- Do I use and value a wide range of assessment strategies?
- Do I engage with colleagues across the education system to develop research informed practices around mathematics education for social justice?

A challenge we know, but one we hope you embrace. A starting point at working on the questions above may be to try out one of the activities that follow and share your experience with one other person.

Activity 1: Gender equality

Introduction

This activity addresses the 5th United Nations Goal, 'achieve gender equality and empower all women and girls.' See www.un.org/sustainabledevelopment/gender-equality. It is useful to explore some aspects of this goal to discuss why this might be an issue of social justice. It can also be linked to global events such as International Women's Day.

This activity is based on research studies that have identified gender stereotypes and the underrepresentation of lead female characters in children's literature. These studies have shown that exposure to gender stereotypes negatively affects girls and boys, limiting the choice of acceptable roles and behaviours and normalising gender inequalities later in life (Filipovic, 2018). Studies have also shown that gender stereo-typing impacts 'children's activity choices, career aspirations, and academic outcomes.' (Filipovic, 2018, p. 311). Female invisibility may lead to the perception that girls are less important, and stereotyping of roles and activities is likely to reinforce the gender system, limiting the aspirations of both girls and boys. Four-year-old children have been found to associate male characters with superiority, whilst female characters are associated with inferiority.

The activity below offers a way to explore the sensitive topic of gender stereotypes in children's books. The activity is written as a bank of ideas and examples of how mathematical learning can be used to explore an issue of social justice. The activity is presented as a problem-solving/seeking task to address a social justice issue and is child centred. We believe it is most effective when teachers use culturally responsive pedagogies and teaching that draws on the knowledge of the children, their own knowledge of statistics, and their personal understanding of the issue of gender stereotyping when planning and teaching. We would also hope that you are able to:

- adopt a 'guided inquiry approach' using key questions to scaffold children's mathematical thinking
- encourage collaborative group work and social interactions between children and the teachers throughout the lesson to support the development of mathematical thinking, problem solving, and dialogue
- draw on your subject knowledge of the data-handling cycle, based on the principles of collecting, organising, interpreting, and analysing data
- draw on your subject knowledge of number, specifically knowledge related to understanding percentages and fractions

Starting point

You can introduce the topic using a cross-curricular approach. For example, you could begin the exploration in a PSHE (personal, social, health and economic) lesson. This will develop the children's knowledge and understanding of the issue to take into mathematics lessons. Begin by presenting children with the problem:

> In a study conducted in 2011 of 5000 children's books, 25% did not have a female character.

Ask children to discuss why this may have been raised as a concern, or 'unfair.'

Take some time to explore what 25% is in relation to the part-to-whole concept, on a number line, out of 100, and fraction equivalent. The problem can become a starting point to understand percentage and finding a percentage of something. Show children different images of 25% or one-quarter of a whole to visualise how many books had no female characters. Alternatively, you can ask the children to draw images of 25% or one-quarter and share these.

Then pose the question, 'How many books would that be?' This problem could be broken down so that you eventually get to work out 25% of 5000 or find one-quarter of 5000. Focus on mathematical thinking and share the strategies the children used to carry out the calculation. You could contextualise the answer by looking at a bookshelf in the classroom and finding out what a quarter of the books on the bookshelf looks like.

Present the children with some more information:

> In another study of 100 best-selling children's books, 53 books did not have a female speaking part (McCabe, 2011).

This statement is another way to explore how to find a percentage of a number. Questions you can ask can include:

- What percentage would that be?
- What is this study telling us? Is this equal? Is this fair?
- How many books had female speaking parts?
- If we use 53 books out of 100 not having female speaking characters, how many books out of 1000 may not have female speaking parts? How many out of 2000, 4000, or 5000?

Ask children to justify their thinking and reasoning on the two studies they have worked on. Discuss the date of the study and ask the children to discuss whether they think this data would be true today. Ask children how they could check.

The two videos below provide another hook to engage with the issue. Teachers can be creative as to how these videos are used either as part of the maths lesson or PSHE lesson. The 'Redraw the balance' video would be an interesting experiment with your children.

- Gender stereotypes in children's books - GENDER ACTION SCHOOLS AWARD.
- (11) #RedrawTheBalance - YouTube.

- https://www.genderaction.co.uk/latest-news/2019/8/27/gender-stereotypes-in-books and https://www.youtube.com/watch?v=qv8VZVP5csA

Discuss the video and how they felt about the outcome. Questions to pose could relate to the importance of providing positive role models for both boys and girls in primary school and ask the question, 'Does our class library of fiction picture books provide equal representation of female and male characters? How do we know and how can we find out?'

Development

Pose the question, 'Does our class library of fiction picture books provide equal representation of female and male characters? How do we know, and how can we find out?' Organise children to work in groups of 5–6, with mixed gender and attainment. We suggest addressing the issue/problem as a whole class, with each group contributing data and following the data-handling cycle below.

Specify a problem

Ask children to come up with questions they could investigate related to previous problems. Collect ideas but have a bank of suggestions to support children's responses, such as:

- Does our class/school library of fiction picture books provide equal representation of male and female lead characters? Or
- Are the number of female and male characters fairly represented in fiction books in our school? Or
- How are male and female characters represented in fiction books?

Plan on how to collect data

Pose questions such as, 'What should our sample size be?' and 'Is the number of fiction picture books in this class enough?' Respond to children's answers and reasoning. A sample size of 100 books might be helpful as you can use this to work out simple percentages, fractions, and calculations. The 100 books could be split between the groups in the class.

Collect data fairly and inclusively

This could be a very exciting way to build up detailed data as a whole class. The responses to each will depend on the question children are answering.

- What are our categories?
- What are we looking for in our fiction books?
- How can we ensure that the data we collect is fair?

Work with the responses from the children.

Process the best way to present the data

As a starting point, the data could contribute to a visual whole-class 3D graph. Collectively generate the data in Excel and share the results with children. Discuss graphing possibilities such as the type of graph that best represents the data, the titles for the chart, the scale, etc.

Interpret and discuss findings

Use probing questions to interpret and interrogate the data. For example, 'What is most common?', 'How many ... than ...?', 'More/fewer?', 'Altogether?', 'Have we answered our main problem question?', 'What have we found?', and 'What story does our data tell?'. The results could trigger further questions being posed and another cycle of data collection, which would be encouraged.

Other possibilities

Below are some examples of several cycles of data.

> Does our class/school library of fiction picture books provide equal representation of lead female and male characters?

Children may suggest does the book have male and/or female characters, which may provide four categories: male characters, female characters, both, or unknown. This can be checked fairly by everyone in the group agreeing with the results.

> What 'roles' do male and female characters have in the stories?

Children may suggest a variety of roles and have their way of classifying the data. This should contribute to a whole-class discussion as to what different roles were found and how best to categorise the data to collect as a whole class.

Continue to develop the categories through questioning.

A final lesson could be looking at the different stories each data collection provided and what it tells us about how male and female characters are represented in 100 fiction picture books in the school. This would involve the children in applying their knowledge of fractions, percentages, and calculations to interpret and discuss findings. They could draw on this knowledge to work on questions such as:

- What deductions can children make about how female and male characters are represented in fictional picture books in school?
- Is a sample of 100 books a fair representation?
- Does the class have any recommendations for the head teacher?
- Does the class have any recommendations for a school librarian?

The activity can also be extended to explore the issue at the local library for a greater impact on the local community.

References

Filipović, K. (2018). Gender representation in children's books: Case of an early childhood setting. *Journal of Research in Childhood Education, 32*(3), pp. 310-325. London: Taylor and Francis.

McCabe, J., Fairchild, E., Grauerholz, L., Pescosolido, B.A. and Tope, D. (2011). Gender in twentieth-century children's books: Patterns of disparity in titles and central characters. *Gender & Society, 25*(2), pp.197-226. London: Sage.

Sovič, A. and Hus, V. (2015). Gender stereotype analysis of the textbooks for young learners. *Procedia-Social and Behavioural Sciences, 186*, pp. 495-501. London: Elsevier.

UN Sustainable Goal #5 Gender Equality - Take Action for the Sustainable Development Goals - United Nations Sustainable Development. https://sdgs.un.org/goals

Activity 2: Race equality

You will see that Activities 1 and 2 follow very similar approaches. We hope that you can use both activities as a way of both developing mathematical skills and aware-ness of the issues of stereotyping and diverse representation in books.

Introduction

The social justice element related to this activity is connected to an anti-racist agenda that acknowledges that racial injustices and ingrained inequalities are apparent in society and evident in education. It is a category that permeates all aspects of the UN Goals and is not fixed on any one, specific UN goal.

This activity is based on several research studies that have identified race and ethnicity in literature in English schools. A key research report to gain some background knowledge of this issue is *Lit in colour: Diversity in literature in English schools* commissioned by The Runnymede Trust. Although the report is heavily aimed at exploring diverse literature in secondary schools, the findings and some reference to primary schools is useful. This study is based on research carried out in England, whereas the majority of the research in this area is based in America. Research carried out by Koss (2015) has shown that diverse litera-ture helps children identify with their culture and the cultures of others that can promote discussions for diversity in the classroom. Studies have also shown that children need to see themselves reflected in the books they read, to see the lives of others and to see them-selves as being able to 'traverse between groups and worlds.' (p. 32). Children's books are powerful learning tools for helping young children understand discrimination. The images we share with children affect their conceptualisation of self and belonging. 'When children cannot identify with a book or see their lives celebrated through stories, it may have a nega-tive impact on their self-image. The message they get is that their lives and their stories are not important.' (Willett, 1995, p. 176, cited in Koss, 2015). Seeing self is critical, but not seeing self is even more critical because children may feel marginalised.

The activity offers you a way to explore diverse representation in picture books using mathematics. Race and diversity are sensitive topics for discussion with children and require careful planning and safe ways to manage the conversation. The activity is designed to offer a bank of ideas and a range of examples of how mathematical learning can be used to explore an issue of social justice. The activity is presented as a problem-solving/seeking task to address a social justice issue and is child centred. We think it is most effective when teachers use culturally responsive pedagogies and draw on the knowledge of the children, their own knowledge of statistics and number, and your personal knowledge of the issue of diversity when planning and teaching. We would hope that you are able to:

- adopt a 'guided inquiry approach' using key questions to scaffold children's mathemat-ical thinking
- encourage collaborative group work and social interactions between children and the teachers throughout the lesson to support the development of mathematical thinking, problem solving, and dialogue.

Prior knowledge that will be useful for children to engage in this activity is knowledge of the data-handling cycle based on the principles of collecting, organising, interpreting, and analysing data. They will also draw on their knowledge of number, specifically knowledge related to understanding percentages, fractions, decimal numbers, and the four number operations.

Starting points

As in Activity 1, you can introduce the topic using a cross-curricular approach to develop the children's knowledge and understanding of the issue to take into mathematics lessons.

Begin by presenting children with the statistical data statement below. The data is taken from the following research study on the diversity of characters in picture books [Koss, M.D., (2015)]. To help with the mathematical calculations, the number 455 is rounded to the nearest ten.

In a study that explored diversity in picture books conducted in 2015, of about 460 picture books, the following data was gathered on the primary and secondary representation of ethnic characters:

White characters: 45% of primary texts and 21% of secondary texts
Black characters: 9% of primary texts and 17% of secondary texts
Other cultures: 5% of primary texts and 12% of secondary texts

Initially you may ask the children to use this data to draw comparison bar charts. You can then offer a series of tasks to support children in understanding the data.

Task 1: Take some time to understand the chart. Ask questions on the type of chart. Ask whether it represents discrete or continuous data. Take some time to discuss the axis and what information the horizontal and vertical axis demonstrates. Take time to understand the key.

Task 2: The chart has some missing information. Working in groups, can children label the x-axis and y-axis, and write a title for the chart? Teachers can provide some labels for children to choose and justify choices made.

Task 3: Discuss the story the bar chart is telling on the ethnic representation of characters in picture books. The other category is an interesting component and useful discussion as to who might be put in that category. The data that non-white ethnic characters are more likely to be secondary characters in picture books rather than primary characters in a picture book is also a useful point for discussion.

This can be followed by a series of tasks focused on developing an understanding of percentages.

Task 1: Develop children's confidence in understanding percentage as out of 100. Use the concept of part/whole to show each of the percentages on a 100 square, as a fraction, its fraction equivalence and so on.

Task 2: The statement, 'Of about 460 picture books the following data was gathered on the primary and secondary representation of ethnic characters,' can be used as a starting point to find a percent of something. Pose the problem: how many books represent each percentage?

- What is 45% of 460 picture books that represented white characters as the primary/main character in the book? Before solving this problem, children may need some practical examples of finding percentage of a quantity. Use the example below to model to children how to find 50% of a quantity (half the quantity), 10% (divide by 10), and 1% (divide by 100). Provide other practical examples to develop fluency in finding 50%, 10%, and 1%

100%	is 460
50%	
10%	
1%	

- Using this information, ask children what other percentages can they find of 460? (They can find 60%, 40%, 9%, ⊹%, 49%, 99%, 51%, or 11%). This is a low threshold and high ceiling (LTHC) task and will give children the opportunity to use knowledge they have and find other related examples. LTHC tasks 'fit nicely with a growth mindset belief. It allows everyone to demonstrate what they can do, without worrying about what they can't do. As everyone is given the same task, no-one's achievement is limited before even beginning' (nRich, 2019) (See https://nrich.maths.org/10345).
- Move onto finding multiples of 10% and finding 5% of 460 by halving 10% of 460:

100%	is 460
10%	
5%	
20%	
30%	
40%	
50%	
60%	
70%	
80%	
90%	

- Provide other practical examples to develop fluency in finding multiples of 10% of different quantities and 5%.
- Once children are confident, can they use the information they have to find the number of books (an approximate) for each percent?
- Can they work out the number of books that had the different ethnic characters as the primary character?

What is 45% of 460 picture books that represented white characters as the primary character?

100%	is 460
10%	
20%	
30%	
40%	
5%	

- Can children find other ways to solve the problem? (Find 50% and subtract 5%.)

100%	is 460
50%	
-5%	

- Repeat with: what is 9% of 460 picture books that represented black characters as the primary character?
- Repeat with: what is 5% of 460 picture books that represented other ethnic characters as the primary character?
- Repeat in finding the percentage number of books that had the different ethnic characters as secondary characters.

The actual number of books that represent each ethnicity might provide another element to the discussion. This could include relating the number of books as a representation of the children in the class. Discuss the date of the study and whether children think the picture books in their school provide a range of ethnic characters as primary or secondary characters. How can we check? Is it important?

Development

How diverse and ethnically representative are the picture books in this school? How do we know, and how can we find out?

Organise children to work in groups of 5-6 with mixed gender and attainment. I suggest addressing the issue/problem as a whole class, with each group contributing data.

Specify a problem – Ask children to come up with question(s) for investigation.

Collect ideas, but have a bank of suggestions to support children's responses, such as:

- Does our class/school library of fiction picture books provide ethnically diverse representation of primary and secondary lead characters? Or
- How ethnically diverse are the fiction books in our school? Or
- How diverse and ethnically representative are the picture books in this school?

Plan on how to collect data - Pose questions such as: What should our sample size be? Is the number of fiction picture books in this class enough? Respond to children's answers and reasoning. A sample size of 100 books might be helpful as you can use this to work out simple percentages, fractions, and calculations. The 100 books could be split between the groups in the class.

Collect data fairly and inclusively - This could be a very exciting way to build up detailed data as a whole class. The responses to each will depend on the question children are answering.

- What are our categories?
- What are we looking for in our fiction books?
- How can we ensure that the data we collect is fair?
- Are we just focusing on the ethnicity of the primary/main characters first?

Work with the responses from the children.

Process the best way to present the data - As a starting point, the data could contribute to a visual whole-class 3D graph. Collectively generate the data in Excel and share the results with children. Discuss graphing possibilities such as the type of graph that best represents the data, the titles for the chart, the scale, etc.

Interpret and discuss findings - Use probing questions to interpret and interrogate the data. For example, 'What is most common?', 'How many … than…?', 'More/fewer?', 'Altogether?', 'Have we answered our main problem question?', 'What have we found?', and 'What story does our data tell?' The results could trigger further questions being posed and another cycle of data collection, which could be encouraged. If you only investigated the ethnicity of the primary characters, you could look into the ethnicity of the secondary characters.

The inquiry could go on to explore the ethnic diversity of the children in the class or that year group. The results of the two could be explored.

The final lesson could be looking at the different stories each data collection provided and what it tells us about how ethnically diverse characters are represented in 100 fiction picture books in the school.

- What deductions can children make about how ethnically diverse characters are represented in fictional picture books in school?
- Is a sample of 100 books a fair representation?
- Does the class have any recommendations for the headteacher?
- Does the class have any recommendations for a school librarian?
- Make other suggestions based on the outcomes and discussions with the children.

Further development

The activity can also be extended to explore the issue at the local library for a greater impact on the local community. Does the class have any recommendations/suggestions for the local library? A similar exercise could be carried out in the local library to see how similar the results would be.

References

Koss, M.D. (2015). "Diversity in contemporary picture books: A content analysis." *Journal of Children's Literature*, *41*(1), pp. 32–42. https://www.childrensliteratureassembly.org/journal.html
Runnymede. (2021). *Lit In Colour: Diversity in Literature in English Schools*. Available at: www .runnymedetrust.org/publications/lit-in-colour. (Accessed: 12 March 2023).

This reference provides access to the Runnymede report and teaching resources aimed at primary and secondary schools. The resource hub encourages an activist approach to diversifying English literature. You can use real data from the report and use the data for discussion and problem solving.

Activity 3: If the world were a village of 100 people

Introduction

This activity is based on the book and accompanying video, *If the world were a village of 100 people*. (See Resources at the end of this section.) The data can be used as an anchor to explore many issues of the inequalities and social injustices that occur globally. The real-life data in the book prompts cross-curricular links with many subjects, particularly PSHE, geography, and science. Links can also be made to the United Nations Goals to explore further some of the ideas in greater depth.

Starting points

As children are introduced to the mathematical concept of equality, the phrase can be expanded to explore equality and inequality in real-world situations. The video opens with the information that the world's population is approximately 7.6 billion people, who share their life on Planet Earth. It then suggests imagining the world's population as a village of 100 people to understand better the world population of 7.6 billion people and the associated data. The data for this activity has been taken from the book (which is more up to date than the video as it is based on the current global population of 7.7 billion people. It is real data.) The activities are designed to expand children's understanding of the world around them and how mathematics can be used to examine issues of social justice.

The lesson can begin with a discussion of very large numbers, asking children to discuss and share:

How do we write 7.7 billion?
What is the value of each digit?
In a village of 100, how many people from the real world would the one person in a village
   represent?

Development

The table below shares some of the data contained in the book and suggests activities for each of the data sets. These could be carried out as a circus of activities with different groups of children working with different areas and presenting their results at the end of the process.

You can also use physical modelling where the children in your class represent the data by occupying different spaces in the classroom or school hall. So, if you have 25 children in your class, each child represents 4%. If you have 33, 3% and so on. You can then compare what the children think the data will show with the actual data. The following are possible activities linked to the different categories in the book.

1. Gender: the data shows 50 men and 50 women
2. Ages of population: the data shows:

- 17 are children under the age of 10
- 16 are between 10 and 19
- 16 are between 20 and 29
- 14 are between 30 and 39
- 12 are between 40 and 49
- Ten are between 50 and 59
- Seven are between 60 and 69
- Five are between 70 and 79
- Three are over 79

Using sugar paper, unifix cubes, and post-its, possible activities include: can you present the following data as a bar chart? Ask students to label the chart and write some true and false statements about the data. They could use fractions, decimals and percentages, and ratio and proportion in their statements.

3. Nationalities: the data shows
   - One Oceania
   - Five North America
   - Nine Latin America and Caribbean
   - Ten Europe
   - 16 Africa
   - 59 Asia
4. Religion: the data shows
   - 33 Christians
   - 21 Muslims
   - 16 do not identify with a religion
   - 14 Hindus
   - 11 practice shamanism, animism, and other folk religions
   - Six Buddhists
   - Eight identifying with another global religion such as Judaism, Confucianism, Shintoism, Sikhism, Jainism, or the Baha'i faith.
5. Languages: the data shows
   - 14 Mandarin
   - Eight Hindi
   - Seven English
   - Six Arabic
   - Five Spanish
   - Four Chinese dialect
   - Three Bengali
   - Three Russian
   - Two Portuguese
6. Health care: the data shows
   - 66 do not have access to safe affordable surgery.
   - 33 cannot afford medicine they need

7. Air and water: the data shows
   - 88 have access to safe water
   - 69 have access to adequate sanitation
   - 12 breathe clean air
   - 22 have no shelter from the wind and rain

An additional activity would be to ask students, 'How many people in the village do not have access to safe water, adequate sanitation and clean air?'

8. Food: the data shows
   - One dying of starvation
   - 11 undernourished and always hungry
   - 33 do not have a reliable source of food and are hungry some or all of the time
   - 22 overweight

Ask students why the data does not add to 100 people. You can also ask students to discuss:

How many people need to be included in the data, and what inferences can you make about those people?

- What is your reasoning for your answer?
- How many people in the real world are dying of starvation?
- How many people in your village have food security?
- How many people in your village do not have food security?
- What are the possible reasons for this?
- Do you think people in England have equal access to food?
- Do you think people in our local community/school have equal access to food?
- How can we find out the answer to the above question? [breakfast, and fruit and vegetable eaten]

9. School and work: the data shows that out of 36 children (aged 5-24)
   - 30 go to school.
   - Three stay at home and work in the house, farms, and small businesses
   - Three are labourers, sell things on street, or even serve as child soldiers

It also shows that, out of 100 people, 86 people can read and write and 14 are illiterate of which 2/3 would be women.

There are 63 adults in the village who could have jobs: of these, 52 can work; six people who want to work cannot find a job; and five are in school. There are also another six people who are retired.

Further developments

1. Use real-life data on the Sustainable Development Goals which can be found at https://sdgs.un.org/goals

Interpret and analyse data. Pick out the goals related to some topics in the video and interpret them. Explore the progress that has been made. Try to predict what will happen in the next 20 years.

Rewrite the book to reflect imagined data from 50 years in the future. Ask the children to justify their assumptions.

2. You can present data on a particular theme and ask children to put the titles and labels on the bar chart, pie chart, pictographs, etc. Children will need to provide a rationale for the choices made. This activity can also lead to some interesting discussions.

3. Using 100 as a percentage, use some of the data to consider the village consisting of a class of 30 children. How many children in the class would be impacted by the social conditions? (The percentages may need to be rounded up to the nearest ten or five.) E.g., If the world were a village of 30 Year X children, 70% would not have access to safe, affordable surgery and 30% would not be able to afford medicine. How many children would that be?

4. Using the idea of 100 as a percentage and the categories presented in the video. Consider the village of the number of children in the school. How many children in the school would be impacted by the social conditions? (The percent may need to be rounded up to the nearest ten or five.) E.g., if the world were a village of X Primary School of children, 70% would not have access to safe, affordable surgery and 30% would not be able to afford medicine. How many children would that be? This activity could form part of a whole-school assembly. It is a great way to demonstrate the power of maths through some interaction with the whole school.

5. The topic can be expanded to explore other real-life lived experiences of the children. Ask children which issues they like to gather information about? Topics could be taken from the other UN Goals.

Resources for this activity

Smith, D. and Armstrong, S. (2020). *If the world were a village of 100 people*. London: Kinds Can Press (3rd Edition).
If the world were a village of 100 people. www.youtube.com/watch?v=A3nllBT9ACg

Activity 4: Nutritious lunches

Introduction

This activity is based on the data taken from The Food Foundation and identifies the role of schools in helping children to get sufficient nutrition to grow up healthy. The social justice element is linked to the United Nations 2nd development goal, 'Zero hunger.' We think it is worthwhile having a broad discussion with your class to explore some aspects of this goal to discuss why this might be an issue of social justice. You can consider this goal at a local level and talk about how some families may not be able to always provide a healthy meal, therefore for some children having a healthy school meal is very important. Dietary inequalities mean that some children, possibly from low-income and other groups, are at risk of poor dietary outcomes.

The activity below provides a blueprint you can use as a scaffold to personalise the activity to your school and setting. The activity is presented as a problem-solving and problem-seeking task, and we would encourage you to present it in a child-centred way. Aim to use culturally responsive pedagogies and teaching drawing on your knowledge of the children, your knowledge of statistics, and your understanding of the issues of hunger and nutrition.

We think that the activity is most effective when:

- Teachers adopt a 'guided inquiry approach,' using key questions to scaffold children's mathematical thinking.
- Collaborative group work and social interactions between children and the teacher are encouraged throughout the lesson to develop mathematical thinking, problem-solving, and dialogue.

The activity will draw on children's prior knowledge of the data-handling cycle based on the principles of collecting, organising, and interpreting data, although children will also develop these skills whilst engaging in the activity.

Starting points

This activity can be taught through making links to other curriculum subjects, such as science, that discuss the topic of food, nutrition, and healthy eating. This will provide some background knowledge and understanding of the topic for application in mathematics lessons. We suggest starting by presenting children with the statement and associated data: *25% of state schools in England and 47% of state schools in Scotland are known to meet school food nutritional requirements (compliance in the rest is unknown).*

Ask students to develop a representation of this data, and ask children to discuss the information it is sharing. Ask them to discuss what the data says about the quality of nutritional food in schools in Scotland and England. What argument or point do they think it is making? They can then discuss the advantages and disadvantages of schools opting for accreditation for 'Food for Life served here.' One way you might do this is through 'hot-seating' and 'role-play' to explore the views of different stakeholders such as children, a school headteacher, school teachers, kitchen staff and parents.

Move on to share the data that, in 2021, England had about 20,200 state schools. Ask the children to work out 25% or one-quarter of 20,200. Ask them to share the strategies they used. Discuss the different strategies that children used to carry out the calculation. Share the following data:

In 2021 30% of primary schools in England were accredited by Food for Life compared to 55% of primary schools in Scotland, and 8% of secondary schools in England were accredited compared to 13% of primary schools in Scotland.

Children can represent this data and then discuss whether it further supports or weakens the point that more state schools in Scotland are known to meet school food nutritional requirements than in England.

Share the data that in 2021 England had about 16,700 primary state schools and 3,500 secondary state schools. Ask small groups to calculate the number of primary schools accredited with good nutrition compared to those not. Again, share the strategies used.

Development

Pose a research problem

Depending on the direction of your data collection. An area for investigation based on this activity could find out whether the school lunches provided by the school meet The School Food Standards, www.schoolfoodplan.com/wp-content/uploads/2015/05/School_Food_Standards_140911-V2e-tea-towel.pdf. Children will need some time to become familiar with the School Food Standards and discuss the different criteria. As a class, come up with a research question/title for investigation.

Plan on how to collect data

Use questioning to find out what data children will need to collect to answer the problem posed. Who would they need to ask? Possibly guide towards asking the school kitchen staff to share what's on the menu each day for a week or access the school's menu for the week.

Collect data fairly and inclusively

Some questions to ask the children:

- What data do we need to collect to answer the problem posed?
- How can we collect the data efficiently and effectively?
- How can we collect the data fairly, so everyone has a similar understanding?

Work with the responses from the children. As a class, you may wish to use previous school lunch menus and classify and organise the food under the following headings (taken from The School Food Standards). For example, each group could look at the menu for one week in January and classify the food items under the heading. Alternatively, ask the cook or kitchen staff to come in and share what is on the menu for the week.

Fruit and vegetables	Milk and dairy	Starchy foods	Foods high in salt, fat, and sugar	Meat, fish, eggs, and beans	Healthy drinks

Process the best way to present the data

Questions to ask the children

- How can we present the data so that it is easier to read? Consider bar charts or pictograms.
- Ask questions about constructing graphs focusing on scale/key, each axis's title and purpose, etc.

Provide time and space for children to present the data they have collected. Ask children to think about how their chart answers or responds to the problem posed.

Interpret and discuss findings

Use probing questions to interpret and interrogate the data. Ask children to come up with some questions they would like to ask of the other groups. These might include:

- What groups of food do children have a lot of access to?
- What groups of food do children have little access to?
- How nutritious are the lunches at this school? How do you know?

Further developments

You can encourage the development of an activist stance by asking children to think about the following questions:

- What recommendations would you make to the kitchen staff and the head teacher of your school?
- What can the school do more of to be accredited for Food for Life? (This will lead to other lines of inquiry)
- What other lines of investigation can be taken to ensure that the food provided by the school is nutritious and follows The School Food Standards? For example, you could investigate how healthy the breaktime snacks are provided by the school or breakfasts.
- How can this class support the local community and families who may experience food inequality and food insecurities?

The activity can also be extended to explore places to buy food on the local high street.

References

School_Food_Standards. www.schoolfoodplan.com/wp-content/uploads/2015/05/School_Food _Standards_140911-V2e-tea-towel.pdf

The Food Foundation. https://foodfoundation.org.uk This contains a wealth of interesting data that can easily be used in the classroom on dietary inequalities

Data presented for this activity has been taken from FF_Broken_Plate_Report 2022_DIGITAL _UPDATED_2023.pdf (foodfoundation.org.uk). This resource can be accessed from the Food Foundation website.

Data on the number of state secondary and primary schools was taken from https://lginform.local.gov .uk/reports/lgastandard?mod-area=E92000001&mod-group=AllRegions_England&mod-metric =2199&mod-period=3&mod-type=namedComparisonGroup#

Activity 5: Water use and conservation

Introduction

This activity is built around the idea of water conservation and how access to water is an essential part of our lives. The social justice element is linked to United Nations Development Goal 6, "Ensure availability and sustainable management of water and sanitation for all." See https://sdgs.un.org/goals/goal6. It will be a helpful to have a class discussion around aspects of this goal and why it might be an issue of social justice.

The activity below provides a blueprint for you to use to help you in your planning. You will want to personalise the activity to your school and setting. The activity is presented as a problem-solving and problem-seeking task and we hope you approach it in a child-centred way using culturally responsive pedagogies and teaching and drawing on your knowledge of the children and your personal understanding of the issues around the sustainable management of water.

We would argue that the activity is most effective when:

- Teachers adopt a 'guided inquiry approach' using key questions to scaffold children's mathematical thinking.
- Collaborative group work and social interactions between children and teachers are encouraged throughout the lesson to support the development of mathematical thinking, problem-solving and dialogue.

The activity will draw on children's prior knowledge of capacity, standard units and non-standard unit for measuring, addition, multiplication, and methods of recording data.

Starting points

This activity is great for making links with other curriculum subjects, such as science and geography, in which you can discuss the topic of water use and conservation. This will provide the children with some background knowledge and understanding of the topic when it comes to the mathematics lessons.

Begin by sharing the story called *The Water Princess* (see Resources below for this activity). Encourage the children to discuss some of the points in the story and come up with their own questions for discussion. Questions might include:

- How does Gie Gie's family use water in everyday life?
- Why do they boil water?
- Why does Gie Gie say that she wants to make it last?
- Why does Gie Gie's mother save one last cup for Gie Gie?
- Where will Gie Gie journey again tomorrow?
- How do you think Gie Gie thinks about water, and why?

Move the discussion on to how children use water in their everyday lives. Have some images prepared (a picture of one of the drinking bottles, brushing teeth, use of toilet, washing hands, shower/bath). Ask children similar questions such as:

- Where does their water come from?
- Is it clean?
- Do they have to think about whether they will have enough water? How much is enough?
- Do they know how much water they use each day, on average? (Explain average.)
- How do they think about water?

Development

How much water do I use in one day?

Children are going to investigate how much water they use each day, on average. All children can begin with their drinking bottle as a unit of measure. You can ask how much water the bottle holds; do they know? How can they find out? (You may get some groups to work with a support teacher so that they can measure the amount of water using a measuring jug.) The teacher may also need to investigate the average capacity of children's water bottles. The average water bottle may have a capacity of 500 ml. The teacher can use this as the basis for the rest of the work. KS1 (Key Stage 1) Children can construct their own way of recording, or they can be provided with the activity sheet. (See companion website.)

Possible questions to explore:

Flushing the toilet

- How many times do you visit the toilet? (On average, it is about seven times and, on average, each flush uses approximately five litres of water, and each flush uses ten bottles of water based on 500 ml as the standard unit).
- Can the class arrange ten bottles of water on a table to understand how much water is used for one flush?
- If one flush is ten bottles, how many bottles of water are needed for seven flushes? Working in groups, can you find a way to work that out? Can you find more than one way to work it out? Encourage children to mark, make, and use pictures.

Brushing teeth

- How many times do you brush your teeth?
- Do you leave the water running when you brush your teeth? Is that good or bad?
- How much water do you use to brush your teeth if you leave the tap running?
- On average, you waste six litres of water every minute. (NHS recommendation is for brushing your teeth for two minutes.)
- Six litres are approximately 12 bottles of water for one minute. How much water are you using to brush your teeth for two minutes?

- Children can visually put 12 bottles of water on a table to understand the amount of water that would be for one minute.
- How many bottles of water are required for two minutes of brushing your teeth in the morning and another two minutes at night? Working in groups, can you find a way to work that out? Can you find more than one way to work it out?

Washing hands

- You use about two litres of water every time you wash your hands. That comes to approximately four bottles of water.
- If you wash your hands ten times every day, how many bottles of water do you use? Working in groups can you find a way to work that out? Can you find more than one way to work it out?

Further developments

How can I save water? Water stress.

Refer to Gie Gie's story and how she and her family used the water very carefully and wisely. Return to Activity 1, and think where children can save water in their everyday lives in school and at home and where they cannot.

Children can be encouraged to take an activist stance by exploring what they can do at school to save water and be water conscious. Ask them to discuss how can they communicate this message to other children and the head teacher.

Stress the importance to health and hygiene of washing hands regularly. Consider how we can wash our hands water consciously. Children can conduct an experiment to save water when washing hands. They can find one strategy to reduce the use of water and use it to determine how much water they use when washing their hands for 20 seconds. This can include running the tap on low and only using water when required. Children can collect the water in a bowl, and measure the usage in a jug, and record it to the nearest water bottle (500 ml). They can record the results using a table and then present the results as a whole-class graph. The table could include:

Saving water: water usage when we wash our hands for 20 seconds	
Strategies to save water	**Capacity of water according to a water bottle (500 ml)**
Turn the tap on very low	
Only turn the tap when needing water to wash my hands	
Can I think of another strategy?	

You can use the graph to answer the following questions. Children will be required to read the graph.

- How much water could you save in school if you washed your hands once, twice, three times four times a day?
- How much water could five people save if they washed their hands four times each day?
- How much water could ten people save if they washed their hands four times every day?
- What about everyone in your class? How would you work that out?
- What about everyone at your school? How much water could the school community save every day if they were water conscious? How would you work that out?
- You can also ask children to think of ways to save water at home. Can they use these strategies to save water at home? What else could they do? Could they speak to an adult at home to talk about how they can save water in the home?

Other related activities

You can add other activities that use water, such as having a shower.

You can generate a number of maths-related activities based on the Water Princess story.

This activity could be done with children in higher classes where they are given the number of bottles, e.g., I drink three bottles of water and they have to find out how many ml of water that would be. They can also convert ml to litres.

References

Countryfile Article on Water Shortages. www.countryfile.com/news/water-shortage-in-the-uk-whats-the-problem-and-how-to-save-water/.

Middlesex University Article on Brushing Teeth. www.mdx.ac.uk/news/2014/05/1-in-3-leave-the-tap-running-while-brushing-wasting-24-litres-of-water-a-day-finds-new-poll#:~:text=According%20to%20waterwise.org%20%27a%20running%20tap%20wastes%20over,is%20used%20in%20the%20average%20modern%20dishwasher%20cycle.

UN Development Goal 6. www.un.org/sustainabledevelopment/wp-content/uploads/2022/07/Goal-6-infographic.pdf.

Waterwise UK. www.waterwise.org.uk/save-water/.

The Water Princess by Susan Verde. www.youtube.com/watch?v=tIWAjQhCIK0.

This is another great story about water conservation. It provides a helpful hook to build some activities for KS2. https://issuu.com/uwebristol/docs/dry_the_diary_of_a_water_superhero

Activity 6: Food miles

Introduction

This activity was created by primary student teachers as part of their 'Advanced Subject Studies' module in the third year of their course. The context provided for the students was critical mathematics education including climate and racial justice. One group put forward this simple and effective classroom activity to involve children in calculating food miles for items they can find in their kitchens. One of the successes of this activity is that children of different ages can take part, especially if it is set as homework where they have the opportunity to work with both their siblings or adults at home.

The mathematics that arises from this activity includes the use of an online food miles calculator and knowledge that can be developed includes distances to planets and beyond in outer space. Classroom discussions can include travel and growing your own food. Some children may already be doing the latter in their own allotments or gardens. Indeed, with the current cost-of-living crisis, this may be more common for many households. Older children can discuss the links to social justice and real-world contexts such as the industrialisation of food, land, and agriculture for an increasing world population. As extension activities, children can calculate 'egg miles' travelled and 'fuel miles' based on different types of transportation used to move food.

There are opportunities for teachers to make connections to personal, social, health (mental and physical), and the spiritual curriculum as can be seen by the pupils at Galmpton Primary school: www.nationaltrust.org.uk/greenway/features/greenways-school-allotment

There is further information for gardening in schools here:
www.swcaa.co.uk/gardening-schools-information-and-guidance

Starting point

Encourage the children to bring two food items into school, with labels indicating country of origin. Lead a discussion on where we purchase our food from. For example, do families use supermarkets that provide labelling, or a local market or butcher's or greengrocer's? Bring in a range of examples of your own including some which have a large number of food miles and others which are local.

For example:

Country of Origin: Costa Rica; Food item: Bananas
The information provided by the website for these bananas states:
'Assuming your food has come from the capital, San Jose travelling to the capital London, it has travelled approximately **5424 miles (8727 km)** as the crow flies.'

Country of Origin: Spain; Food item: Cucumber
'Assuming your food has come from the capital, Madrid travelling to the capital London, it has travelled approximately **787 miles (1266 km)** as the crow flies.'

Discuss what food miles are with the children. Make connections to geography and find out if children are aware of both the countries where food comes from but also where these countries are. A displayed map of the world may be useful here. This discussion can develop into where ingredients are sourced from; so, if we are purchasing a pizza made locally, children can consider whether the mozzarella cheese that has been used for the topping has been made locally or travelled from Italy, for example. Another aspect for children to think about is where waste food travels to, both in terms of landfill or home compost. The latter can be linked to the benefits for our gardening and biodiversity.

Pair up children in your classroom to work together using the online food miles calculator (See Resources below for this activity). You could provide each pair with an empty table on paper, for them to enter their results. For a whole-class discussion, circulate and collate these on the classroom board as the children are working. Once collated centrally, ask the children, "What do you notice about the food miles calculations?' and 'What are the effects of food miles on the environment?" to encourage discussion on the environmental effects such as pollution of travel by air (plane), sea (boat), and road (lorry). Considering the mode of transport is important. For example, bananas travel a large distance although are relatively environmentally friendly because they are generally imported by ship. However, some other fruit that comes from closer to home is imported by lorry or even by plane and so works out as having a greater carbon footprint.

Pollution has many facets such as noise and oil spills which have consequences for plant life and creatures, including humans. In my own experience of using this activity with primary-aged children, it has generated enthusiasm in collecting items from the home fridge and discussing the findings with family members. This enthusiasm can spill into the classroom as children share responses with their peers.

Development

Secondary mathematics student teachers have discussed ideas for class projects such as getting children to calculate the food miles in their meals from the evening before; asking what the most efficient meal in terms of food miles is; and asking if we can purchase the same foods locally from farmers to reduce miles. We can make the link to emissions and eating seasonal produce. Other school project ideas include calculating how much coffee/tea is consumed by teachers each year and how many miles this is and how many food miles are created by the lunchtime from the school canteen on any one given day. The children could interview school dinner staff and discuss ways in which to reduce food miles.

Resources for this activity

Food miles calculator at www.foodmiles.com/.

Activity 7: Plastic waste

Introduction

This activity explores how levels of plastic waste and pollution, including micro- and nano-plastics have increased over time. It provides opportunities for students to explore solutions, share ideas and take an activist stance by writing to their local members of parliament about the issues raised.

Students are encouraged to interpret data and graphs to draw, make predictions for the next decades, and highlight inequalities in waste and disposal around the world. They will access information on the internet and so require the use of computers. It is helpful to create groups of students with different experiences of mathematics, interests, and previous learning, so that discussion is rich and with a wider range of perspectives.

Starting point

Begin by getting the class to consider the quantity of plastic in their classroom and school – including for example, the canteen area – and in their homes. Children can make a list of common plastics found in these places and estimate the numbers for each type. For example, a list might include pens, ring binders, chairs, play equipment, plates and cutlery, bottles and food containers, bins, packaging etc. Encourage them to reflect on recycling processes that may operate at home for their local council and what they as a family put in the recycling bin. Some schools now have 'Eco Councils' where children are nominated to become 'Eco Ambassadors,' regularly meeting to make positive changes in the schools and beyond. For example, after-school clubs have included litter-picking activities; those children who may have been involved could share their thoughts on the types of items 'picked' including quantities of plastic.

For an insightful discussion, learners could consider the following:

- Are there any recycling facilities at our school, and if so, is plastic recycled?
- If we recycle at home, what are the most common plastic items that go into the recycling bin?
- Are there alternatives to plastic packaging, especially on food products in the school canteen and home?

Development

Provide students with the information below showing how much plastic enters the world's oceans in terms of understanding the scale of the problem. This information is taken from the 'Our world in data' website (see Resources for this activity below):

270 million tonnes of plastic is produced a year.
275 million tonnes of plastic is thrown away.
99.5 million tonnes is discarded within 50 kilometres of the coast.

31.9 million tonnes mismanaged (stored in inappropriate containers).
Eight million tonnes of plastic end up in the ocean each year.

Ask learners to reflect on this information. (For example: Why is the figure for waste higher than the figure for production?) and what might be the most effective interventions for reduction of plastic in the world's oceans. Ask students to discuss the following questions in small groups:

- What do you notice about this data?
- What might be effective ways to reduce the amount of plastic in the world's oceans? How can global plastic waste be greater than the plastic production for any year?
- How might the plastic waste be entering the oceans?
- What are the implications of plastic waste for people living near coastlines?
- Once plastic enters the oceans, where could it end up?

Follow these ideas with a thought-provoking task of exploring how much plastic the world has produced since 1950 onwards.

Further development

Different groups/pairs of learners could then focus on aspects of the problem, for example, some could explore plastic waste disposal methods, global plastic production since 1950 (this could include an opportunity to widen the conversations with elderly relatives such as grandparents and their memories of alternatives to plastic such as cloth/beeswax products that have returned), and which industrial sectors produce the most plastic. Allow children to choose the area they wish to explore and then present them with the data from the same site, as above, which relates to their topic. For example, children exploring plastic disposal methods could look at how this has changed over time in terms of the amounts that are discarded, recycled, or incinerated:

Move on to ask students to discuss which industrial sectors they think produce the most amount of plastic and approximate how much. Then share the data below taken from 'Our world in data' and showing the uses of plastic.

Packaging	146 million tonnes
Building and construction	65 million tonnes
Textiles	59 million tonnes
Other sectors	47 million tonnes
Consumer and institutional products	42 million tonnes
Transportation	27 million tonnes
Electrical and electronic	18 million tonnes
Industrial machinery	3 million tonnes

Ask students to write down some questions that they want to ask their partner about this information. When this activity has been used with students, some questions they have posed included:

What specific packaging might this refer to?
What might be 'consumer and institutional products' be?
What types of textiles might this include?'

Students could then share their questions with partners and listen to the responses. Ask them to think about whether they agree or disagree with their partner. Pairs can then share their discussion with the rest of the class.

Other possibilities

These conversations could prompt wider discussions with senior managers such as head teachers, about ways to improve the plastic recycling facilities within the school. Also, children may continue the conversations with family members, offering opportunities to change shopping habits, such as choosing alternatively packaged products to those often encased in plastic, for example, cheese or chocolate.

Students could be given the opportunity to present their results to their peers and teachers in a variety of ways, using the tables and charts provided in the source, sharing their findings and thoughts on these, and responses to the questions posed. Peers could provide feedback on these oral presentations, including their own questions about the data. Links could be made to other school subjects such as geography and science, with teachers from a variety of subject specialisms ideally providing insight into the issues surrounding plastic production and waste. The cross-curricular opportunities that this activity lends itself to could be explored through the data on countries producing the most total plastics waste, those that produce the most mismanaged waste and those that emit the most plastic into the oceans, which rivers transport waste into oceans, and the oceans with the most plastic waste.

Students could research alternatives to plastics being invented around the world, including plant-based products. For a class presentation, organise the students to write down their ideas in a way ready to share with other groups and the class, with diagrams or photographs that they have found through researching.

Resources for this activity

Our world in data: https://ourworldindata.org/plastic-pollution

Activity 8: Wildfires

Introduction

Fire is considered a living thing by many Indigenous cultures, a living entity that must be handled with respect or there will be severe repercussions. Knowledge exchange where we learn from Indigenous communities in a reciprocal and respectful manner offers opportunities for us to understand the deep and personal connection that the ancestors had to their home territories. They knew things like weather patterns, wind directions, historic events, and environmental nuances based on generations of experience. This allowed them to make decisions with a level of accuracy that is difficult if not impossible to reproduce today (See Resources below for this activity).

This activity explores the global wildfires that arise from the rising temperatures on Earth. The context provided was news reports from summer 2022 about the wildfires in Spain, France, Italy, Morocco, the UK and the USA. I have shared the following activity, in their first term, with student teachers of initial teacher education, who made links to the topic of number sequences.

Starting point

As a starting point, you can play the short video on forest fires from Association of Teachers of Mathematics UK (see Resources for this activity below). This will lead to discussion around number patterns, prediction, conjecturing, justifying, and writing algebraic formulae for the number of fires over time measured in hours. To encourage discussion, you can pose questions such as:

- What number patterns can you see in your table?
- How can you use the table to predict the number of fires in ... one day, two days, four days, six days ...?
- Can you write a formula that will help us to work out the number of wildfires after a given time?

You can then draw on news items from the BBC to encourage students to consider the statistics on Australian bushfires and the area of bush destroyed in January 2020 (see Resources). There are impactful visuals here in terms of speed of fires spreading and data on homes destroyed and people who have died as a result. Students can also explore the estimated number of animals that have been affected, including koalas, kangaroos, sheep and endangered species such as the dunnart, the black glossy cockatoo, pygmy possums, Ligurian bees and the southern brown bandicoot, as reported on the webpage. Once the types and numbers of animals affected have been listed in simple tables, children can show the data in representations of their choice such as bar and pie charts. This leads onto discussing the amount of area affected. Give the students the information that the Australian fires covered an area of 100,000 square kilometres. Using a map of the UK ask them to represent this area. For example, you might choose the site of your school as the centre of a circle which represents an area of 100,000 square units. There is much work to be done here on using scale to calculate the radius of the circle needed.

Students who worked on this activity discussed the large size of this region and attempted to locate their home city within the UK diagram. They discussed their awareness of the American and Japanese regions in relation to the size of those countries. To practice their geometry skills and make cross-curricular links to geography, learners could, wherever they are on Earth, locate their home residencies and, using a pair of compasses, draw circles of a given radius to represent the amount of land affected by wildfires.

Development

The next part of the activity can focus on the speed of fires using the information below:

The average speed of a person running is 6.12 mph
The average speed of a forest fire is 6.7 mph
The average speed of a grass fire is 14 mph

Students could be asked to produce an infographic of this information. They could include other speeds.

Students exploring this activity reflected that the speed of the grass fire was more than double that of an average person's running speed. They stated it was important for people to keep away from grass in the event of a fire. They also remarked that it is unlikely that people could survive if attempting to run. Teachers may like to discuss mistakes and misconceptions in reading the decimal for the speed of the average person, for example, 'six point one two' rather than 'six point twelve.'

This data can be compared to speed of animals, including those mentioned earlier and affected by these forest fires. Students can work in groups to research the speed of animals affected including koalas, kangaroos, sheep, and endangered species such as the dunnart, the black glossy cockatoo, pygmy possums, Ligurian bees and the southern brown bandicoot. They then use this research to ask further questions such as:

- Which animals are likely to escape and which not?
- How can we protect those animals that cannot escape?
- How much time should emergency authorities give for people to leave their homes for safety?
- Write down any other thoughts that you have about how we can use mathematics as a tool to help the problem of forest fires. Have a spokesperson to share your ideas with the rest of the class.

Other possibilities

Students can research the impact of fires in moorland in the UK.

Resources for this activity

Association of Teachers of Mathematics: The Forest fires activity can be found at www.youtube.com/embed/IgNxjJKi8uo?feature=oembed
BBC News reports on bush fires
www.bbc.co.uk/news/world-australia-50951043
www.bbc.co.uk/news/world-australia-51102658
Indigenous Fire Safety: the webpage https://indigenousfiresafety.ca/ offers educators and teachers lesson plans for children up to the age of 11.

Activity 9: Fair choices

Introduction

This activity is based on ideas generated through the 'Primary mathematics and social justice' research project, which aimed to explore how primary school teachers can build on their interest in addressing social justice issues through teaching mathematics. In particular, the focus was on developing effective strategies that can be used by teachers in primary schools to enhance students' critical understanding of mathematics and collective mathematical agency, that is, their ability to work collaboratively in applying mathematics to solve real-life problems. We are grateful to Caroline Hilton, Joel Kelly and the six teacher researchers (who cannot be named due to research ethics principles) who contributed to the development of this activity.

The primary teachers participating in the project felt constrained in what they were able to do during designated mathematics lessons as both schools involved in the project had adopted externally produced mathematics schemes of work which were quite prescriptive. However, the flexibility of the wider primary curriculum, which routinely incorporated cross-curricular projects, provided opportunities to apply the mathematics learnt during routine mathematics lessons to solving real-life problems.

There are often times in a primary classroom when a decision needs to be taken collaboratively, for example, electing a member of the school council or deciding how to spend 'golden time.' Using mathematics to explore different ways of voting provides plenty of opportunities to consider how numbers can be used to assign value to different potential outcomes and hence arrive at the fairest way of arriving at a decision through consensus. Discussions around the relative merits of different ways of doing this can raise similar questions to those that need to be resolved when considering which voting system to adopt to ensure a fair democratic process in real-life elections.

Using numbers to assign value in making decisions offers opportunities for students to engage in data handling, for example, considering different ways of displaying the outcomes of a vote, calculating ranges and averages, using ratios and proportion, and exploring different sequences of numbers.

Starting point

You might start with a scenario such as wanting to decide as a class how to spend 'golden time' and offering a choice between which game to play. Start by inviting students to propose three or four possible games to choose from and display these on the board. Label a box with the name of each game, and give each student one counter. Now allow students to place their counter in whichever box they wish to choose. When everyone has voted, involve the students in counting the number of counters in each box and presenting the results in different ways, e.g., bar chart, pictogram (what picture you would you use, and would each picture represent one counter?) and pie chart (if appropriate). Discuss the relative merits of each way of presenting the results, e.g., a pictogram gives you some idea of what the totals (frequencies) are representing.

Now discuss with students whether it would be fair to spend the whole of golden time playing the game that got the most votes. You could encourage them to consider the following questions to prompt discussion:

- What if two of the games got the same number of votes?
- What if all three (or four) games got the same number of votes?
- What if one game got only slightly more votes than another (e.g., 15 and 12 votes)?
- What if one of the games only got one vote?

Try to come to consensus within the class about what the 'fairest' outcome would be. It might be that students decide to allocate time proportionally to those games that got a minimum number of votes. If so, get them to work out which calculations they would need to do to work out the time to be spent on each game. They should consider how accurate they need to be and whether an approximation would be desirable. Whatever happens, make sure that the decision taken by the class is put into action – this will reinforce students' appreciation of how mathematics can be a powerful tool for solving problems collectively.

The issues that arise are likely to mirror those in the debate between whether to adopt a 'first-past-the-post' electoral system or a form of proportional representation. There are other issues that might be discussed including whether people's votes might be influenced by seeing how others had voted or by knowing that they can be seen by others. Consider how these issues might be resolved.

Development

You might go on to explore whether it would be fairer to give each student more than one counter and allow them to allocate these to different games. You could discuss different ways of doing this and get them to predict whether the outcome would be the same (before testing their predictions by trying them out). For example, what might happen if half the class chose 'Aliens' but also liked 'Teddies', whilst the other half chose 'Dragons' but also liked 'Teddies'? Encourage students to come up with their own variations and explain the reasons behind their choice (perhaps working in groups). Acknowledge different ideas that students come up with, and assign ownership to these ideas.

Here are some suggestions if needed:

- What if each student gets three counters and can allocate two counters to their first-choice game and one counter to their second-choice game?
- How many counters would there be if we wanted to allow three choices or four choices? (This is a good way of generating triangle numbers.)
- How else could we allocate the counters? What difference would it make?
- What if students were able to decide how many counters to allocate to each choice?
- What would be a good number of counters to use?
- What if the game with least votes after the first round was eliminated?

- What if students worked in groups of three, with each group having the same number of counters to allocate?
- What if the groups were different in size? How many counters should each group get?

Other possibilities

The teachers involved in the project returned to this idea of considering the fairest way of reaching a class consensus when tackling a range of different social justice issues. These included the following:

- Voting on the extent to which different factors (such as deforestation, pollution, climate change) can threaten biomes (such as rainforest, grassland).
- Carrying out a survey of how students travel to school and then choosing between a number of options of whether people should be taxed for using electric cars, petrol cars, buses, etc. (related to ULEZ, the Ultra Low Emission Zone, in London).
- Choosing between which different polluters should pay for the damage caused to the environment and how much they should pay.
- Students work in groups to present their idea on a particular theme and all students then vote for which idea they thought was best.

7 Mainly secondary

As we suggested in the opening to the previous chapter, we realise that for many readers who teach in secondary schools this will be your starting point. And that readers will bring with them a range of experiences and understandings around teaching mathematics for social justice. This is exactly how it should be. As a group of people interested in social justice, the authors believe that all groups of learners are enhanced through diversity. Diversity of experience allows us to learn with each other, to draw on each other's experiences and so, in a sense, learn for each other.

Our aim for this section is that the activities that follow will allow you to act in the space in which you have some agency: your classroom. We understand and experience the many constraints on those of us who aim to work towards a more just and equitable society through our mathematics teaching – but we have also experienced the joy and energy which working for social justice can bring to colleagues and to the students we work with.

Whilst we hope that you find the activities which follow useful, and we would love to have feedback from you on the ways in which you have used these activities in your practice on the companion website, we want to start the chapter with a reflection on the broader pedagogical approaches which we think support the move to a more socially just mathematics education.

On page 26 Pete Wright proposed four essential elements of mathematics teaching for social justice. A useful starting point might be to reflect on these elements before planning to teach any of the activities which follow. Does your chosen activity:

- Employ collaborative, discursive, problem-solving, and problem-posing pedagogies which promote mathematical sense-making and the engagement of all learners with mathematics?
- Promote mathematical inquiries that resonate with learners' real-life experiences and that help them develop greater understanding of their social, cultural, political, and economic situations?
- Facilitate mathematical investigations that develop learners' individual and collective agency, enabling them to take part in future social action for the public good?
- Challenge common myths surrounding school mathematics, expose processes that lead to the marginalisation of some learners, and open up to scrutiny what it means to be successful?

So now it is over to you. We would encourage you to try out one of these activities with a group of students that you teach. Maybe agree as a department that you will each teach the same activity so you can discuss the lessons afterwards. It would be great to involve your students in these discussions.

DOI: 10.4324/9781003361466-9

Activity 1: Child labour

Introduction

This activity is based on UNICEF's Child Labour report from as recently as 2021. Children are often interested in those of similar ages around the world, whatever their backgrounds and circumstances. We hope this activity will engage and motivate learners in the class-room to consider the situation of other children across the globe, to promote discussion and mathematical thinking. There are clear links to Personal, Health, Social and Economic education to be made.

This activity has been shared with students and adult learners. They made links to geography, creating a wall display that included a world map, their findings, ideas for reducing child labour and powerful photographs taken from the report.

The mathematics that arises from this project includes reading and interpreting real-world data; learning new mathematics terminology and vocabulary; making predictions and estimating; and extrapolating data by drawing graphs.

Starting point

To set the context for a discussion with learners, ask them, in pairs or threes, to discuss the following statements presented in the Executive Summary of UNICEF's Child Labour report (2021):

- Child labour remains a persistent problem in the world today.
- Global progress against child labour has stagnated since 2016.
- The global picture masks continued progress against child labour in Asia and the Pacific and in Latin America and the Caribbean.
- Continued progress was registered over the last four years among children aged 12 to 14 and 15 to 17.
- The Covid-19 crisis threatens to further erode global progress against child labour unless urgent mitigation measures are taken.
- Involvement in child labour is higher for boys than girls at all ages.
- Child labour is much more common in rural areas.
- Most child labour – for boys and girls alike – continues to occur in agriculture.
- The largest share of child labour takes place within families.
- Child labour is frequently associated with children being out of school.

Prompt your learners to consider the reasons behind these facts. You may wish to simplify any terminology according to your learners' needs. To encourage and support dialogue, consider presenting some of the powerful photographs of children from the report, along-side these statements.

Development

For learners to understand the statistics behind child labour, divide the class into groups of three or four to discuss the following data sets. There are 11 in total. You may choose to allocate data to groups and ask each group to report back after their discussion. A starting point should be that the groups represent the data in some form. Each set of data is followed by a series of questions to discuss.

1. **Child labour** (All figures in millions. Children aged five to 17.)

   2000: 16% in labour, 11.1% in hazardous work
   2004: 14.2% in labour, 8.2% in hazardous work
   2008: 13.6% in labour, 7.3% in hazardous work
   2012: 10.6% in labour, 5.4% in hazardous work
   2016: 9.6% in labour, 4.6% in hazardous work
   2020: 9.6% in labour, 4.7% in hazardous work

Discussion

- What does this information tell us about child labour?
- What might 'hazardous work' mean?
- Can you write a headline to say what the data is showing?
- What do you estimate the percentages and numbers of children will be for the next four, eight, 12, 16, and 20 years? Give reasons for your estimates.
- How confident are you that your prediction will come true? What would you need to know to be more confident?

3. **Comparison across regions**

Sub-Saharan Africa:	2008: 25.3%	2012: 21.4%	2016:22.4%	2020: 23.9%
Asia and the Pacific:	2008: 13.3%	2012: 9.3%	2016: 7.4%	2020: 6%
Latin America and the Caribbean:	2008: 10%	2012: 8.8%	2016: 7.3%	2020: 5.6%

Discussion

- What does this data show?
- What is the percentage gap between the highest and lowest percentages? In which year(s) is the gap of percentages the widest and why? Why do you think this is?
- What does that tell us about the trend of children in child labour?
- What predictions would you make, based on this graph, for the next four, eight, 12, 16 and 20 years?

- How confident are you that your prediction will come true? What would you need to know to be more confident?
- **Comparison across regions in 2020**

Sub-Saharan Africa	23.9%
Central and Southern Asia	5.5%
Eastern and South-Eastern Asia	6.2%
Northern Africa and Western Asia	7.8%
Latin America and the Caribbean	6%
Europe and Northern America	2.3%

Pose the following questions

- What does the information tell us?
- What might be the reasons for the highest and lowest percentages, based on the regions?

Sub-Saharan Africa:	2008: 65.1	2012: 59	2016: 70	2020: 86.6
Asia and the Pacific:	2008: 113.6	2012: 77.7	2016: 62.1	2020: 48.7
Latin America and the Caribbean:	2008: 14.1	2012: 12.5	2016: 10.5	2020: 8.2

(All figures in millions)

Discussion

- What information does this data tell us?
- What might be the reasons for the declines and increases of the number of children in child labour?
- Extend this graph over the next 12 years to show what you think the picture will look like in 2032.

To develop the activity further, suggest that students explore the regional trends. The report helpfully provides a synopsis of the ways in which to reduce child labour, and learners can research these areas in the following groups:

- Poverty reduction
- Levels of informality
- Social protection
- Education exclusion
- Population growth
- Other challenges

They can share their own ideas of what these mean for reducing child labour and display them on post-it notes as part of a wall display. This conversation would then lead into exploring three aspects of child labour:

- Labour across the ages
- Boys and girls in child labour
- Child labour in rural and urban settings

One suggestion is to divide the class into three groups according to their needs, suitability, and interests, each exploring the data on one of the three aspects above. Each group would be provided with the corresponding sets of charts from the report. Once all three groups have worked on their theme, each could present the findings to the rest of the class. Throughout the activities, learners could continue to contribute to the wallchart display of the class project, pooling together different thoughts, explanations, and solutions. Learners can share their expertise across the groups and have a voice/role.

The first group, exploring child labour across the ages, could be asked to write down what they think the proportion of children in child labour are, between the ages of 5-11 years, 12-14 years, and 15-17 years. After showing them the information below, ask them:

How accurate were your predictions? Is there anything that surprises you about the data?

Percentage of children in child labour across age groups

5-11 years	9.7%
12-14 years	9.3%
15-17 years	9.5%

Learners may express surprise at this data, especially those who are similar ages to the children presented here, and/or those with older and younger siblings. Ask learners what they feel/think about the largest proportion of children in child labour represented by the data above, especially if they are of a similar age.

This group would then look at the data over the last 12 years, for these age groups:

5-11 years	2008: 10.7%	2012: 8.5%	2016: 8.3%	2020: 9.7%
12-14 years	2008: 16.9%	2012: 13.1%	2016: 10.5%	2020: 9.3%
15-17 years	2008: 17%	2012: 13.1%	2016: 11.7%	2020: 9.5%

Ask the students to discuss reasons which might explain the increase in child labour for the youngest of children and why might the figures of older children in child labour be declining?

For the second group exploring boys and girls in child labour, ask them to discuss:

- Globally, who do you think is involved in child labour more, boys or girls?
- Do you think it is older or younger girls or boys involved in child labour?
- Give reasons for your ideas on these.

Once students have had the opportunity to discuss their thoughts, provide them with the following data and ask:

- What information does this data give?
- Do these figures surprise you?
- What might explain the differences in the numbers of boys and girls in the age groups?

Depending on your learners' and as appropriate to their needs, you may like to discuss gender fluidity and non-binary identities.

Child labour: Comparing boys and girls

5-11 years	Boys: 10.9%	Girls: 8.4%
12-14 years	Boys: 11%	Girls: 7.5%
15-17 years	Boys: 12.2%	Girls: 6.6%
All ages	Boys: 11.2%	Girls: 7.8%

For this data, ask learners whether this surprises them and why boys may account for the largest share of children in child labour. Ask the group to write down three statements to summarise the information, to display on the post-it notes and add to the classroom wall display of the project. Either the same group of pupils or another group can explore the data below which compares child labour amongst boys and girls across different regions.

Share of child labour across the regions (by sex)

World	Boys: 60.7%	Girls: 39.3%
Sub-Saharan Africa	Boys: 56.1%	Girls: 43.9%
Northern Africa and Western Asia	Boys: 65.1%	Girls: 34.9%
Central and Southern Asia	Boys: 67.5%	Girls: 32.5%
Eastern and South-Eastern Asia	Boys: 65.3%	Girls: 34.7%
Latin America and the Caribbean	Boys: 67%	Girls: 33%
Europe and Northern America	Boys: 62.3%	Girls: 37.7%

Using the statistics in the next data set, learners could make predictions about the decline of child labour amongst boys and girls using the following data. They could extrapolate the graphs to make predictions about how the trends might continue.

Decline in child labour

Boys 2000: 23.4%   2004: 21.3%   2008: 21.4%   2012:18.1%   2016:10.7% 2020:11.2%
Girls 2000: 22.5%   2004: 19.9%   2008: 16.9%   2012:15.2%   2016:8.4% 2020:7.8%%

The data below shows rates of child labour in rural and urban areas. The activity could begin by making estimates of child labour, prior to presenting the world data. Teachers can prompt learners to discuss their own local urban or rural settings to provide a context. Before showing the students the data, ask them to discuss if they think there will be differences in the number of girls and boys doing child labour in urban and rural areas?

Child labour in rural and urban areas

Total	Boys: 13.9%	Girls: 4.7%
Rural	Boys 16.1%	Girls: 11.6%
Urban	Boys 5.7%	Girls: 3.6%

After sharing the data with learners, ask them to discuss:

How accurate were your estimates?
Does this data surprise you?

They can then write their thoughts on post-it notes to add to the class wall-display project. Finally, this group could explore the following data, making comparisons across regions, explaining differences around urban and rural settings around the world. Ask them to write down three statements they can make about the data. They could locate the regions on a world map and add their statements to it.

Child labour in rural and urban areas by region

World	Rural: 76.7%	Urban: 23.3%
Sub-Saharan Africa	Rural: 82.1%	Urban: 17.9%
Northern Africa and Western Asia	Rural: 69.2%	Urban: 30.8%
Central and Southern Asia	Rural: 75.2%	Urban: 24.8%
Eastern and South-Eastern Asia	Rural: 75.2%	Urban: 24.8%
Latin America and the Caribbean	Rural: 51.3%	Urban: 48.7%
Europe and Northern America	Rural: 47.3%	Urban: 52.7%

Other possibilities

This could lead to an activity based on writing headline news for a school newspaper or children's magazine, which uses these statistics, graphs, and charts. They could go even further by engaging in persuasive writing to write a letter to their local Member of Parliament putting forward the global issues of children in labour and how government might address it. Further discussions could include the impact of Covid-19 and future pandemics. The report includes solutions that could be researched by more experienced students, for example, registration of every child at birth; ending gender norms and discrimination; child protection; decent work; improving rural livelihoods; child labour in domestic and global chains; conflicts and disasters; and international cooperation and partnership.

Plan a whole-school awareness day at which the students share their research. Invite relevant charities and other workshop leaders to work with staff and parents on the issues raised by this activity.

Resources

UNICEF Child Labour Report is available at www.ilo.org/wcmsp5/groups/public/---ed_norm/---ipec/documents/publication/wcms_797515.pdf

Activity 2: Counting the votes

Introduction

This activity is based on an idea from the *Teaching mathematics for social justice* book published by the Association of Teachers of Mathematics (Wright, 2016). It was generated by secondary mathematics teachers working with Pete on a collaborative research project. The original activity (including the resource sheets) was designed for use with secondary school students (age 11–16). However, in this version, the notes are targeted for use with student teachers, although they could be adapted for use with secondary school students. They are based on Pete's experiences of using this activity with PGCE Mathematics students. They are based on the principle that student teachers should begin by trying out the tasks for themselves, taking on the role of learners, whilst the tutor models how the tasks might be introduced by a teacher. The student teachers and tutor then step out of these roles to discuss the purpose of the activities, the pedagogic rationale used in introducing them, and how they might be used or adapted in the classroom.

The original activity was designed to promote understanding of different voting systems and an appreciation of the mathematical principles and ideas on which they are based. In doing so it highlights how mathematics can be applied in real-life contexts and provides an example of a strong link between mathematics and social justice issues. Understanding how a voting system works can empower students to use their own vote wisely in future life. The mathematical content includes the properties and characteristics of arithmetic progressions, geometric progressions and other sequences, calculating the nth term, and working systematically with combinations. It highlights how choosing a particular voting system can influence who, and which type of candidate, is subsequently elected. This can lead to interesting discussions around which voting system is fairest, which can also be used to consider choosing a fair or suitable method for electing class representatives or members of a school council.

The activity is also designed to promote discussion amongst students and to generate productive group work. There are also opportunities for investigative work, e.g., by encouraging students to explore different voting systems that are used in various elections around the world or to come up with their own 'fairer' systems for counting the votes. Student teachers should be prompted to discuss how to introduce the tasks to make the most of these opportunities.

Starting point

Resource Sheet 1 is a good starting point as it poses an interesting problem for students to consider that they can relate to their own experiences (after all most of them are unlikely to have voted yet in a formal election). The problem involves three friends choosing from five films that are on offer at a cinema, assuming that they all want to go and see the film together. This leads naturally into a discussion about assigning scores to preferences, which serves as a good introduction to the 'Borda points' voting systems (based on applying different types of mathematical sequences) which are introduced in Resource Sheet 2. It is possible to make a strong case for choosing *Cleopatra*, *Bobby*, or *Tango*, depending on how much weight students think it is fair to assign to different preferences. Students can be prompted to conduct a debate around which of these films to see and why.

Counting the Votes - resource sheet 1

Preference Voting

Imagine that three friends, Yaline, Brad and Alex, are going to the cinema together but they can't agree which film to see.

There are five films altogether to choose from.

They decide to write down their preferences:
'1' for their first choice film, '2' for their second choice film, etc.

Each friend's preferences are shown below:

Brad's preferences:

Film	Preference
Cleopatra	5
Wheels	4
Bobby	3
Tango	2
Cosmos	1

Yaline's preferences:

Film	Preference
Cleopatra	1
Wheels	5
Bobby	4
Tango	2
Cosmos	3

Alex's preferences:

Film	Preference
Cleopatra	2
Wheels	4
Bobby	1
Tango	3
Cosmos	5

Group discussion:
• Which film should they see?
• Use only the information shown above.
• Justify your decision to others.

Figure 7.1 Preference voting

Counting the Votes – resource sheet 2

Borda Points

One way of deciding who wins in an election is to assign points for each preference.
Jean-Charles de Borda (1733-1799) was a French mathematician, physicist and political scientist who designed a preferential voting system that is still in use today.

Borda served as a ship's captain in the French navy and fought against the English in the American Revolutionary War in 1777-1778. As an engineer, he developed new instruments and methods used widely for navigation. He also constructed the standard metre that was used as the basis for the metric system of measurement.

After the French Revolution in 1789, there was an attempt to extend the use of the metric system to time and navigation. It was decided that a right angle should be divided into 100 degrees and a day should be divided into 10 hours, each hour being 100 minutes long. Borda was an enthusiast for the new system and constructed navigational instruments for use with the new units.

The new units of time didn't catch on and Napoleon abolished the Republican Calendar in 1806. However, the 'gradian' (one hundredth of a right angle) is still used today in engineering and the French military.

Borda had a ship, an island, a cape, an asteroid and a crater on the moon named after him. His name is one of 72 names inscribed on the Eiffel Tower.

Borda's preferential voting system:
Voters in an election express preferences for each candidate, '1' for their first choice, '2' for their second choice, and so on.
A mathematical sequence is then used to award points for each preference.
The points awarded to each candidate are then added together.
The candidate with the largest total wins.

Borda count with arithmetic weighting:
The sequence used is an arithmetic progression, for example 1, 2, 3, 4, 5, 6, …
If there are 5 candidates, then 5 points are awarded for each 1st preference,
4 points for each 2nd preference, and so on down to 1 point for each 5th preference.

Borda count with geometric weighting:
The sequence used is a geometric progression, for example 1, 2, 4, 8, 16, 32, …
If there are 5 candidates, then 16 points are awarded for each 1st preference,
8 points for each 2nd preference, and so on down to 1 point for each 5th preference.

- Use Borda's preferential voting system to decide the winner in an election (you could use it to decide which film the friends should see in *Counting the Votes 1*).
- Discuss whether Borda count with arithmetic or geometric weighting is a fairer system to use for your chosen election. Justify your argument.
- Which other mathematical sequences could you use and how fair would they be?

Figure 7.2 Borda points

Students could go on to propose their own titles of films, perhaps conducting an election in class around which is the 'best film of all time' and exploring what happens when different voting systems are used to determine the winner. This leads to an interesting dilemma about whether it is ethical to deliberately nominate a sequel to a film in order to split the vote and ensure it doesn't win, e.g., nominating *Jaws 2* and *Jaws 3* to reduce the chances of *Jaws* winning.

After trying the task for themselves, student teachers could be encouraged to consider what questions they might ask students to prompt discussion in class around the links between mathematics and social justice issues.
Here are some suggestions:

- Why can't you consider only 1st preferences in this case?
- Should more 1st preferences or fewer 5th preferences be considered more important?
- Should one 1st preference or two 2nd preferences be worth more?

Students are likely to suggest adding the preferences and looking for the film with the lowest total (or the lowest mean score). You could compare this to the 'Borda points with arithmetic weighting' method (see Resource Sheet 2) and consider why the two sets of calculations are directly related and will lead to the same outcome. Generalising this result can lead to some nice algebraic reasoning. The argument that 1st preferences should be given more weighting than other preferences could be related to the 'Borda points with geometric weighting' method (see Resource Sheet 2), and students could be encouraged to consider why it has this effect. It is also interesting to explore what the effect would be of applying other sequences to assigning weight to preferences, such as square, triangle numbers, prime numbers, or numbers in the Fibonacci sequence. Alternatively, consider different arithmetic/geometric progressions by changing the first terms and common differences/ratios. This can generate an appreciation of how quickly different sequences grow. Student teachers should be encouraged to explore these ideas further and consider the opportunities they open up for extending the task.

Development

Resource Sheet 3 introduces three more methods for counting the votes which are based on mathematical applications. Again, encourage student teachers to work in small groups to try out the activity for themselves. Enlarging the ballot papers onto A3 paper and cutting them out will facilitate group discussion. Asking each group to start with a different voting system, before moving on to others, will ensure that every method is explored by at least one group. This is an ideal task for getting student teachers to appreciate the value of providing prompt questions for students at an appropriate time so that they are able to tackle the problems independently whilst choosing productive pathways. After completing the task, encourage student teachers to consider the types of question they might ask, whether they pose these to all students at the start, use them as prompts for some groups when circulating, or save them until discussing the task with the whole class at the end.

Here are some suggestions:

- How would you arrange the ballot papers to help you keep track of who is eliminated? (Particularly relevant to Method 2.)
- What might you need to record to help you work out who wins? (Particularly relevant to Methods 2, 3, 4, and 5.)
- Is there always a clear winner? Why? How many pairs of candidates would there be in an election with three candidates, four candidates, five candidates, six candidates, ... n candidates? (Particularly relevant to Method 5.)

In discussing the rationale for the task, student teachers are likely to highlight how each of the four candidates wins under at least one of the five methods, emphasising how important the choice of the method is for counting the votes. This begs the question about who decides which voting method to use in real elections and how transparent this choice might be. It is worth highlighting that, in a real-life election, it is quite likely that the same candidate will be elected under different voting systems, although it is sometimes possible for two different methods to give different outcomes. This task has been designed deliberately (with careful manipulation of the preferences on the ballot papers) to highlight that this is not necessarily the case. The fact that the ballot papers are not 'typical' (hence the title of the task) should be emphasised to student teachers.

An interesting aside is that the four names of candidates were chosen as they are all former female presidents who were elected democratically in their countries (Malawi, Ireland, India, and Brazil respectively). It is common for students (and student teachers) to use male pronouns when discussing the voting methods and this can be highlighted at the end as an example of unconscious bias.

Counting the votes – resource sheet 3

An unusual ballot

These eleven ballot papers are from an imaginary election carried out using a preferential voting system:

Ballot paper	1
Write '1' for your 1st choice, '2' for your 2nd choice, etc.	
Banda	*3*
McAleese	*4*
Patil	*1*
Roussef	*2*

Ballot paper	2
Write '1' for your 1st choice, '2' for your 2nd choice, etc.	
Banda	*2*
McAleese	*1*
Patil	*4*
Roussef	*3*

Ballot paper	3
Write '1' for your 1st choice, '2' for your 2nd choice, etc.	
Banda	*1*
McAleese	*3*
Patil	*4*
Roussef	*2*

Ballot paper	4
Write '1' for your 1st choice, '2' for your 2nd choice, etc.	
Banda	*3*
McAleese	*4*
Patil	*1*
Roussef	*2*

Ballot paper	5
Write '1' for your 1st choice, '2' for your 2nd choice, etc.	
Banda	*2*
McAleese	*3*
Patil	*1*
Roussef	*4*

Ballot paper	6
Write '1' for your 1st choice, '2' for your 2nd choice, etc.	
Banda	*3*
McAleese	*1*
Patil	*4*
Roussef	*2*

Ballot paper	7
Write '1' for your 1st choice, '2' for your 2nd choice, etc.	
Banda	*1*
McAleese	*2*
Patil	*4*
Roussef	*3*

Ballot paper	8
Write '1' for your 1st choice, '2' for your 2nd choice, etc.	
Banda	*3*
McAleese	*4*
Patil	*1*
Roussef	*2*

Ballot paper	9
Write '1' for your 1st choice, '2' for your 2nd choice, etc.	
Banda	*2*
McAleese	*1*
Patil	*4*
Roussef	*3*

Ballot paper	10
Write '1' for your 1st choice, '2' for your 2nd choice, etc.	
Banda	*2*
McAleese	*3*
Patil	*4*
Roussef	*1*

Ballot paper	11
Write '1' for your 1st choice, '2' for your 2nd choice, etc.	
Banda	*3*
McAleese	*4*
Patil	*1*
Roussef	*2*

- Cut out and use the 11 ballot papers to decide which candidate would win the election under each method for counting the votes shown below.
- Discuss which method you think is fairest for counting the votes and why.

---

1. Relative majority (or 'first past the post'):
Count only the 1st preferences and ignore all other preferences.
The candidate with the most 1st preferences is elected.

2. Absolute majority (or 'alternative vote'):
The candidate with the fewest 1st preferences is eliminated and their votes are redistributed according to the next available preference marked on the ballot papers.
This process is repeated until one candidate has more than half of all votes.
In the event of a tie, results of previous rounds should be taken into account.

3. Borda count with arithmetic weighting:
See *Counting the Votes resource sheet 2* for an explanation of this method.

4. Borda count with geometric weighting:
See *Counting the Votes resource sheet 2* for an explanation of this method.

5. Condorcet Pair-Wise Counting:
Take each pair of candidates in turn and decide which of the two is preferred by considering only the preferences for those two candidates on the 11 ballot papers.
If a candidate is preferred to all other candidates, then that candidate is elected.

Figure 7.2 An unusual ballot

Other possibilities

All of the methods in Resource Sheet 3 are recognised preferential voting systems (see the Electoral Reform Society website at www.electoral-reform.org.uk) and are (or have been) used in real-life elections, e.g., the alternative vote is used in the Irish presidential elections and the Borda count is used for the NBA's Most Valuable Player award. There are many more methods in use; however, these five have been chosen as they depend largely upon mathematical reasoning. Student teachers could be encouraged to explore other voting methods (and the related mathematical ideas) used to elect a single member to represent a group of people, e.g., a mayor or general secretary of a trade union. There are a lot more than five methods in use around the world, and there is an even greater variety of methods used to elect a group of people to represent a larger population (which includes various methods of proportional representation).

The life story of Jean-Charles de Borda (see Resource Sheet 2) can be used to draw attention to the socio-political and fallible nature of mathematics. Of particular interest is the combination of being a mathematician and political scientist, and the way that Borda engaged with revolutionary ideas relating to replacing units of measurement, some of which endure to the present day. Student teachers could be encouraged to research other real-life historical figures (especially women and people of non-Western heritage) whose life stories challenge orthodox (and hegemonic) views of mathematics.

References

1. Wright, P. (2016) *Teaching mathematics for social justice: Meaningful projects for the secondary mathematics classroom.* Derby: ATM Publications.

Activity 3: Housing and community

Introduction

This activity is based on ideas generated by members of the Teaching Maths for Social Justice Network (TMSJN), which is a network for teachers of mathematics in all school phases committed to addressing issues of equity and social justice in the classroom established in April 2021 (www.mathsocialjustice.org). It explores social issues, such as housing, within students' own local communities. It provides an opportunity for students to develop their mathematical agency through engaging with meaningful data that relates to their own situation and personal experiences.

Students are encouraged to develop an appreciation of how statistics can be used to quantify and represent social issues relating to their home environment. They will extract, collate, and analyse real-life data relating to the area in which they live and consider how to represent this data in novel and innovative ways. They will be working with secondary data from the StreetCheck (www.streetcheck.co.uk) website during this activity, so you will need to arrange access to a computer suite, or a class set of laptops, and check beforehand that your school network allows access to this website. It will be useful for this activity to have multiple printed copies of local maps (showing postcodes / street names and covering the school's catchment area) and coloured pencils or highlighter pens. The activity works best if students work collaboratively in pairs.

We would like to acknowledge the contribution of the following colleagues from the TMSJN who drew on their experiences of trying out similar ideas in the classroom: Maria Esteban, Ali Ford, Ladan Sadjadi, and Max Aantjes.

Starting point

Begin by facilitating a whole-class interactive discussion around issues relating to housing in the local area. Explain to students that they are going to explore the data available on housing to answer the following questions:

- What proportion of homes are houses/flats?
- What proportion of homes are owned/rented by their occupants?
- To what extent does this vary from one neighbourhood to another (within the local area)?

Discussing these questions is likely to prompt questions about the ambiguity of the language used, for example:

- How is a 'home,' 'house,' 'flat,' 'own,' 'rent,' or 'neighbourhood' defined?
- How would a sub-divided house be categorised?
- What about a 'shared ownership' scheme (part rent, part buy)?
- What about where the homeowner sub-rents a room to a friend or family member?

Students should come to a class consensus about how the ambiguities highlighted above might be resolved. This should take account of the practicability of different definitions for finding and extracting data (see below). You could display the diagrams below (also included in Resource Sheet 1) which can be generated from the StreetCheck website (www .streetcheck.co.uk), by carrying out a 'Search' for the postcode 'BN41 2FD' (Easthill Drive, Portslade, Brighton) and then clicking on the 'Housing' tab. You can prompt a discussion using these diagrams and the following questions:

- *Would 'Residence in Commercial Building' be categorised as 'house' or 'flat'?*
- *Would 'Shared Ownership' and 'Rent Free' be categorised as 'owned' or 'rented'?*

(a)

Housing Types	
Detached	4
Semi-Detached	96
Terraced	4
Flat (Purpose-Built)	12
Flat (Commercial)	12
Residence in Commercial Building	1
Total	**129**

(b)

Housing Types	
Detached	2
Semi-Detached	46
Terraced	2
Flat (Purpose-Built)	50
Flat (Commercial)	1
Total	**101**

Figure 7.3 Housing types and tenure

The reliability and subjective nature of data is an important issue in statistics that, whilst often overlooked, is crucial when it comes to interpreting the findings of statistical analyses. The implications of decisions taken by the class should be discussed, and students should refer back to these when interpreting the findings.

Ask students to predict what they think the proportion of homes that are houses and owned by their occupants might be for their local area and how these might compare to other areas. Keep a record of their predictions to refer to at the end (you could use a short paper or online survey to do this). Comparing initial predictions to the findings from their research will enable students to appreciate the power of mathematics to generate insight into their own situation and understanding of social justice issues relating to their local community.

In this activity, the proportion of homes that are houses (rather than flats) and the proportion of homes that are owned by their occupants (rather than rented) are used as 'proxy measures' of the relative affluence of a particular area. Proxy measures are commonplace in education, e.g., the percentage of students who are 'pupil premium' or 'free school meals' are used as proxy measures of disadvantage in schools. The following questions will help students develop their appreciation of the concept of a 'proxy measure' (which is alluded to in Resource Sheet 1):

- Do you think people who live in a flat are generally better off than those who live in a house? Why? Can you think of any exceptions to this rule?
- Do you think people who own their own property are generally better off than those who rent? Why? Can you think of any exceptions to this rule?

Development

Now get students to use their own postcode to collect data on 'Housing Types' and 'Housing Tenure' for their local area from the StreetCheck. They should calculate the proportion of homes that are houses (rather than flats) and the proportion of homes that are owned by their occupants (rather than rented) for their local area. Note that students can see the local area that is generated by their postcode in StreetCheck by clicking on 'Show census area covered' under the streetmap that appears on the summary page. For example, this is the local area that includes BN41 2FD (Easthill Drive, Portslade, Brighton):

Figure 7.4 Local area

Map data: ©OpenStreetMap, StreetCheck

They can also calculate these proportions for the wider area in which they live (defined by those areas sharing the first half of their postcode, e.g., BN41 for the example above) by clicking 'view information for the whole of BN41 here.'

The following questions can then be used to prompt a whole-class discussion:

- How do your results compare with those of your partner? Those of other students?
- How do the results for your local area compare with those for the wider area in which you live?
- Were the results what you expected? If not, why do you think this is the case?

You can now encourage students to collate the data for other areas which they might be interested in exploring, e.g., those neighbouring the local area in which they live, the school's catchment area, or the town/city/county in which they live (they will need a street map with postcodes to do this). Where appropriate, they can pool their results with each other. Challenge them to identify the largest and smallest proportions for local areas within their school's catchment area and within their local town/city/county. They might also consider two contrasting areas in different parts of the country.

You might need to highlight the need to aggregate the data when combining areas and discuss why taking the mean of the separate proportions will not work. You could display the following diagram (See Table 7.1) and calculations to stimulate such a discussion.

Encourage students to discuss different ways of representing these proportions using various statistical diagrams (e.g., bar chart / pie chart). You might use these questions to prompt discussion (note there is not necessarily a 'correct' answer to these questions):

- Which diagram would be more appropriate?
- In what contexts would a different diagram be more appropriate?
- What can you conclude about the data from one diagram but not from the other?
- Why do you think pie charts are used on the StreetCheck website?
- Which diagram would be best for highlighting inequality in housing? Why?

Challenge students to think up their own ways they could display contrasting proportions of houses/flats and homeowners/renters for different areas on the same street map. This would be an ideal activity for generating a stimulating display (make sure students include their names on any display work to foster ownership of their ideas). Whilst you should encourage students to come up with their own ideas, here are some suggestions for those that struggle to do so:

- Draw an 'appropriate statistical diagram' within each aggregated area on the map.
- Shade each aggregated area with a different colour to represent the proportions.

Finally, encourage students to reflect on their findings. You might use these prompts:

- How close were the actual proportions to your own initial predictions?
- What about the class's initial predictions? What might account for any differences?
- What do the findings tell us about inequality in our local area?

Table 7.1 Proportion of houses

BN41 2FD		BN41 2FU	
Housing Types		**Housing Types**	
Detached	4	Detached	2
Semi-Detached	96	Semi-Detached	46
Terraced	4	Terraced	2
Flat (Purpose-Built)	12	Flat (Purpose-Built)	50
Flat (Commercial)	12	Flat (Commercial)	1
Residence in Commercial Building	1	**Total**	101
Total	129		

Proportion of houses in area including Easthill Drive (BN41 2FD)

= 104/129 = 80.6%

Proportion of houses in area including Foredown Road (BN41 2FU)

= 50/101 = 49.5%

- Mean of the two proportions above = (80.6 + 49.5)/2 = 65.1%
- Proportion of houses in both areas combined = 154/230 = 67.0%

- What else do they tell us about our local community?
- How might this compare to other communities in different parts of the world?

Other possibilities

Explore whether there is a correlation between the proportion of houses and the proportion of homeowners in different areas:

- How will you collect the data you need? (Two-column table with a row for each small postcode area?)
- What statistical diagram will you draw? (Scatter-graph and line of best fit?)
- What are the implications of any correlation? (Relate to inequality in housing.)

Explore other data available via StreetCheck (people, culture, employment, crime):

- What questions could you explore? How might these relate to inequality?

You could use the following example (included in Resource Sheet 2) to prompt a whole-class discussion focusing on how statistics can sometimes be used deliberately to mislead people:

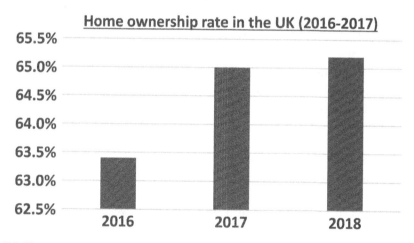

Figure 7.5 Home ownership rate in the (2016-2017)

Prompt questions:

- In what ways might this diagram and headline be misleading? How do you know?
- What would be a more transparent way of presenting the data?
- Compare the diagram to the following diagram which includes the same data.
- Can you see any other ways in which the original diagram was misleading?
- How accurate was the headline: 'Home ownership rates in the UK are rising fast!'?
- What would be a more accurate headline?

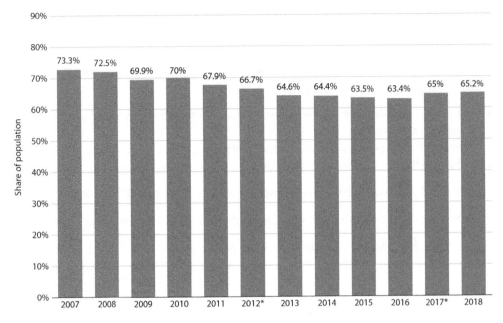

Figure 7.6 Home ownership rate in the UK (2007 to 2018)

Encourage students to reflect on their own statistical diagrams that they generated earlier in the activity. Ask them whether they might be considered misleading in any way and, if so, how they could be improved.

Online resources:

- Local community Resource Sheet 1
- Local community Resource Sheet 2

These resources can be found on the book's companion website: www.routledge.com/9781032421636

Activity 4: Investigating earnings

Introduction

This activity is based on ideas generated by members of the Teaching Maths for Social Justice Network (TMSJN), which is a network established in April 2021 for teachers of mathematics in all school phases committed to addressing issues of equity and social justice in the classroom (www.mathsocialjustice.org). It explores inequality in earnings between different ethnic groups and how this has changed over time. It provides an opportunity for students to develop their mathematical agency through engaging with real-life data, posing their own questions, analysing, and presenting their own findings.

Students are encouraged to develop an appreciation of how statistics can be used to quantify and represent levels of inequality relating to ethnicity. They will engage with time-series graphs and consider how to calculate and describe trends over time. They will be working with secondary data on the internet during this activity so you will need to arrange access to a computer suite, or a class set of laptops. The activity works best if students work collaboratively in mixed attainment groups of three or four.

We would like to acknowledge the contribution of the following colleagues from the TMSJN who drew on their experiences of trying out similar ideas in the classroom: Hafsa Farhana; Vinay Kathotia; Azadeh Neman; and Kate O'Brien.

Starting point

Begin by facilitating a whole-class interactive discussion around issues relating to inequality in earnings between different ethnic groups and how these have changed over time. Ask students to make predictions about what they might find from exploring these issues and keep a record of their predictions to refer to at the end. This will encourage students to reflect upon their own preconceptions around the issues and help to address common misconceptions. It will also enable them to appreciate the power of mathematics to generate insight into real-world social justice issues.

You could encourage them to consider some of the following questions:

- Which ethnic groups do you think might earn the most on average?
- How do you know? What might be the reasons for this?
- How big do you think the difference will be? Has it changed over the last five years?
- Do you think the pattern will be the same in different occupations? Why?
- How much inequality in earnings is there between different occupations? Why?
- How might this be related to difference in earnings between ethnic groups?
- Do you think people are better off now than they were 20 years ago? Why?

Explain to students that they are going to explore some of these ideas for themselves (in groups) and get each group to come up with their own question or hypothesis that they would like to investigate. Encourage them to discuss with each other why this question or hypothesis is of interest to them and to keep a record of this, as they will be reporting back on their thinking, and justifying their choices, to the whole group via a poster presentation.

The two statistical diagrams below (also included in Resource Sheet 1) can be used to prompt discussion amongst students. Ask them to describe the key features of each diagram and what it shows. You could encourage students to come up with their own headlines, e.g., 'Pay gap narrowed since 2012' (as used by the ONS for the second diagram), and the extent to which the available evidence supports these. Also consider what the diagrams don't show, e.g., how many people are in each group. Encourage students to ask their own questions about the data, e.g., *What is a 'quintile' and why choose the top/bottom two? How are the different groups defined? Why are these groups used? Is there any duplication in the data? (E.g., 'Bangladeshi' is a subgroup of 'Asian.') What is the difference between the 'median' and the 'mean'? Why is median used to represent average pay and not mean?*

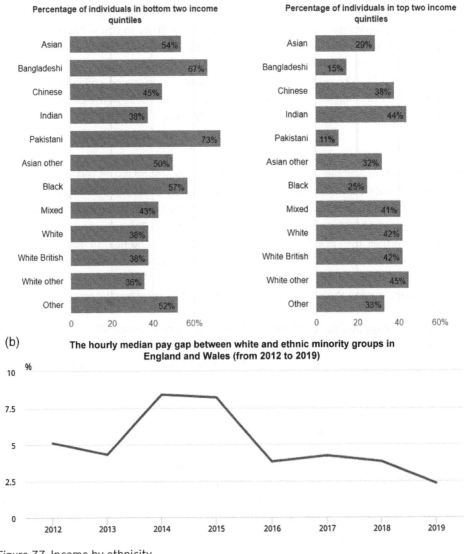

Figure 7.7 Income by ethnicity

Development

Once each group of students has decided on a question/hypothesis to investigate, get them to spend some time planning how they will go about answering their question before they collect any data (this is likely to save time in the long run by enabling students to be more focused). The following questions might be useful at this point (or at a later point in their investigations):

- What data do you need to collect to answer your question/hypothesis?
- Where will you find it? How will you search for it? What 'key words' will you use?
- What problems might you encounter with your data? How might you address these?
- What will you do with the data? What calculations might you need to make?
- How will you organise your data? How will you present it to others?
- What statistical diagrams will you use to present the data?

Students can then work in groups to collect data, analyse their data, and consider how they should present their findings to others. A poster is a good way of facilitating this and provides an opportunity for students to talk about how they went about conducting their investigation with others. Encourage students to annotate their poster with explanations of the decisions and choices they made, e.g., why they chose to use particular statistical calculations or diagrams, what difficulties they encountered, and how they resolved these. Make sure students include their names on their posters to foster ownership of their ideas.

Students can either take it in turns to present their poster, or the posters can be displayed in a gallery for other students to view in turn. Whichever way you organise this, be sure to provide opportunities for other students to pose questions to the group about their approach, as focusing on the process that students follow in conducting their investigations will help to develop mathematical agency. You should be prepared to facilitate this by modelling questions to ask. The following are examples of questions that might be useful:

- Why did you decide to ...? Why did you choose to use ...?
- What difficulties did you encounter ...? How did you resolve these?
- What would you do differently next time? Why?

You might want to intervene at various points in the investigation where the need arises, such as when you judge it would be useful to consider different ways of representing data, when these would be used and for what purpose. Below are two examples you could use (with accompanying questions) to prompt a discussion around the key features of, and the rationale for using, pie charts / bar charts (also included in Resource Sheet 2) and line graphs (also included in Resource Sheet 3).

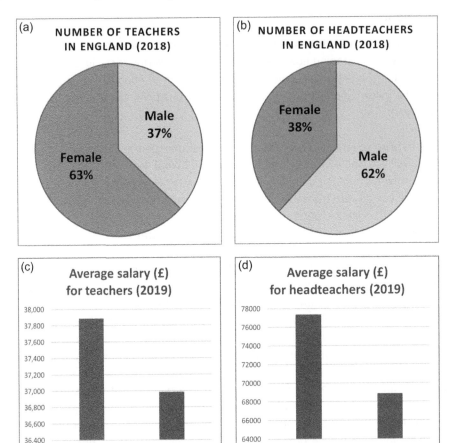

Figure 7.8 Male and female salaries for teachers and headteachers.

Questions to prompt discussion:

- What are the distinctive features of a bar chart/pie chart?
- What does each diagram show (that the other one doesn't)?
- When would it be appropriate/inappropriate to use each diagram?
- What can you infer about the situation for male/female teachers from the diagrams?
- What can't you infer from each diagram?

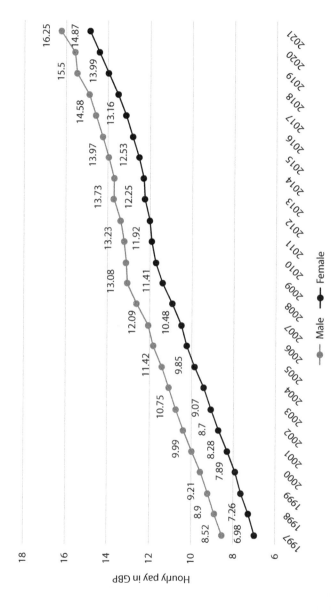

Figure 7.9 Median hourly earnings for full-time employees in the UK by gender (1997 to 2021).

Questions to prompt discussion:

- What are the distinctive features of a line graph?
- What does a line graph show you that other statistical diagrams can't?
- When would it be appropriate to use a line graph?
- How many time series could you display on one line graph?
- What can you infer about the situation for male/female employees from the line graph?
- What can't you infer from the line graph?

Other possibilities

You might want to highlight to students how different ways of presenting data can lead to very different interpretations, some of which can be deliberately misleading. Fostering a critical understanding of statistics, and how they can be used to mislead, is an important aspect of developing mathematical agency. You could use the diagrams below, and the accompanying questions, to facilitate this:

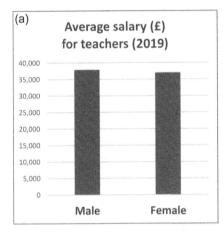 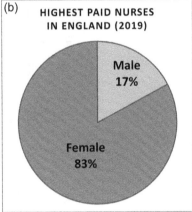

Figure 7.10 Misleading statistics

Questions/prompts to facilitate discussions:

- What is different about the way the data has been presented in the bar chart above and the way it was presented in the bar chart in the earlier section 'Male and female salaries for teachers and headteachers'?
- Which of the following statements would you say was most accurate?'Male teachers on average get paid significantly more than female teachers.''There is little difference between the pay of male teachers and female teachers.'
- Would it make a difference if you were only shown one or other of the bar charts?
- To what extent does the pie chart above support the following statement?'Women are more likely than men to be promoted to the highest paid nursing jobs.'
- What other data would you need to know to be able to test if this statement is true?
- The statement is in fact false as, in 2019, 11% of all nurses in England were male and 89% were female.

Inequality in earnings is a complex issue. For various socio-historical reasons, differences in earnings between ethnic groups are closely related to the differences in earnings between different occupations and differences in representation of ethnic groups in different occupations. Each of these offers a different line of inquiry and included below are possible data sources and suggested questions to prompt discussion that can be used for guidance:

Average weekly pay by employment sector (from 2000 onwards): www.ons.gov.uk/ employmentandlabourmarket/peopleinwork/earningsandworkinghours/datasets/average weeklyearnings

Discussion prompts:

- How much inequality in earnings is there between different occupations?
- How has this changed over time? Why do you think this is the case?
- Can you predict what will happen in the future?
- Which years shall we look at? Why?
- Which measure shall we use for 'average' earnings? Why?
- How might we present the results? Why?
- How can we quantify the increase over time?
- How can we measure inequality (compare the gap) between occupations over time?

Median pay (Table 1), unemployment (Table 2), occupation (Table 3), sector (Table 4) by ethnicity (2004-2019): www.ons.gov.uk/employmentandlabourmarket/peopleinwork/emp loymentandemployeetypes/adhocs/14006medianhourlypaybyethnicityandethnicitybrea kdownbyoccupationsectorandselfemploymentuk2004to2019

Discussion prompts:

- Which data will you use from the data that has been provided?
- How will you collate it? How will you analyse your data?
- Which statistical methods will you use?
- How will you represent your data? Which statistical diagrams will you use?
- How will you draw conclusions from your data?

The following prompt questions will help to draw out links between the different dimensions of inequality in earnings described above:

- Which ethnic groups are better/worse off than they were 20 years ago? By how much?
- Which occupations are better/worse off than they were 20 years ago? How does this relate to ethnicity?

Online resources:

- Investigating earnings Resource Sheet 1
- Investigating earnings Resource Sheet 2
- Investigating earnings Resource Sheet 3

These resources can be found on the book's companion website: www.routledge.com/ 9781032421636

Activity 5: Measuring inequality

Introduction

This activity is based on an idea from the *Teaching mathematics for social justice* book published by the Association of Teachers of Mathematics (Wright, 2016). It was generated by secondary mathematics teachers working with Pete on a collaborative research project. It involves students exploring inequality in income earned by different groups within a population, e.g., the UK or the World. It highlights how understanding some social justice issues, in this case inequality, requires students to be confident in applying highly mathematical ideas and concepts.

Students are encouraged to generate their own measures of inequality from statistical tables and to compare these to measures commonly used by economists, including the Lorenz curve and Gini coefficient. This involves developing an appreciation of calculating ratios and proportions, dealing with cumulative data, drawing smooth curves, and identifying a range of strategies for estimating irregular areas. Students are able to see clearly how mathematics can help them develop their understanding of an issue that is of particular interest and concern to them. Throughout the activity, be ready to engage with students' questions about inequality and social justice. (They are likely to be surprised, and perhaps outraged, by just how much inequality there is.)

Starting point

Begin by presenting students with some data representing the distribution of income amongst a population. The example in Table 7.2 (included on Resource Sheet 1) shows the percentage share of total income earned by each decile of the world's population in 2011.

Table 7.2 Global inequality by income in 2011

Decile of world population	Percentage share of total income
1st decile (poorest 10%)	0.6
2nd decile	1.0
3rd decile	1.4
4th decile	1.9
5th decile	2.8
6th decile	4.3
7th decile	6.5
8th decile	10.6
9th decile	19.6
10th decile (richest 10%)	51.3

Rather than resorting to teacher explanation, a good way of checking that students understand the data is to ask them to explain to each other (and then to the class) the meaning of one particular value, e.g., '19.6' in the table above. This is likely to generate discussion around the meaning of the word 'decile' and the distinction between percentages and actual amounts. A good way to conceptualise the 'deciles' is to imagine everyone is lined up in order from the least wealthy to the wealthiest (by household income) before being divided into ten equally sized groups. The ninth of these groups (counting from the least wealthy) will then earn 19.6% of the total global income between them.

Now get students to work in pairs or groups and to discuss the following question (based on the information in the table): *What single measure could you use to compare the level of global inequality with other years?* Then ask groups to present their ideas to the rest of the class and collate these on the board, being sure to write down the names of the students, e.g., *Yaline and Brad: Share of richest 10% − share of poorest 10%.* Make sure you keep these ideas for later (see below). Encourage students to explain their reasons for choosing their measure. The rationale here is to develop students' sense of ownership and collective agency (see Chapter 3) by acknowledging and recognising their contributions publicly.

Those who engage with this activity usually choose either a single measure, e.g., the percentage share of the richest or poorest 10% (these being considered the most significant values) or a combination of values as a difference or a ratio (leading to a rich discussion about the distinction between additive and multiplicative reasoning in this context and the language associated with these concepts). Other ideas have included aggregating the deciles, e.g., comparing the percentage share of the richest and poorest 50%.

Development

At this point students can be introduced to the ideas of a Lorenz curve and Gini coefficient. Explain that these are methods that economists 'commonly use' to represent and measure levels of inequality. It is important to be careful with your use of language here and to emphasise that this does not mean that they are any better than the measures that the students themselves came up with (which are likely to be more meaningful and easier to understand how they relate directly to the data). When the opportunity arises, you might like to discuss with students the merits of different measures, e.g., the Gini coefficient is a standard measure and is therefore more comparable with other populations that have already been measured in the same way and for which data are available.

The first step is to generate a cumulative table for the data shown in Table 7.2. This is shown in Table 7.3 (also included in Resource Sheet 2). You might get students to generate this for themselves using Table 7.2. If you show them the completed table, then make sure they understand the meaning of the data, e.g., by asking: *Where does the '48.7' come from and what does it mean?*

Table 7.3 Cumulative data for global inequality by income in 2011

Percentage of world population (cumulative)	Percentage share of total income (cumulative)
0	0.0
10	0.6
20	1.6
30	3.0
40	4.9
50	7.6
60	12.0
70	18.5
80	29.0
90	48.7
100	100.0

Show students the corresponding Lorenz curve shown in Figure 7.11 (also included in Resource Sheet 2) and invite them to discuss and explain how it is drawn, and its characteristics and features. If they have come across cumulative frequency graphs before, you might want to make a distinction between these and a Lorenz curve (which represents proportions rather than frequencies). Ask students to describe what they think the curve would look like if the world were less equal (more unequal) or more equal (less unequal). Ask: *What would perfect equality look like?* (This is important for calculating the Gini coefficient as we will see later.)

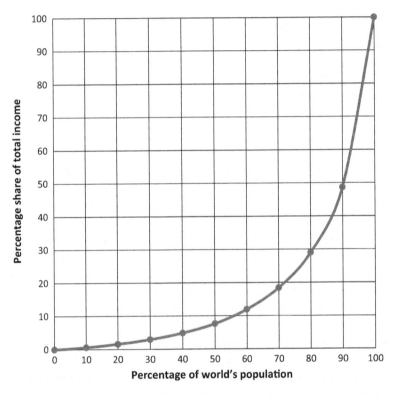

Figure 7.11 Lorenz curve for global inequality in 2011

An interesting issue that has arisen in discussion here is that, if it were possible to have perfect equality, i.e., if every household earned exactly the same income, then it would not be possible to order the population or divide it into deciles. Hence the 'line of perfect equality' is a theoretical construct, and it might be better to think about it as a 'line of *almost* perfect equality.' It will be a diagonal straight line joining (0, 0) and (100, 100), because 10% of the population will earn 10% of the total income, 20% will earn 20%, etc.

Once students have understood the important characteristics of a Lorenz curve, they can now be introduced to the Gini coefficient. This is a ratio and is defined as the area of the shape bounded by the 'line of perfect equality' and the Lorenz curve, divided by the area underneath the 'line of perfect equality' (which will be a right-angled triangle). Figure 7.12 (included in Resource Sheet 3) shows how to calculate the Gini coefficient from a Lorenz curve for UK inequality in income in 2011 (the same year as the data for global inequality presented earlier).

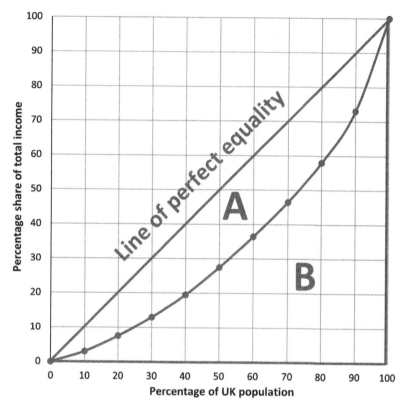

Figure 7.12 Calculating the Gini coefficient from a Lorenz curve for UK inequality in 2011.

In this diagram, the Gini coefficient is defined as:

$$\text{Gini coefficient} = (\text{Area of A}) \div (\text{Area of A} + \text{B})$$

It is worth discussing the following questions with students: *What happens to area A if there is more inequality?* (It gets bigger.) *What happens to the Gini coefficient if there is more inequality?* (It also gets bigger.) *What are the smallest and largest possible values for the Gini coefficient?* (0 and 1 respectively.)

The Gini coefficient for UK inequality in income in 2011 (the data represented in Figure 7.11) was 0.34.

The challenge for students now is to find ways of working out the Gini coefficient for themselves by finding an estimate for the area of A (the area of A + B is relatively easy as it is a right-angled triangle). You should leave plenty of time for students to explore this problem as it is potentially very rich and there are a variety of different methods they might employ. Students can work with the Lorenz curve for global inequality in 2011 (using Resource Sheet 2). Leave them to discuss their own methods in groups and, once they have done so, encourage them to find different ways of doing it. By comparing their answers using different methods, and by comparing their answers with different groups, they can consider how confident they are in the accuracy of their results.

You might ask groups to present the methods they used to calculate the area of shape A to the rest of the group, once again recognising and acknowledging contributions from different students. Emphasise how all methods give an approximation and, where appropriate, you could ask whether their method will result in an over- or underestimate for the Gini coefficient. The following methods are the most common methods used by students.

Students might use a counting squares method (the Lorenz curve in Resource Sheet 2 has been produced deliberately on a cm square grid). This might involve counting whole squares, any half squares on the diagonal and then counting the irregular 'part squares.' The issue is what to do with the part squares, and there are various legitimate ways of counting these systematically: match each large part with a corresponding small part to make whole squares; count all part squares and divide the total number by two; only count part squares that are more than half a square.

The other approach is to use vertical lines to divide up shape B and approximate its area by using trapeziums, e.g., by joining (10, 0.6) to (20, 1.6), or by using rectangles, e.g., draw a horizontal line halfway between 0.6 and 1.6. This approach is interesting as it might be a precursor to introducing calculus (where the trapezium rule is used to derive the integral of a function and hence find the area under a curve).

One thing to note is that the Gini coefficient is a ratio and therefore it does not matter which units are used to calculate A and A + B (as long as the units used for the two areas are consistent). Students tend to come up with answers between 0.63 and 0.65 for the Gini coefficient for global inequality in 2011. This can lead to a rich discussion in which students are invited to compare the Lorenz curves (Resource Sheets 2 and 3) and Gini coefficients (0.34 and 0.64) for UK inequality and global inequality respectively. You might pose the question: *Why is the Gini coefficient for the UK significantly lower than that for the whole world?* Note that it is a recognised phenomenon that equality tends to be greater in less wealthy countries.

Other possibilities

Students might be encouraged to draw their own Lorenz curves and calculate the Gini coefficients for data they can find on the internet when researching into income inequality. They might even generate their own data by carrying out a survey of their classmates on how much 'spending money' they are given each week (although care needs to be taken with this task to safeguard any vulnerable students, perhaps by getting students to complete an anonymous survey).

Students might explore changes in the Gini coefficient in UK (or in the World) over time. You might encourage them to identify trends they can see in the data, come up with headlines to describe these, and discuss whether there are historical events or changes in policy that might explain them. There is quite a lot of data available on the Gini coefficient in UK, e.g., the graph in Figure 7.2 (also included on Resource Sheet 3), which illustrates that there may be more than one way of calculating incomes, is taken from a House of Commons report.

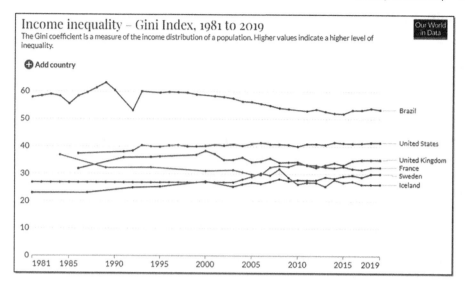

Figure 7.13

Source: Our world in data (2022) https://ourworldindata.org/grapher/economic-inequality -gini-index

Students might also like to research how inequality in the UK compares to other countries around the world. The 'Our world in data' website includes an interactive tool (see Figure 7.13 and Resource Sheet 3) that allows students to select any countries in the world they might be interested in comparing with the UK.

You might want to stimulate a discussion around equality by considering the question: *Would it be fair to everyone to earn exactly the same income?* Some students will commonly assert 'yes' to this question (based on principles of equality) whilst others might argue that people should be paid according to how much work they do, how much responsibility they take on in their jobs, or how long it takes them to qualify. This is likely to develop into a philosophical debate around ethics, and students should be encouraged to discuss their ideas openly whilst listening carefully to others' opinions and respecting each other's views and sensibilities.

Online resources:

- Measuring inequality Resources Sheet 1 (Global inequality)
- Measuring inequality Resources Sheet 2 (Lorenz curve)
- Measuring inequality Resources Sheet 3 (Gini coefficient)

These resources can be found on the book's companion website: www.routledge.com/ 9781032421636

Activity 6: Refugee journeys

Introduction

This session was first run at a workshop at the Association of Teachers of Mathematics (ATM) Conference. It was the third in series of workshops exploring learning and teaching mathematics drawing on drama education techniques. In particular the process called the 'Mantle of the expert', developed by Dorothy Heathcote. A previous workshop had involved designing and building refugee shelters. The focus of this workshop was the refugee journey and refugee education. The workshop is outlined in brief in Chapter 1, page 13. I worked with my partner, Helen Toft, a drama educator on designing and running the workshop.

We were struck by the similarity of the aims of the professional organisations to which we belonged. The Association of Teachers of Mathematics has as a guiding principle:

> The ability to operate mathematically is an aspect of human functioning which is as universal as language itself. Any possibility of intimidating with mathematical expertise is to be avoided.

The National Association for the teaching of Drama (NATD) has as a guiding principle:

> We are committed to developing a child-centred, humanising curriculum with an internationalist perspective. We are constantly asking ourselves what does a child need to know in order to be at home in the world?

We felt these two guiding principles placed social justice at the heart of the work of the associations. A specific aim of the workshop was to develop a greater understanding of the information available about refugees, and in particular to challenge some of the misinformation leading to misconceptions around numbers of refugees arriving in England. This seems to be a story which repeats itself with the Home Secretary in the UK Government talking about an 'invasion' of refugees on the South Coast in the autumn of 2022.

Starting point

The participants were all teachers at the ATM conference and so had not worked together previously. The ATM and the NATD also have within their guiding principles a commitment to cooperative and social learning so we chose to open the session with a series of drama games. These were selected to focus on the idea of oppression, support, and space. The first game was 'Bomb and shield.' Participants spread out around the room, and each person chooses one person to be a 'bomb' and another to be their shield. These choices are not revealed. Participants then move round the room and 'after a countdown from ten to one, the participants stop and try to have their shield between them and their 'bomb.' We discussed how language has changed. 'Bomb and shield' comes from Augustus Boal's work;

we would use alternative language such as 'Alien and defender' when working with young learners today.

A second game, 'Touching the floor', asked participants to play in groups of four. I would shout out a number. Each group, whilst remaining in contact with the floor, had to make sure only the given number of body parts were touching the floor. So, for numbers greater than eight, body parts other than legs had to be touching the floor, and if I shouted three or less, at least one person had to be supported by the rest of the group. If the first game had spread the group around the room, this brought people very closely together.

We now moved into the main activity for the workshop. This began by asking each group of four to make 20 small clay figures. We asked for these to be one twentieth the size of the average person. We were asked what we meant by 'average' - this led to an interesting discussion about averages - and we left the final decision to each group. We had asked for 20 per group as there were five groups and we needed 100 clay figures as we were going to work with percentages. Whilst the groups were working on the clay figures, we asked them to calculate how long it would take to walk 4,320 km. We did not reveal why we had chosen this distance, or indeed what we were going to use the clay figures for. Groups again had to make decisions about the assumptions they would make: How fast would a person walk; how much rest would they need; would they take rest days - and so on. We agreed that this journey would take a minimum of three months. At this stage we revealed that 4,320 km is one estimate of the distance from Aleppo in Syria to Calais. We also explained that what we would move onto next was to map the refugee journey from Aleppo to Calais by creating a map of the journey, to a scale that would fit into the room, and then use the figures to create an infographic of the percentages of refugees in each country on the journey.

We used the three fact sheets below to support the students in mapping and representing the journey.

Distance from Aleppo to border of	In km
Greece	1500
North Macedonia	2000
Austria/Germany	3100
Germany/France	3700
Calais	4320

People displaced by war in Syria: April 2016

Population of Syria 22.8 million

6.6 million people displaced within country; 4.8 million displaced to other countries

Country	Number of Syrian refugees
Turkey	2.8 million
Lebanon	1.5 million
Jordan	1.5 million
Germany	500,000
North Macedonia	400,000
France	10,000
UK	8,000

These figures were the most recent figures available at the time of the workshop. We recommend that you use the most up-to-date figures if replicating the workshop. The website https://data.unhcr.org/en/countries/ contains such data.

As the figures were placed on the map, the atmosphere changed in the room. This activity was giving us a new empathetic insight into the refugee journey. The last act in this section was to calculate the width of the Channel between Calais and Dover. It was approximately the width of one of the tape measures we had been using. The whole group gathered to look at the 0.1% of a person (represented by an arm of one clay figure) on the scale map. One of the participants looked back at the journey, and said, with tears in their eyes, 'If you have walked all that way and that is the final part of the journey, of course you will try to cross.'

The final section of the workshop moved on to introduce a drama technique called 'The mantle of the expert.' This also allowed us to model ways of supporting learners in becoming active, in changing their world through coming to an increased understanding of the world. 'Mantle of the expert' was developed by Dorothy Heathcote and is described as a dramatic-inquiry based approach to teaching and learning. The big idea is that the class do all their curriculum work as if they are an imagined group of experts (see www.mantle-oftheexpert.com).

When engaging in a mantle, learners take on responsibility for running an enterprise in a fictional world. This role is developed sufficiently so that they care enough about the long-term goals of the fictional client to engage in activities through which they begin to imagine the fictional world that they have been presented with. Learners and teachers interact, predominantly as themselves whilst interacting as experts, imagining that they are interacting as other people in the fictional world. Over time, learners engage in activities that, whilst they are curriculum tasks, appear as professional practices in the fictional enterprise. In any mantle, the teacher positions the learners as knowledgeable and competent colleagues.

The enterprise that Helen introduced was a business that recycled shipping containers for a range of other uses. Drawing on images of actual uses for old shipping containers, she showed how the fictional business had supported the creation of pop-up shops in Shoreditch, London, and worked to create shelters for the homeless in Brighton. In her role, as Chief executive officer (CEO) of the charity, she told the group that the charity had decided to take a new direction. She read out the following letter that she had received from a boy in a local primary school. He had written this letter as a result of a visit to the school by UNICEF to talk about the plight of child refugees. When working with children, we would use a handwritten letter that could be passed around the groups:

> We are writing because we are very sad. Children like us are dying in the sea. We saw it on TV. Children cannot get to go to school. We want to help. Somebody left an old container on the road near our school. We think it would make an amazing classroom for our friends in Calais. Bill came to talk to us from UNICEF and we do not like what is happening at all. Please help us make a nice warm fun place for them to learn like us.

Helen, in her role as the CEO, then described how she had become inspired by this letter to reform the business as a social enterprise that would recycle shipping containers. The shipping containers would be transformed into mobile classrooms that could be transported to any area of the world where children were being deprived of education. The participants were invited to become a member of one of the following teams.

- Accountancy team
- US offices team
- Marketing team
- Asian offices team
- Donor negotiations and communications team
- Design team

Individuals made their own choices of role by selecting a role card labelled with the particular job they were volunteering for.

New groups were formed that contained a number of these roles. Individuals introduced themselves explaining what skills and experiences they had that had led them to make this choice. This is the point at which individuals could decide how much of a character they wanted to create and inhabit. Once the groups had introduced themselves, they discussed a name and a logo for the social enterprise. After sharing and discussing, a logo and name were adopted.

The final activity for the session involved the groups working with shoe boxes as scale models of containers. The shoe boxes were about 1/20 of the size of a shipping container, so the groups picked up their models from the scale map at the back of the room and placed them in the classrooms that they had constructed.

Development:

The ideas underpinning this workshop could be used to represent any of the refugee journeys or to compare the response to different refugee crises. For example, the current disparity between the numbers of Ukrainian refugees offered free passage to the numbers of Afghani, Syrian, or Eritrean refugees.

It could also lead to links with refugee charities. Several of these charities offer online teaching for children in the camps, and teachers in the UK can easily take up this challenge.

An earlier version of this section appeared as 'Teaching mathematics through drama', in *Mathematics Teaching 263* published by the ATM in September 2018

Useful websites

Association of Teachers of Mathematics (ATM): www.atm.org.uk
National Association of Teaching through Drama (NATD): www.natd.co.uk
The mantle of the expert: www.mantleoftheexpert.com
Data on refugees: https://data.unhcr.org/en/countries/

Activity 7: Epidemics

Introduction

I first came across this activity at a conference in Durban, South Africa. The activity had been used be mathematics educators working in rural South Africa in areas afflicted by AIDS. UNICEF still reports that Eastern and Southern Africa 'carry the largest share of the global burden of HIV' and that whilst much progress has been made the gains are 'fragile.' UNICEF states that over 60% of children and adolescents worldwide living with HIV are in Eastern and Southern Africa.

I always used the activity with teacher education students on World AIDS Day, 1 December. I have sometimes combined this with the activity, "Counting to six million" (See page 10). The World Health Organisation report that about 40 million people have died of HIV since the beginning of the epidemic.

When the Covid-19 pandemic hit and schools were closed down globally, I shared this activity with many teachers around the world as I ran several series of webinars with international audiences. It is a clear example of how we can use mathematics to interpret the world, but also how our developing understanding of mathematics can impact on our actions on and in the world. It is also an example of how understanding mathematical models can save lives.

Starting point

The activity is best with reasonably large numbers of participants. If I am working with a lecture hall of teacher education students or an assembly containing a whole year group at a school, I will select 30 to come to the front. If I am working with a class of school students, I will work with the whole class. I have previously prepared small pieces of paper – one for each participant. One piece of paper has a cross on it, the rest are blank.

These are folded up, so no participant knows if they are the 'carrier' of the virus. The participants move around the space until I say 'stop' – you can even use music and, when the music stops, the participants pair up and secretly open the paper. If a participant is paired with someone with a cross on their paper they are 'infected' and write a cross on their piece of paper. I repeat this process four or five times.

I then invite the whole group to discuss and then estimate how many people will be infected. I will ask groups to estimate quickly – without giving them time to consider the mathematics and then to have an extended discussion exploring what the maximum and minimum number of infected participants will be in order to revise their estimate. We then open up the pieces of paper and see how the 'virus' has spread across the group.

The next stage is to add an intervention. Depending on the virus you are modelling this could be mask wearing, hand washing, vaccination or taking other precautions. I suggest that the first intervention reduces the risk of infection to a 50% chance. The simulation is repeated but this time each participant has a six-sided dice. If a participant pairs up with someone who is infected, they roll the dice. They are only infected if they roll an even number. The discussion phase is repeated.

Finally, another intervention which I suggest reduces the chance of infection to one in six. So, now, you only 'catch' the virus if you roll a six.

Development

This can lead to discussion of creating mathematical models which allow us to explore the world. We also explore the accuracy of the model that we have created by referring to data. For example, a recent UK government report suggests that the booster vaccination for Covid-19 reduced the risk of infection to 86%, which reduced to 69% after a year. Students can consider how to model this mathematically.

There are many rich sources of data for students to explore. The government coronavirus dashboard breaks data around infection, vaccination, and deaths into age groups and regions. This can lead to many rich data-handling activities. These data can be used to develop infographics such as those discussed in 'If the world were a village' on page 48-49.

Other possibilities

This approach to data handling can be used to examine many situations involving inequality. Mathematical models which progressively model interventions as way of moving towards a less inequitable world illustrate the effectiveness of direct action.

Useful websites:

Coronavirus Dashboard: https://coronavirus.data.gov.uk/
UNICEF: www.unicef.org/esa/hiv-and-aids#:~:text=The%20numbers%20are%20stagger-ing.,cause%20in%20the%20same%20year.
World Health Organization: www.who.int/data/gho/data/themes/hiv-aids#:~:text=Since %20the%20beginning%20of%20the,people%20have%20died%20of%20HIV.
World AIDS Day: www.worldaidsday.org/

PART 3
Possible ways forward

This final section seeks to acknowledge the difficulties for all teachers in introducing activities such as the ones we have shared in the previous section. As you will understand from what you have read, all the authors have used these activities in a range of contexts across different ages and stages of learners. And we have all encountered challenges, both at a curricula level – people may question how these activities fit into the curriculum – and at a system level. Colleagues may be concerned that working for social justice in our classrooms does not always fit the current government agenda and that our institutions may be penalised for this. We would hope that sharing the discussions that follow will support you in working for social justice through your teaching by understanding that it is not a journey you undertake on your own.

In Chapter 8, Pete Wright talks to two colleagues, Shaila Gosrani and Lauren Hennessy, as part of an evaluation of a work group on participatory action research and teaching mathematics for social justice. Shaila and Lauren were teaching in secondary schools at the time. In Chapter 9, Manjinder talks to secondary student teachers that she has worked with on the teacher education course and, similarly, in the next chapter, Balbir talks to a primary student teacher from one of the courses she teaches on. Finally, Tony has a discussion with teacher educators and teachers who attended a workshop he ran around teaching mathematics for social justice.

We are all in awe of the commitment of these teachers to working for social justice in their mathematics classrooms. They inspire us. We hope these reflections inspire you too.

DOI: 10.4324/9781003361466-10

8 Teaching mathematics for social justice
Reflecting on practice

Pete Wright

In this section, I use extracts from a reflective discussion I held with practising teachers to explore how some of the theoretical ideas from Part 1 of this book can be translated into classroom practice. The online discussion was with Shaila Gosrani and Lauren Hennessy, two participants in an 'innovations work group' organised through (and funded by) one of the regional Maths Hubs in England. The work group ran from September 2019 to July 2020 and was focused on 'teaching mathematics for social justice' and 'participatory action research' (see Chapter 2). At the time, Shaila was in her 8th year of teaching and Lauren was in her 3rd year of teaching, in secondary schools in the Bristol area in England. Coincidentally, both were also studying on the same Masters' Level university course in mathematics education. The reflective discussion was part of an evaluation of the work group carried out with ethical approval from University College London Institute of Education. We are grateful to Shaila and Lauren for giving consent for their data to be used in this section of the book.

The following extract from the discussion suggests the significant level of interest that exists amongst mathematics teachers in exploring issues of social justice in their classrooms. However, it also demonstrates how this aim is rarely given high priority in schools, with most professional development geared towards raising attainment in high-stakes examinations. There are significant constraints to be overcome for those colleagues who wish to pursue such an interest.

Pete: Why did you choose to participate in the work group? ... What was your motivation for wanting to take part?

Shaila: I can start just because I've got the answer, I've already thought about it. Was it last September? I don't know, but I'd started at a new school. And my boss ... I think she used to work for the Maths Hub. And she just sent round all the different options, and she was like 'choose one.' And I couldn't believe it, because in my last school, I think they were quite tight on budgets. So, I was just so excited that I could do some CPD [continuing professional development].

Shaila: And to be honest, I'd never even thought about teaching mathematics for social justice. Well, I had thought about it, but I didn't think there'd be a work group on it.

Shaila: So, when I saw that, I like instantly wanted to do it. And I was almost a bit worried that they'd say no. Because they'd be like 'oh, can you do something a

DOI: 10.4324/9781003361466-11

bit more relevant, like teaching maths at GCSE [General Certificate of Secondary Education], the new GCSE, or something like that?' ... So, when I saw that, I was just very intrigued by it.

Pete: What about you, Lauren?

Lauren: Yeah, same ... I think I must have signed up to the Maths Hub mailing list. So, I must have got it that way.

Lauren: Because, you know, I was a fairly new teacher, just in my second year of teaching and really keen to develop my skills. And I was also doing the Masters ... I was already in that mindset of like doing multiple things. I was teaching part time, studying part time. Whereas I found a lot of teachers who are teaching full time didn't really look out for CPD options because they were just so busy with their teaching schedule. Whereas I was really like: 'OK, great, I'll fit in some other things.'

Lauren: It happened to be that this group wasn't on any of my days off. But I was really lucky that my school let me have the four days off to do it, which I didn't think they would because I was only a part-time new member of staff. I didn't think they'd give me it ... I think, partly because other people didn't request time off, I was able to get it, that CPD.

Lauren: And I have to say, when I initially saw it, all I saw was 'maths and social justice,' and I had no idea what the rest of it meant, if I'm totally honest. I didn't have a concept of 'participatory action research' [PAR]. Yeah, so it was literally the maths and social justice that drew me in and then it was only through the work group that I came to understand what PAR was all about.

Pete: OK, right, thank you. It's quite interesting that you said you're surprised to see that as a title, Shaila. Because, I mean, I was approached by [the Maths Hub Lead] to run a work group. And I was really surprised that somebody would want to run a work group on this topic, because it's, kind of, government funded. And I thought 'are they really going to go for this?' And I was even more surprised, after I'd written a proposal, that she came back and said 'yes, we got the go ahead to do it.'

Lauren: Right, yeah. It is rare.

Teaching is a collegiate profession and teachers are often very keen to share good practice, innovative approaches, and teaching resources with others. The work group provided an opportunity for participants to collaborate with colleagues in different schools and exchange ideas that, in turn, prompted dialogue within their mathematics departments. The teachers welcomed the opportunity to engage with research findings, particularly those from the field of critical mathematics education which they had rarely come across before, and to reflect on how these related to existing practice.

Pete: OK. And what did you hope, or expect, to get out of it [the work group]?

Shaila: ... What did I hope to get out of it ...? To be honest, when I say I've never thought about teaching mathematics for social justice ... Actually, when I was teaching Core Maths at Sixth Form, I did try and like ... it was great because I did try and, like, get in some ethical issues and, actually, it was really good.

Shaila: So, I guess I wanted to learn how to incorporate more of it into my teaching. And, yeah, I guess it's the sort of thing where I could have just bought books, and slowly got recommendations for books, and really slowly incorporated it into my teaching myself. But you realise at some point that's never going to happen.

Shaila: So, yeah, I was like wanting the collaborative approach ... I wanted to learn how to incorporate social justice issues into my teaching. That's what I wanted.

Lauren: Yeah, I was the same. And I think, developing on what you said [Shaila], ... it wasn't just that I wanted to learn it for my own practice, although I did. But I wanted to have the backing of saying 'well, I've been on this work group' and I've come back and I've brought something to the department that felt a little bit more ... rather than me, as this new member of staff saying 'oh, I've got this idea how we could teach maths,' like I've actually gone on a CPD. And I've been given the time to do that, and then I've come back and brought something to the department that feels like it's backed up by research evidence, rather than just me proposing my own wacky ideas.

The participatory nature of the work group was welcomed by the teachers and was seen to be in marked contrast to much of the professional development they had encountered in the past, which tended to be more prescriptive. The work group encouraged teachers to reflect more critically on their own pedagogy and practice, to ask themselves new questions about the nature of mathematics and to challenge some of the assumptions about teaching and learning that they had previously taken for granted. These revelatory considerations spilled over into the conversations they had with their friends, family, and colleagues. The ongoing and sustained nature of the work group, which involved trying out ideas between workshops and collecting data to evaluate their impact, was welcomed as an effective way of bringing about genuine transformations in teachers' thinking and classroom practice.

Pete: To what extent did your experiences match your expectations? ...

Lauren: I think this kind of links back to my first answer, which is that, actually, I didn't have any expectations of the PAR process, because I didn't really know anything about it. So, I suppose the experience was like quite a different experience [from] what I expected. Because I was kind of imagining we'll just come there and learn some techniques and then go off and do the techniques, which is what we did. But actually, we were so involved in the process of, you know, actually thinking about a research question, thinking about how to collect data, thinking about how to report back on the data we've collected.

Lauren: ... It was a much wider experience than I'd imagined. And really, really useful, especially because we were, you know, me and Shaila, we were both doing the Masters, and kind of entering into the world of research. ... So, it was much richer than I'd even expected because I hadn't really anticipated that whole element of building, designing the research together. So, it definitely matched my hopes, in terms of coming away with concrete ideas of things to do in the classroom and being able to bring them back to the department, like it ticked that box. But it was also a lot more because of the research aspect.

Shaila: ... Yeah, it met my expectations. But I hadn't really predicted what or how I was going to ... I knew I wanted to learn how to teach mathematics for social justice, but I hadn't imagined how I would do that.

Shaila: I was thinking it was going to be very resource based and, actually, ... some really valuable things I've learned from this course is that it's not just about your resources. It's about the pedagogy that you use, but it's not just about the resources. And it's like you could have an amazing resource to do with social justice, but if you still teach it in a traditional power imbalanced way then, for me, that's not teaching mathematics for social justice. ... I'm really glad that I've learned that.

Shaila: ... the number of conversations I've had with friends and family, like adults, about this ... and it has just been so interesting, like everyone around me is so interested in this. And I don't think they've ever been interested about anything else to do with teaching or maths that I've ever talked about. ... This group gave me the idea of what to do my dissertation on. I didn't know I was going to do my dissertation on this topic.

Shaila: Back to what [Lauren] said about ... a lot of CPD, you just kind of like turn up, passively take it all in and then go away. You do learn stuff, but sometimes you don't always have time to implement it. I did think it was a bit intense at first, when we actually had to like do these things and do interviews and stuff. But, actually, I realised ... that's actually a good thing.

Shaila: I've been doing quite a few sessions on other things in school like, I don't know, like antiracism stuff. And the person running the session has been like, you know, 'you can't just sit here passively, you've got to go away and do reflective tasks and stuff in between, because you have to do the work.' And I think, with teaching maths for social justice, I think it's the same. It's not just something you can learn ...

Shaila: It would just be great if this could just be like an ongoing thing, if this was like a group that was just ongoing. So, we met up three times every year ... and constantly, like, shared our experiences and resources.

Pete: Lauren, did you want to come back in and say something?

Lauren: I do, actually, ... that's a great idea, Shaila, and I think that should happen.

The teachers described how the activities they tried out, which included the 'Counting the votes' activity in Part 2, impacted positively on the engagement of students with mathematics, on their mathematical agency, and on their attitudes towards the subject. Their students were generally excited to try out new ideas and to be asked to provide feedback on their experiences. They found that the impact of the work group went beyond the lessons they taught with a social justice focus and significantly influenced their general approach to teaching mathematics. It also had an indirect impact on colleagues.

Pete: What impact has the project had on your practice and your students?

Shaila: So, at the beginning ... when I tried out a couple of the lessons ... I think I just did the voting one ... I can't remember now ... I think it's had a big impact on my practices in that I've talked about it informally quite a lot with some of my colleagues ... lots of maths teachers that I know that are my friends ... I guess, the whole teaching mathematics for social justice, in terms of like your classroom pedagogy and stuff, I think it's definitely affected my practice.

Pete: Do you find yourself teaching differently even if you're not doing one of the social justice [activities]? ... How did your practice change then?

Shaila: I guess I always tried to be like this, but I just made it even more obvious. So, I don't know ..., like if a student spotted a pattern, but it wasn't the pattern that I wanted them to ... it wasn't the pattern that was the main aim of the lesson, I still tried to big it up as loads as I could.

Shaila: I saw something years ago that was like, when a student gives you an idea, you can like write things up like 'Bobby's Theorem' or 'Rosie's Theorem,' and then there's like 'Pythagoras's Theorem.' And just bigging up all their ideas, like everything they come up with is really important ... trying to make them all feel like mathematicians and being amazed by their answers. ... That's all I can think of right now.

Pete: Let's hear from Lauren and then, if you think of anything else, we can come back to you.

Lauren: So, I think, for me, it's a thing that will sort of embed slowly over time, kind of build up so that I feel confident using ... Yeah, like Shaila says, it's not just these specific resources, but the kind of ideas that we've talked about, and you can apply that in different lessons and just in, you know, the way you present tasks.

Lauren: But I think for me ... it doesn't just happen overnight from doing one lesson, and I was starting to get there specifically with one of the classes that I used to collect the data from. And it did feel that it was sort of changing my relationship with that class because they were really interested in ... as a group, overall, they were enthusiastic, and they were interested in this research project. And I think, in some ways, they ... felt proud to be part of it, that I'd selected them as the class. And then, unfortunately, everything changed with the lockdown [after the outbreak of the Covid-19 pandemic in March 2020] ...

Lauren: And now, of course, for me it's a strange time because ... I'm working as a supply teacher ... I planted those seeds, but now it's something I'll have to come back to ... But it's definitely something I'll come back to when I am in more of a stable maths teaching job. And once I've felt like I've been able to embed it myself, that's when I want to share it with other colleagues, which is something I'm really excited about. And I'm pretty sure, Shaila, that's your plan too? We want to get this in our school's scheme of work.

Shaila: Yeah.

The collaborative and participatory nature of the work group allowed teachers to provide each other with mutual support, raised their levels of perseverance, motivation and confidence, and offered legitimacy to their efforts to address social justice issues in the mathematics classroom. They described how the work group enabled them to re-engage with, and re-focus on, the humanistic beliefs, values and ideals that were the motivation for them to come into teaching in the first place.

Pete: OK, so the last question, what are the implications for the future development of your practice? ... I don't know if there's anything you want to add in terms of where you go next?

Shaila: ... So, when I did the first resource, like the 'Counting the votes' one, I realised that, if it's like a change and the children don't get it, they're not going to be enthusiastic, and I think trying those things out, you just get really disheartened because you'd be disappointed. And, actually, you'd just want to go back to the 'safe mode.'

Pete: Children don't like change, do they?

Shaila: But then, because I knew I was doing this work ..., because I knew that these resources, I didn't make them, so I knew they were trustworthy. So, then it made me just change the way I spoke to the students as well. So, instead of being frustrated, I realised that I just had to calmly and kindly continue to convince them. And, if they responded with any form of frustration, I made sure to try and respond with a way that made it make sense, rather than being frustrated myself. So, yeah, the implications for the future development of my practice is ... yeah, having this group has given me confidence in like sticking by my aims and goals and ideals.

Pete: Do you think those aims and goals and ideals ... are they something that have been there all the time or are they new or ...?

Shaila: No. To be honest, I think they're probably ... like when I originally decided to become a teacher, I reckon they were probably the strongest ideals that I had. Oh, and by the way, totally agree with what [Lauren] said ... I haven't just like flourished into like a teacher that can teach mathematics for social justice. Like, it is a really slow process. But, yeah, I really like slow processes, so my practice is slowly changing, yeah.

Pete: OK. So, Lauren, do you want to add anything about implications for the future? Or do you think you've covered it all?

Lauren: ... I will just add, actually, like Shaila was saying about how, when we had the lockdown and things, suddenly we might have had a bit more space and time to reflect. And I thought, now, because I'm not actually teaching in a school regularly, ... I'm going to take some time to actually work on building up some resources of my own, and like really put some energy into that. And particularly with a focus on sustainability issues and climate change, because that's a big passion of mine. ... And you know, I've got my reflective journal and all my notes to come back to, and I'll pick back up and keep developing that thinking.

Our reflective discussion highlights the potential of participatory approaches, that focus on teaching mathematics for social justice, for transforming the experiences of both teachers and learners. Whilst designing and sharing resources is vital, the discussion emphasises the importance of giving equal attention to pedagogical considerations, in other words, not just what we teach but how we teach it. The work group prompted teachers to reappraise their relationships with students, with the aim of fostering their mathematical agency, and to seek to embrace more dialogic, collaborative, investigative, and culturally responsive teaching approaches that enhance students' engagement with mathematics. The dialogue demonstrates the power of critical reflection for generating insight in this area.

Since being involved in the work group, Shaila and Lauren have continued to develop their own ideas around teaching mathematics for social justice and influence the practice of others, including through their active participation in the Teaching Mathematics for Social Justice Network. The network, which is targeted at teachers of mathematics in all school phases who are committed to addressing issues of equity and social justice in the mathematics classroom, was established in April 2021. Its principal aim is to share teaching ideas, resources, and practices with other members, and to provide mutual support and encouragement. Find out more at www.mathsocialjustice.org.

9 Teaching mathematics for social justice
Reflecting on practice

Manjinder Kaur Jagdev

In this chapter, I reflect on a mathematics lessons planned and taught by Drew (a pseudonym), a student teacher at York St. John University (YSJU) and lesson ideas created by Year 2 Primary undergraduate student teachers at YSJU. Drew completed his school placement in a mixed state school in Yorkshire at the start of 2023. In my role as his tutor, I had the privilege of visiting him to observe his teaching of a lesson to Year 10 class (15-year-olds). Alan (also a pseudonym), his mentor and an experienced mathematics teacher, was also present in the lesson. Every such school visit involves post-lesson feedback, with reflections from the student teacher, his mentor and I. The lesson was designed to meet the English mathematics national curriculum objectives around data handling and statistics. This lesson explored these objectives in the context of climate change.

Drew opened the lesson by sharing a video which included graphs and other data relating to fossil fuel consumption. Students made comments about the 'positive correlation' they noticed in the data and made links to their learning in geography lessons. The students seemed engaged whilst watching the video about the island of Tuvalu and worked on an activity exploring correlation and lines of best fit in the real-life context of climate change. The students were positive about their mathematics learning, saying that they valued working on mathematics in a real-life context, as well as seeing an application of mathematics. One student mentioned the importance of learning mathematics in order to challenge misleading or 'fake' news.

At the end of the lesson, Drew asked the students for feedback. A female student talked about the need for electric cars, a male student suggested that he thought more renewable energy sources are required. Other students argued that statistics can be used to back up arguments that people are making when they talk about how to impact climate change and that statistics and data can be used to support these suggestions even further. Two powerful comments from the students in the lesson were:

> I wonder if the progressing extreme heat will affect our animals and even human beings. Will this affect us in dangerous ways? For example, will we die from heat stroke, will the water sources dry up, and the animals die of thirst? These are my wonders for this graph.

> I already knew climate change was a problem, but understanding the statistics behind it allows me to see the scale of the problem and how it will affect our lives in the future.

DOI: 10.4324/9781003361466-12

In the post-lesson feedback, Drew reflected on the following aspects of his teaching. I have used the usual proforma we use to reflect in an observed lesson:

Behaviour and high expectations	*Classroom had a very good working environment; all groups participated and were engaged. Expectations of equal contributions and collaboration made at start of lesson. Some off-topic conversations: I think this was mainly due to a bit of a struggle to access some of the material but once students understood what was needed they all worked very well.*
Pedagogy	*Video used to engage students. Used homework to firstly motivate and prepare students for the lesson. Students were very engaged and worked collaboratively. The exercise should be streamlined and the lesson should have more of a focus on the criticality of mathematics and statistics and in turn more debate and discussion in the class.*
Curriculum	*Critical maths education and looking at relevant real-life mathematics. Cross-curricular links to Science and Geography.*
Assessment	*Plenary allowed for deep and critical reflective thinking that spark an excellent discussion after in which students gave amazing answers.*
Professional behaviours	*Good classroom environment and students voluntarily help by handing out books. The class was put into groups...*

My own feedback to Drew, relating to these five aspects above, highlighted that all students were engaged in the task. This unusual lesson was positively received by the children which signals an opportunity to do group work and focus on mathematics related to climate justice / ecology more regularly. The strong planning of group work enabled the pupils to respond positively to the teamwork. One student commented on how the experience was like being in future employment – all coming together to work on a task. This was perceptive, making good links to potential skills required in the workplace. Many students stated that they liked the group work set-up because it was a different way of working in mathematics lessons, in terms of sharing ideas. One student stated that often, when working on their own, they get stuck and do not know what to do. In this lesson's scenario, it was better because they could discuss their ideas. As they suggested, 'teamwork helps us work it out.' The mentor, Alan, commented that it felt like an unpressurised environment in which to learn mathematics.

Alan also suggested that there was no competition between the students, only collaboration in this lesson. He thought the students showed high levels of criticality and deep thinking on the use of statistics in the context of climate change. The students made links to other curriculum subjects including science and geography. Drew could follow this up with those subject leads for cross-curricular projects on climate justice and ecology. In terms of meeting curriculum objectives, there were clear links to data-handling objectives with students identifying correlation and using lines of best fit to make predictions. They plotted graphs and could explain and interpret what the data showed, suggesting, for example, 'as time goes on, we have less ice caps.' Drew's background is in statistics and so he has subject expertise in data handling and can use this to plan further opportunities for children when teaching data-handling topics in real-life contexts.

Climate change is an urgent and complex issue that is already plaguing our world. It is a multifaceted problem that requires an interdisciplinary and critical approach to fully understand and address. Therefore, it is vital for the next generation to be able to comprehend how mathematical models and statistical analyses are used to study climate change and its impacts, but also how these methods are limited and uncertain. Additionally, students must explore the dimensions of climate change, including the unequal distribution of its impacts and the role of power and influence in shaping policy and action.

10 Teaching mathematics for social justice
Reflecting on practice

Balbir Kaur

This interview is between me, Balbir, in my role as a primary mathematics lecturer and a primary PGCE student teacher, and Ruth, a PGCE student. The interview explains how Ruth plans a unit of maths work and applies her approach to teaching maths for social justice (SJ) in a primary school setting into practice. She discusses how she addressed the balance between focusing on the mathematics subject knowledge and integrating the social justice issue.

One of the assessments on the PGCE programme requires students to plan a curriculum project where they take pedagogical, subject, and curriculum knowledge and integrate SJ principles in how they approach the teaching of the curriculum. The learning, teaching, and assessment are modelled on the many principles for TMSJ (teaching mathematics for social justice) discussed in this book. It provides an excellent example of how mathematics subject knowledge is enhanced and pedagogy is developed by incorporating real-life problems linked to the United Nations Sustainability Goals that address social justice issues in society.

Ruth chose the SJ theme 'Understand and tackle food poverty through maths education' in her mathematics curriculum project, which she shared with a Year 4 class (8–9 years). The curriculum plan was linked to the UN Sustainable Development Goal #2, Zero Hunger. The topic was selected because it is topical in the current climate and the rising cost of living across the country, with many people needing support to buy nutritious food. The topic was also appropriate for the local community, as the school is in Brent, London, with many children from financially disadvantaged backgrounds. The student became aware that over the last few years, there had been an increase in the use of food banks accessed by the local community, the Trussell Trust being one of them. Ruth indicated how the TMSJ issue was relevant to many pupils' lives and linked well to the maths topic of money. It opened up discussions, conversations, and activities on how children were going to use maths to help them make informed choices about how they shop for food, how much of a household budget needs to be allocated and budgeted for food, and what they were willing to spend to donate to food banks.

Balbir: Can you talk me through your motivation for selecting the TMSJ curriculum enhancement module?

Ruth: Okay. I chose maths because it's my weakest subject. I felt going into teaching it would be the subject that I would need the most support with. I felt English and all the

DOI: 10.4324/9781003361466-13

other subjects I'm fine, but maths was the one subject I was not confident in. I actually left school without a GCSE in maths, so I had A and B's in all my other subjects, but I did not have a maths GCSE qualification. And I think when I got to university, and I did the maths identity professional learning activity that really helped me and got me thinking about why I felt I wasn't good at maths and how that's led me to where I am today. I had a difficult journey with maths in school, and that's why I left without a GCSE. I just sort of gave up on maths in school, and I thought, it's not for me. I'm not going to do it. But then realising I am actually capable of doing it, but I just didn't have the opportunity or the support that I needed in school.

I worked in schools as a support assistant before I did the PGCE and I saw how maths could be taught differently, and how children enjoyed maths. I felt I really missed out on that experience, so I thought, definitely as soon as I get to the PGCE that's the subject that I would like to focus on, because I know I have maths anxiety. I know I brought that into the course and I don't want to pass that on to the children I'm teaching because I've had those negative experiences, and I felt that just throwing myself into this module would be a good opportunity to face that anxiety head on and build a lot more confidence. This module has definitely done that for me. I've left the PGCE really enjoying teaching maths. I think it's one of my favourite subjects to teach, because I'm learning a lot with the children and also identifying my own areas of weakness and knowing what I need to work on. What I wanted to get out by choosing this module is what I did get out of it. I'm really, happy the focus of that module was TMSJ.

Balbir: What was your initial understanding of teaching maths for social justice?

Ruth: Well, I got SJ. We hear it a lot, and you sort of know it's all about equity in society. But I had never really thought about how it links to maths. I thought what does that look like? I know, if we're talking about SJ and English, for example, I know what that looks like. It's through the text that we're reading and discussing, the themes that we're picking up from those texts. But I thought in maths, I didn't understand how that would actually work. But once we sat down in lectures and we saw examples and we thought about how we use maths in every aspect of our lives and how it helps us understand the world, it sort of became the obvious thing. Why aren't we doing this? Because this makes sense! It makes sense for everyone's lives. It makes sense to the children. I didn't have a clear understanding going into it. I had no idea of what it would look like, but once we got started it just seemed like an obvious choice.

Balbir: And how did your understanding of TMSJ develop or change during the course of the module?

Ruth: I think, with the practical examples that you shared in lectures, and really looking at how we can break down a SJ issue using maths and using the maths to better understand that SJ issue. Once I started seeing the connections, how it becomes a lot more relevant to the pupils and how it helps them understand the maths topic more. Also how it's helping prepare pupils that we're sending out into the world with these maths skills to have real practical use of the subject. We tend to think about maths so much more in terms of engineering, but we never think about it in some of the other ways maths can be used. So like from a sociological viewpoint, and I thought thinking about it from that side of the story makes a lot more sense as well. There's a lot of sociological issues that we don't unpick with maths. Finding that element through this course was really interesting, and it just gave me a better understanding of how we understand society and the issues in society.

Balbir: Was there anything from your school experience that contributed to your understanding of TMSJ?

Ruth: I think probably the assignment that we did, and how you could take a topic and put it into practice, and give it a go with the children. I think that made me realise that it is possible. Again, there's limitations because there are other pressures in the school, but also starting to see the possibilities and seeing the difference it makes for children as well, because they enjoyed it. It's not just a maths lesson. It's a maths lesson with a story behind it, and that really resonated with a lot of the pupils, it makes sense. I think actually putting what I learned in university sessions into my practice.

Balbir: You speak a little bit about some of the challenges of doing this work. Can you share any challenges that you experience in your attempts to incorporate SJ principles in your maths teaching?

Ruth: I think schools sometimes having a rigid structure, that they're reluctant to go off course especially with schemes. For example, my school used White Rose, and they were very sort of rigid with their White Rose, they followed that structure a lot. I wasn't allowed to deviate too much from White Rose and the worksheets. I found that challenging. Rather than focusing on the worksheets, I kind of incorporated this work as independent practice at the end of the lessons. I planned a lot of maths talk throughout the lessons and got children working in teams on the work that linked to the SJ issue I prepared. So I think that was the hard part, having the freedom to deviate from the maths scheme and to try to work the SJ issue into the maths work that schools are expecting to see in children's books. I think that was sort of the main challenge.

Balbir: Were you doing TMSJ alongside the maths schemes?

Ruth: Yes, I had to go back to what the scheme needed covering, how the questions were phrased, do the required worksheets children were expected to complete: that was really challenging. But I think I did manage to build that in. I planned a lesson on the Monday morning before we started the money maths topic, like a sort of a PSHE lesson to set the scene to discuss the SJ issue on food poverty. We talked about food poverty, about their experiences, thought about the experience of other people, I mean their communities, or what they know from listening to the news or food poverty in other parts of the world. So, once we had that discussion when we got into the maths lessons, children knew where they were going with the work, and they responded quite well, because they had previous understanding of the SJ issue, but they also had that introductory lesson which gave them information that they might not have known beforehand. [An example of the planning is given below.]

Programme of study: Estimate, compare and calculate different measures, including money.

Lesson 1: Recognise and convert pounds and pence (TMSJ: Recognise the value of
    money)
Lesson 2: Compare and order money (TMSJ: Know that 'own brand' and offers can make
    money go further)
Lesson 3: Estimate using money (TMSJ: Make food choices based on need and budget)
Lesson 4: Add using money (TMSJ: Which products are good value for money)
Lesson 5: Subtract using money (TMSJ: Which products are good value for money)

So, I think, going into the maths lesson they were focused on the topic, food poverty. They were able to make the links, they were able to say, 'oh, we discussed this earlier.' In maths lessons I found opportunities to bring the learning back to the SJ issue. I used the context of food poverty in maths lessons quite a bit; that's how I sort of drew it in. I would have visuals that linked to the SJ issue in front of them, and then, once they did the maths related to the SJ issue, they would go and do the work for the maths scheme that would go into their book.

Balbir: What kind of ideas of maths mastery did you bring in your TMSJ lessons?
Ruth: I think it was variation of presenting the maths in a different. I also planned in a lot
    of maths talk and I was mindful of how I grouped children, making sure the groups
    had children who would model good maths language for those who needed that
    modelling. We did reasoning as well in the problems I designed. But, yeah, they
    would have to do the reasoning and break the problem into small steps. This is
    where I do appreciate White Rose, because I think it sort of also guides our teach-
    ing in that it does help you think about how you're breaking down the learning. So,
    because I had to use it in conjunction with my teaching, I would follow those steps
    stated in White Rose. So, for example, with money we have to start with recognising
    money, and then we moved to estimating. Then we moved on to comparing, order-
    ing, and then to addition and subtraction. So having that guideline from White Rose
    that breaks the learning down in those steps. I think that was also quite effective.
    We built fluency because we would sort of recap learning every day, and also based
    on formative assessments from the previous lesson, we would see what we needed
    to come back to, recap on the learning to help children sort of commit to long-term
    memory, and that tends to build up.
Balbir: Did you notice a difference in engagement from some children in your TMSJ
    lessons?
Ruth: I could see a lot more interaction. I'm just thinking about a couple of boys in particu-
    lar: they enjoyed talking, they enjoyed interacting. Because of how I grouped some
    of the children, the fact that they could be with their friends while they were talking
    about maths, I think they enjoyed that, so they weren't always realising that they
    were doing the maths work. They felt like it was a more fun lesson, I suppose, but they

were getting down to the maths. In that regard, I think maybe they responded more positively, even though they may not have recognised that themselves, that they were engaging with the maths a lot more than they normally do.

Post TMSJ lessons we had a couple of children who would bring up the topic of Food Poverty. I had one child who designed a poster in her own time that wasn't prompted or anything. So again, it was her having those thoughts. I don't know so much if she had pulled the maths into that, but I know she was thinking about it.

Balbir: What resources did you draw upon to support your planning, design, and teaching of TMSJ lessons?

Ruth: It was what was signposted to us. I looked at some NRich activities. I think the hard part was trying to maybe find an activity that I could have adapted or used in that context and trying to find ideas that you could use to incorporate into your lesson. I was just trying to pull together all of these things and create my own resources. From what I've sort of seen in some of the resources I've been signposted to from you [tutors] that my mentor might have suggested. There were a couple of interactive maths websites as well.

Balbir: How did the teachers, mentor and other school colleagues respond to your TMSJ?

Ruth: I think teachers are so busy to be honest, I feel like they say 'Oh, that's interesting. That's nice.' But because they have so much more to do, they're not going to be too engrossed in what I'm doing, because they're always constantly trying to focus on keeping up with their own responsibilities. Because they've decided or determined how maths is already going to be taught, they're not open to having these new sorts of elements influence change. The school I was in was very strict on how they implemented the maths teaching. They already knew where they were going with this, so they were not open to those sorts of influences. I think my mentor thought it was interesting that we could do that, but I often feel sometimes with mentors, although, you appreciate all the input, the advice and the help I sometimes feel like they are teaching you to teach in their way. But they're not always open to sort of helping you build your own teacher identity, or what you want to sort of bring into teaching, or the new ideas and research that you sort of want to build into teaching. It might not be that they are open to it, it's just feels like they have an established way of doing things that they sort of want to continue with. So I feel like sometimes mentors need to remember that you're trying to also bring in your own learning and experiences, and you want to sort of take your teaching in a different direction. Sometimes I feel like they're teaching you to teach just as they do.

Balbir: I just want to go back to the SJ principles we discussed during taught sessions. Did you have a theoretical framework for your work? What SJ principles did you consider when you were TMSJ?

Ruth: I used both Pete Wright's Social Justice principles (see Chapter 2 in this book), and I focused on encouraging pupils to have a sense of responsibility to their communities. I think by discussing the food banks in our area we had a Trussell Trust just around the corner. So by talking about that, just thinking about it in their own communities and their roles and responsibilities within their community. Helping them think about their own agency, or empowering them to think about how they can make a difference in their community.

That was something that I really tried to build into the lessons. And then also again, the obvious one, equipping them with the mathematical skills to go out and be agents of change by helping them make informed decisions. For example, a lot of them had unrealistic ideas of what food costs. They didn't know because they don't do the bills, but I think they need to start knowing these things and thinking about it and have a realistic understanding of how much things cost. So, having those examples in our maths lesson, how much does a packet of pasta actually cost? How much does a pint of milk cost? Giving them the mathematics skills that if they're out in the shops and they have ten pounds, and they need to get breakfast, what are they going to get with that ten pounds? How are they going to add up all the items they need to get? How much change are they going to have left over? So those mathematical skills and also giving them a chance to explore some of the complexities in society. So, understanding, why do we have food poverty? What are the reasons? The solution is so just getting them to ask those bigger questions and try to make connections to the different things happening in the world around them, their world but also the larger world around them.

Balbir: Having done this work, what have you learned about yourself and your positionality whilst engaging in TMSJ?

Ruth: Well, I've learned that I'm capable, I'm able. I need to have a lot more confidence in my ability to make a difference and in my ability to learn, because I think it's a learning process, and I can learn to teach effectively. It's a matter of time, bringing the energy and focus as well. My positionality as well, I hope it doesn't get dampened as I start my Early Career Teacher year because you start off with these really high hopes and these big ideas, but then the reality of being in the job sometimes I feel like crushes it all. But I feel like coming from the background I've come from I want to be that teacher that makes a difference. I really..., genuinely, that's what I want to do, and I feel like I want to go into schools where I can help children sort of use their maths learning or whatever teaching they are using to help them feel empowered to make a difference in their own lives, even if it's their own lives, not even thinking about the wider community. How can they better their own lives, their own opportunities? So I think that's really where I would like to go with it.

Balbir: How did you develop your maths subject and pedagogical knowledge whilst planning and TMSJ?

Ruth: I think it's a lot of watching experienced teachers. Just seeing some of the strategies they use in class, and how some of them are effective. I think that's invaluable because they do have a whole bank of knowledge that they use, different skills, and how they adapt in the moment to respond to how pupils are responding to the lesson. That sort of helped me build up some of my pedagogical strategies, or how I am going to teach on different topics and different elements. Also thinking about while observing them how I might change it slightly if I was the person teaching the lesson. Once you get a chance to teach it sometimes it's not as easy as it looks. So thinking about how you would do it differently the next time. Reflection is always a big one, and, I think, having the chance to teach it. Someone can tell you how to do it, but it's very different when you actually get to do it yourself, and you have a feel for it, then you think, oh, well, that definitely didn't work, and you can sort of sense it. You can assess as you go along knowing what you would do differently each time, and also build on the subject knowledge as well, because I feel like with Maths, the big part of the confidence is, if you don't know what you're talking about, you're not going to be able to explain it confidently or pick up on the other ways of doing things that pupils have, because we all think differently, and some pupils might have a totally different way of approaching the same problem, but if your own subject knowledge is not strong enough to identify that they're still going to get to the same endpoint, you might sort of squish that because it is not how you want children to work it out. So again, I feel like just making sure you've read around the topic, and you're focusing on the key learning, especially for someone with my maths background. I'm still learning quite a lot. And yeah, that's … I feel like that ties into the pedagogy as well, because for you to teach it effectively, you've got to know yourself what it is you're trying to teach. So I think, yeah, just starting researching myself has helped with that.

Balbir: Was there any aspect of the principles of TMSJ that you found more challenging to incorporate in your maths teaching?

Ruth: I think the discussions are always hard because of time limits. I feel because we talk a lot about the theory in teaching and what we know we should be doing, we should give them time to talk and to explore. But we don't have the luxury of time in the classroom. It's the time to really unpick these topics and do it effectively, and I'm hoping that with experience I'll be able to do it a lot more effectively, because I feel like I've got an idea now, but it's going to be a real steep learning curve trying to balance how I do it effectively.

Balbir: So how do you think primary maths education can contribute to social justice issues?

Ruth: I think a big one is the quote that you shared, you used a lot in the lectures as well, about reading the world with maths and writing the world with maths. Everywhere we look there's a way to understand the world through maths, and I think if we look at SJ issues through statistics and number, for example, like if we look at food poverty just looking at the percentage of children who are going hungry in this country and understanding what that percentage equates to in actual numbers. These are actual, real people. It is this many 100,000s of children who are going hungry: it gives you an idea of the scale of the problem. So I think it's those maths skills that help you understand the scale of problems of certain SJ issues. It makes it feel a lot more real; rather than just saying people are going hungry, you actually understand. If it's one person going hungry, it's one person too many, but if we're talking about 500,000, you know, it's just unacceptable. So it helps you really understand the scale of the problem whatever the SJ issue is.

Balbir: Okay, thank you very much. I have no other questions. I don't know whether you'd like to share anything that maybe I've not asked you.

I hope that, as this sort of idea spreads, and we have a lot more training teachers doing this, that, as more people [are] coming to schools with this idea and this way of thinking or this way of teaching, that schools will a lot be a lot more open to doing it. So I'm hoping in the next few years we actually see it being on the schemes and we see TMSJ tie into the other areas of the curriculum that we're studying. We talk about linking the curriculum and doing these cross-curricular learning, but I sometimes feel like maths is too much of a standalone. So it would be really nice in the next few years, if we can see how we're really linking all of those other SJ issues we're learning in other subjects into our maths learning. And I'm hoping this really spreads and takes off because I've enjoyed it. Going into my school, I would like to find elements of how to do this. I'm definitely going to. I want to keep the momentum going, because I feel like if I don't, it's very easy to just put it to the side and forget about it. So I want to try and make a conscious effort to do that. And I'm hoping in the next few years there'll be a lot more people teaching in this way.

11 Teaching mathematics for social justice
Reflecting on practice

Tony Cotton

In the spring of 2023 I (Tony) ran a morning workshop for a group of teachers and teacher-educators in Nottingham, in the Midlands of England. As part of the workshop, I shared some of the activities that appear in Section 2 of the book. I asked the participants if they would be interested in reflecting on their experience of teaching mathematics for social justice (TMSJ) with readers of this book. Fortunately for you and me, Bekah Gear, Tazreen Kassim-Lowe and Marks Simmons responded. I used similar prompt questions as Pete and Balbir in earlier chapters in this section. As with the previous chapters, I leave Mark and Tazreen's comments to speak for themselves. I hope that it supports readers in reflecting on their own experiences.

How would you like to be described in the book?

Tazreen: I am a former Primary School teacher and Mathematics Lead teacher. I am currently a PhD candidate at the University of Nottingham and an accredited Professional Development Lead with the National Council for Excellence in Teaching Mathematics (NCETM).

Mark: I am a mathematics teacher educator at the University of Nottingham School of Education. I am married with two children.

Bekah: I am a primary teacher educator at Nottingham Trent University (NTU), with a mathematics subject specialism (accredited NCETM Mastery specialist). I am married with a baby on the way!

Why did you particularly want to follow the workshop up? Why do you think issues of teaching mathematics for social justice are important?

Tazreen: If we are not teaching to make the world a kinder, caring and more equitable place, then why are we teaching? I think Tony touched on the importance of the human element in mathematics both in terms of humanising mathematical contexts through statistics which demonstrate inequalities for example but also valuing and validating individual's mathematical superpowers as contributions to classroom culture. I think issues of TMSJ are important as mathematics can often seem separate and

DOI: 10.4324/9781003361466-14

distinct from other curriculum areas such as 'humanities' (which literally has the word human in it!) but really, I think mathematics is more social than we give it credit for and shapes the experiences and interactions we have throughout our life (perhaps because I was a sociologist before I was an educator!).

Mark: I would like to think that humans are capable of creating a more just world, although it clearly presents us with an enormous challenge. Education should inform a person and equip them to think critically about their life and their world. We are entering a new era, where homo sapiens' activities and population needs have palpably brought them into contact with environmental/planetary limits. In this context, teaching mathematics for examination test scores simply will not do.

Bekah: Tony's session enabled me to reflect deeply on my previous practice, particularly whilst I was working in schools as a mathematics leader for my group of schools and NCETM Mastery Specialist. It made me consider how often within mathematics the purpose of education can be missed. Whilst in school, I felt that 'teaching for mastery' became a mask for teachers to hide behind. Sometimes this phrase creates a misconception of what equity is and thus sometimes we (educators) ignore the fact we have a duty to create a culture where all children feel and believe that they are mathematicians. It's a rite of passage that must not be ignored. Tony challenged the notion that mathematics is simply mechanical and the social nature it presents as an educational experience.

How would you characterise TMSJ?

Tazreen: Teaching mathematics for social justice, I think, is twofold: meaningful contexts and classroom interactions. One aspect is using mathematics as a tool to discuss challenging systemic social issues, such as Tony's activity where we represented the population of the continents of the world in a space in the workshop. The other aspect is how we organise our classrooms (I am an advocate for mixed-experience pairings) or learning spaces, interact with our learners, and trust our learners' ways of thinking. Actually, I think there is a third hidden aspect, which is acknowledging our own relationship with mathematics and others. For example, I am often aware of being the only person of colour with a disability in education settings and how I might be perceived as 'less.' Less of a mathematician, less of a person. On the other hand, my mathematical superpower is a hyperawareness of the second principle of how we interact with our learners, particularly those from groups who are often considered less, but I think of them as underserved. I also acknowledge my privilege as someone who has been fortunate enough to be given opportunities in my life and the role that mathematics has played in my own success. So, in conclusion, meaningful contexts, meaningful interactions, and meaningful reflexivity!

Mark: Humans have created a society deeply run though with ingrained injustices. TMSJ is an opportunity to comprehend these through the use of mathematics as a way of seeing the world – via statistical interpretation and representations of facts such as proportions.

Bekah: Teaching mathematics for social justice for me is about how we value and validate all learner's experiences and interactions. Creating immersive mathematics experiences that invite noticing, conjecturing, and debating is at the heart of this. It is about developing the whole child within the concept being taught, and it takes courage and creativity to apply it into practice. It is about going beyond the curriculum and thinking hard about our pedagogical choices. We also have to be courageous in how we challenge the view of labels and assessment 'boundaries' that categorise children. We have to be open and ready to feel uncomfortable and challenged.

Had you used any of the activities previously? Have you tried any since the workshop? What about activities of your own that you would see as impacting on TMSJ?

Tazreen: I haven't used them directly but have shared the book *If the world were a village* by David J. Smith with previous classes and with participants in Maths Hubs work groups [See Chapter 6, Activity 3]. I thought the book was a good opportunity to notice both the mathematical and the social. I have, however, downloaded some of the lessons from the TMSJ website [see https://mathsocialjustice.org/] and am particularly interested in the lesson on 'misleading graphs.' Tony's activity about the exponential spread of Covid really made me think about how we consume and interpret data to make sense of ourselves in the world [see Chapter 7, Activity 7]. I recently had a conversation with a taxi driver who believed that there was no way that the increased rate of Covid in late 2023–early 2024 could be predicted and instead believed that there was someone or some organisation that was purposefully spreading Covid to eliminate certain societal groups. Instead, I suggested that they would have used previous statistics, current statistics and 'done some maths' to create that data. He was not satisfied with this answer and nor was I, and it made me want to understand this better myself and bring this context into a maths session with my current tutees. I have also read *Mathematics for Human Flourishing* by Francis Su multiple times since Tony's talk and have recommended it to everyone I know, whether they consider themselves to be 'mathematical' or not!

Mark: I used the human population distribution activity at the start of this PGCE term. I have previously used 'If the world were a village' and also used Gapminder [see www.gapminder.org/] dynamic scatter graphs in a mixed subject session with geography: pairs agreed on a graph to tell the story, presenting this from a mathematical and a geographical standpoint in collaboration.

[I also created the activity in Figure 11.1, following a recent General Election.]

2019 Election Proportional Reasoning/Rounding task

Party	Votes (thousands)	MPS	Rate:
	13966	365	
	10269	202	
	3696	11	
	1242	48	
	866	1	
	644	0	
Others	975	22	

Can you name the parties, calculate rates and round them to easy-to-U extent?
Any noticings?

Figure 11.1 Election proportional reasoning/rounding task

Bekah: I have used story books within CPD sessions as part of a NCETM Research Innovation Work Group as well as a Leadership Development group. As part of this, I used the book *If the world were a village*. I used story books to demonstrate how you can create real life contexts within mathematics lessons and use these to facilitate experiences within teaching and learning.

What was your experience of working on activities such as these? What were the learners' responses? What about colleagues?

Tazreen: My experience of working with activities such as these is that I have to really think about whether or not I want to make the mathematics the 'star' or the context. At a recent TMSJ reading group we read Laurie Rubel and Andrea McCloskey's 2021 paper: 'Contextualization of mathematics: which and whose world?' I particularly appreciated the idea of considering what is in the foreground and background.

Mark: Learners enjoyed the activities for themselves and could imagine children engaging well with them and potentially learning some things about the world through a mathematical lens, as well as discovering a genuinely relatable and useful application of maths. Colleagues have been a little wary at times. My mathematics colleagues are institutionally senior to myself and can be more worried about compliance issues, though they are committed to social justice as a matter of principle.

Bekah: I found it took a lot of encouragement to support the teachers and leaders I was working with to think creatively about how they could bring this into practice. However, it was also noted that practitioners in the EYFS (early years foundation stage) settings were more susceptible to the idea. I have previously used storybooks in my mathematics teaching. I have noticed how using a 'book' as a context empowered more children to talk and share their thinking. It also felt that it took away the 'high stakes' experience that some mathematics lessons can create for children who feel that they 'can't' and 'won't' be mathematicians.

What challenges did you face?

Tazreen: We discussed the challenges of time, resources, support (as with a lot of worthwhile endeavours in education). But one participant mentioned that they found being explicit about who is experiencing injustice and why was rather uncomfortable. At the start of the pandemic, my partner was working in intensive care and had noticed the rate of patients of colour dying early on. I was still a class teacher at this time and when my students would ask me why the rate of deaths in certain communities was higher than others, there was no clear-cut answer without upturning histories of oppression, geographies of colonialism, economics of housing even. How far should we delve into this, especially with very young people where the cause and effect of something is not clear cut?

Mark: There is the challenge of limited contact time on the teacher education course I work on and a professional qualification to teach people towards.

Bekah: It was evident that both teachers and leaders alike feel the strain of the curriculum expectations, and often it was a question of 'well where does this fit into the curriculum?' It felt that the curriculum and assessment model in school is impeding teachers' and leaders' creativity to embrace new ideas that can enhance their practice and celebrate equity and TMSJ.

What are the implications for your future practice?

Tazreen: Through individual stories, Tony demonstrated the power of care. I think TMSJ starts with care which may evolve into equality, maybe equity, and, hopefully, justice. Anne Watson's book, *Care in Mathematics Education*, has reignited my appreciation for the word. So, I will continue to care, continue to be a part of groups and conversations which prioritise care in Mathematics Education, continue to care ethically for the individuals I work with, teach and research with, and use care as a vehicle for social justice.

Mark: I aim to use any opportunities afforded by the timetable to include more such activities and further discussion around the issues in this year's course.

Bekah: Previously, during a values week session at NTU, I brought in a TMSJ session. However, I would like to encourage this to be brought into the taught content. I have recently read *Care in Mathematics*, by Anne Watson and she has further prompted my thinking in how I model these traits to our trainees. I want to continue to support the narratives around TMSJ and hopefully support teachers (at all stages of their journey) to notice how they too, can develop equitable practices within mathematics teaching.

Bibliography

Smith, D. and Armstrong, S. (2003) *If the world were a village*. London: A and C Black.
Su, F. (2020) *Mathematics for human flourishing*. London: Yale University Press.
Watson, A. (2022) *Care in mathematics education: Alternative educational spaces and practices*. Cham: Palgrave Macmillan.

Useful website

The website of the Teaching Mathematics for Social Justice Network in the UK can be found at https://mathsocialjustice.org/

12 Some final thoughts

How to summarise or conclude a book such as this? We have acknowledged throughout the text how we understand the competing pressures that teachers are under, in whatever phase or wherever in the world they work. For all of us, you, the reader, or us, the writers, there is a belief that education can change lives for the better, whether that is through achieving good grades in high-stakes examinations or through gaining a clearer understanding of the world, which allows us to act differently. You will have your reasons for picking this book up, for being intrigued by the title. We all hope that by this point you will have tried out some of the activities and begun reflecting on the effectiveness of this approach. So, we thought we would 'conclude' by sharing our hopes for the text as we release it into the world.

And, of course, this is not a conclusion. It is a stopping-off point for all of us, wherever we are on our journeys.

Tony Cotton

This is likely to be the last academic book I contribute to. It feels like the time to hand over whatever batons I have been carrying to others. In some ways this is a culmination. It brings together theoretical perspectives I have been exploring for the last 45 years with activities that I have been planning, using and sharing for, perhaps, the last 40 years. One of the joys of getting older is that you meet people that have seen you as their teacher, in some form or another, and remember learning with you. That is why I know that some of these activities will last and can have an impact. So, my simple aim for the book is that it will engage you enough to try out something and that through that simple act you will be encouraged to continue to work for social justice in your classroom. I truly believe that most teachers work for social justice through their teaching whether they are overt about it or not. I also believe that structures imposed by governments often act against this and that this is what leads to teacher frustration and anxiety. Perhaps this book will reduce this tension. My less simple aim for this book is that it will, in some way, support the creation of a more just education system for my grandchildren and great-grandchildren and for your children and great grandchildren. As Paulo Freire, in his great work *Pedagogy of the oppressed*, said, 'I work, and working I transform the world.'

DOI: 10.4324/9781003361466-15

Balbir Kaur

I hope the ideas and examples in this book offer the reader the courage to rethink and critically evaluate how mathematics can be used to teach students to transgress against racism, sexual and class boundaries and address the many global issues as outlined in the UN Goals. The book has demonstrated how the theoretical ideas of teaching for social justice can be translated across a mathematics curriculum throughout all phases of education with the vision that, regardless of the age group, phase of education, or length of teaching experience, you can use teaching as a space for change and enact critical pedagogies in how mathematics is taught. Although the book provides many messages, and each reader will take away the message that speaks loudly to them, I wish to highlight the following as possible starting points or extensions to this book. Firstly, to actively participate in the difficult work of dismantling oppressive structures that create inequities, teachers must engage in critical self-reflection to construct new and transformative forms of knowledge. Recognising the privileged status you bring to the profession can only be a starting point to understanding better the complexities of our identities within the larger socio-political context. Secondly, work with partnerships and maths communities to create communities of practice that will confidently empower teachers to shift school culture for a whole-school responsibility to TMSJ. And finally, engagement with practitioner-based and participatory research that can enable transformative pedagogies centrally positioned towards multicultural and social justice education. I want to end this section by echoing the words of Ruth, who describes TMSJ as a means to understand the world better, how TMSJ makes sense for everyone's lives, and it just seemed obvious. Why aren't we teaching maths this way?

Manjinder Kaur Jagdev

I hope that one of the impacts of this book is that students and school-based mentors will confront the anthropocentric thinking, challenging assumptions of human superiority. We can embed ecofeminist principles into our classroom practices that consider the natural world, for example, biodiversity, deforestation, wildlife species (butterfly, bee, and bird populations), rather than only humans in it. Freedom, justice, and peace would shape our thinking about real-world contexts and practices of mathematical reasoning for our classrooms. The real-world contexts such as caretaking, relationships across places, and histories and futures can be integrated into our teaching and learning. In this way, those who have previously been excluded, such as Indigenous communities, people of colour, the poor, children, and women, can be included. As we expand this participation, we create opportunities for greater diversity in terms of who asks questions and whose real-world problems get solved with mathematics (and how) (Solares-Rojas et al., 2022). The resolution for my own teaching practice is to develop such classroom contexts, curricula and pedagogy that reflect complexity and interconnectedness, in terms of gender, social roles, race, and racism. Angela Davis (American author, scholar, and activist) proposes a theory that holds people accountable and believes that they can change, be radical and active. The intentions and purposes of my work in this book are that learners, students, and teachers are active in collaboratively creating ideas that allow them to reflect, learn, and adjust practices, responding to injustice and building positive ways of living. This educational process should be natural and organic.

Reference:

Solares-Rojas, A., Arellano-Aguilar, O., González, M. M. G., López-Vargas, M. R., Coles, A. and Serrano, A. M. (2022) Mathematics education and social-environmental crises: An interdisciplinary proposal for didactic innovation with rural communities in Mexico, *Research in Mathematics Education*, 24:2, 202-223, DOI: 10.1080/14794802.2022.2062781

Pete Wright

I hope that this book will impact practitioners in two ways. Firstly, for those who are already convinced of the need to address issues of social justice in the mathematics classroom, I hope it will provide guidance on how they can translate some of their ideas, values, and beliefs into practice. In my experience, there are significant numbers of teachers who are keen to transform their practice, if only they could find the time and energy to overcome the constraints they face on a day-to-day basis. Many teachers come into teaching because they want to make a difference to young people's lives and to make society a better place. Unfortunately, it is all too easy to lose sight of these aims given the pressures teachers face in schools. I hope that this book will reassure these teachers that they are not alone in their aspiration and provide them with the confidence to share ideas with others and to re-engage with the reasons why they came into teaching in the first place. Secondly, there are likely to be readers who are intrigued by the idea that teaching mathematics is inherently linked to issues of equity and social justice. They may not have given this much thought in the past and may only be starting to appreciate the links for the first time. I hope that this book will encourage practitioners to reflect critically on existing practice (both their own and that of others), to re-examine their previous beliefs and assumptions, and to start questioning some common practices and discourses related to the mathematics classroom that are too often taken as given. Whilst I was a practising teacher, my ambition was to promote learners' agency, to encourage students to pose their own questions and make decisions about how to use the mathematics they had learnt to generate a fuller understanding of the world around them. As a teacher educator, my goal is now to promote agency amongst teachers and to encourage them to challenge discourses and myths that are associated with teaching and learning mathematics. By doing so, I hope that, as a profession, we can transform classroom practice and bring about a socially just mathematics curriculum that contributes towards addressing some of the current challenges we face as a global society.

Final Reflections

Over To You

INDEX

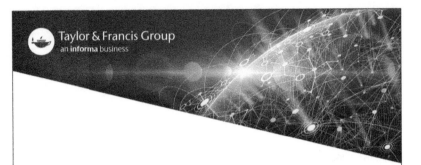

For Product Safety Concerns and Information please contact our EU
representative GPSR@taylorandfrancis.com Taylor & Francis Verlag GmbH,
Kaufingerstraße 24, 80331 München, Germany

Printed and bound by CPI Group (UK) Ltd, Croydon, CR0 4YY

08/06/2025

01897005-0019